TRANSFORMATION PROCESSES
IN EGYPT AFTER 2011
– THE CAUSES, THEIR COURSE AND
INTERNATIONAL RESPONSE

TRANSFORMATION PROCESSES IN EGYPT AFTER 2011 – THE CAUSES, THEIR COURSE AND INTERNATIONAL RESPONSE

Edited by

Radosław Fiedler,
Przemysław Osiewicz

λογος

Berlin 2015

Reviewer:
Prof. UŁ dr hab. Radosław Bania

Coordinators of the publishing project:
Professor Radosław Fiedler

English language consultancy:
Katarzyna Matschi and Graham Crawford

Typesetting and cover design:
Ryszard Skrzeczyński

Photography:
Radosław Fiedler

Publication financed by NCN – the Polish National Science Centre
(decision numer DEC-2012/05/B/HS5/00510).

Logos Verlag Berlin GmbH

Gubener Str. 47, 10243 Berlin, Tel.: 030-42851090

www.logos-verlag.de

ISBN 978-3-8325-4049-0

Bibliographic information published
by the Deutsche Nationalbibliothek

The Deutsche Nationalbibliothek lists this publication in the
Deutsche Nationalbibliografie; detailed bibliographic data
are available in the Internet at http://dnb.d-nb.de.

CONTENTS

FOREWORD

The Arab Spring in North Africa and the Middle East came as a surprise to scholars dealing with this region. There were enthusiastic opinions about young, Arab people who staged a revolution using their mobile phones, the Internet and Facebook. A young Egyptian, Wael Ghonim, who organised a protest campaign on Facebook observed: "if you want a free society, give them access to the Internet." From the present perspective, however, the situation has become significantly more complicated. The transformation process in Egypt has come to a halt, and after 2013 we can actually note some symptoms of authoritarianism being reinstated in Egypt.

The ousting of the authoritarian leaders in Egypt, Libya, Yemen and Tunisia in 2011 has not solved the economic, social and political problems. It can even be said that some of them have become aggravated. Regional security has been adversely influenced by the civil war in Syria, chaos in Libya and Yemen as well as the threat posed by Islamic State.

The present publication is the outcome of the research project *The European Union towards the Transformation Processes in Egypt after 2011*,[1] conducted by the Faculty of Political Science and Journalism at Adam Mickiewicz University in Poznań, Poland from January 2013 till May 2015. The project was co-ordinated by Professor Radosław Fiedler.

The main objective of this publication is to analyse the course of the Arab Spring in Egypt and its outcomes in the internal, regional and global dimensions. In order to achieve their objective, the authors sought to answer the following research questions:
– What were the causes and course of the Arab Spring in Egypt?
– What are the international consequences of the transformations in the Middle East and North Africa after 2011?
– What terminology should be used when talking about the events in the Middle East and North Africa after 2011?
– What are the main threats to the transformation process in Egypt?
– How is the transformation process in North African countries perceived in terms of the priorities of Polish foreign policy?
– How have the events in Egypt after 2011 influenced the policies of the USA, the European Union, the Russian Federation and China towards Egypt?

[1] The project has been financed by the National Science Centre on the basis of decision number UMO-2012/05/B/HS5/00510.

– How have the transformations in Egypt influenced its relations with other states in the region?

– How have the transformations in Egypt been perceived by both moderate and radical Islamist fundamentalists?

– How have 'social media' influenced the process of transformations in Egypt?

The publication presents a multifarious and critical outlook on the Arab Spring in Egypt and its internal consequences, as well as the influence it has exerted on regional and international contexts.

The interdisciplinary nature of this project had a direct impact on the research methods applied in the course of its implementation. Key significance was attributed to the methods typical of political science (with particular emphasis given to studies in international relations) as well as history and law. The studies were conducted on the basis of an analysis of legal texts (as regards legislative acts laying the foundations for the influence on the transformation process in Egypt) and an analysis of the institutional aspects concerning the assessment of political initiatives and decision-making processes in Egypt. The following methods were applied in the course of research: descriptive and comparative methods allowing for the causes, course and effects of the transformations and international involvement to be retraced, systemic and factor-related methods (facilitating the presentation of the determinants of the transformations and processes shaping the phenomena analysed within the framework of the project). A significant stage of the research was constituted by surveys conducted in Egyptian institutions and other selected centres.

The authors of successive parts of the publication developed their research questions on the basis of selected elements, such as the determinants of EU and international involvement, the role of individual countries involved in Egypt, the range of activities and the consequences of the Arab Spring for the transformation in Egypt. This defined and limited range of topics allowed us to indicate the changes in terms of politics, as well as show the factors regarding the Arab Spring in Egypt.

The publication is divided into two parts. One presents international response to the Arab Spring in Egypt, both from global and international governance, represented by major players, such as the United States, Russia and China, and regional ones, such as Israel, Turkey or Iran. The other part encompasses an academic analysis showing the course of transformation in Egypt: both the causes and course of the political transformations in Egypt, the military factor in Egyptian politics and the role of new media and social mobilisation in ousting president Hosni Mubarak; also the democratic transformations in Egypt as perceived by the representatives of the global jihadist movement and the main impediments and threats to democratisation in Egypt are discussed in this part. Noteworthy, the authors present a new perspective on the transformation in Egypt and a critical analysis of the terms applied as regards the Arab Spring in North Africa and the Middle East.

The range of studies presented addresses this publication at a wide circle of readers, in particular experts on European integration and international relations. The project team sought to draw particular attention to the dynamics of the process of shaping mutual relations and to emphasise the diversity of determinants that affected this process.

Egypt has already witnessed two replacements of governments since the 2011 events. After Mubarak was detained, the Military Council took power, and the tension in Egypt increased the longer it continued to maintain power. In 2012, the citizens of Egypt elected new president, Mohammed Morsi, a moderate Islamist with connections to the Muslim Brotherhood. After one year, he was deposed by the army, officially acting on behalf of discontented citizens and in order to defend the republic. In 2014, Abd Fattah el-Sisi was appointed President, but the situation continues to be highly unstable, as it was in the years following the Arab Spring. As this book is being released, the Egyptian Administrative Court has decided to delay the parliamentary elections scheduled for March and April, due to a judgment passed by the Constitutional Court. The suspension of the electoral process confirms the political dysfunction and social tensions in Egypt.

This publication is not exhaustive, but lays the path for further attempts to tackle the multiple aspects and complexity of the issue of EU-Egypt relations and their development in the immediate future.

The authors would like to extend their particular thanks for support they obtained in the course of the project from the following:

Mr. **Reda Abdelrahman Bebars**, Ambassador of the Arab Republic of Egypt in Warsaw; Mr. **Tamer Mohamed Kamal Elmiligy**, Counsellor of the Embassy of the Arab Republic of Egypt in Warsaw; Mrs. **Nikola Gillhoff**, Policy Officer Middle East I-Egypt, Syria, Lebanon, Jordan, European External Action Service; Mr. **Filip Kaczmarek**, Member of the European Parliament 2009–2014; Mr. **Marwan Hobeika**, External Consultant European Endowment for Democracy; Mrs. **Geneviève Vercruysse-Toussaint**, the Senior adviser in European Affairs at the ICRC Brussels delegation.

Radosław Fiedler, Przemysław Osiewicz

Poznań 20 April, 2015

Part I

TRANSFORMATIONS IN EGYPT

Marcin TARNAWSKI

Jagiellonian University, Krakow

THE ARAB SPRING
– REMARKS AND IMPLICATIONS

INTRODUCTION

Starting at the end of 2010 in Tunisia, the process of socio-political changes in Arab states has aroused tremendous interest worldwide, not only due to the ease with which long-reigning dictators were relinquishing their power, but also because of the domino effect which set off a chain of events across virtually the entire Arab world. The mere fact of shifts in power at the highest levels might have been foreseen, since such changes occurred in the past and will continue happening in the future; however, the ease with which 'revolutionary ideas' spread across the Arab world came as a surprise even to analysts. It is not just the fact of leaders who had often ruled for several decades yielding power. Most of the rulers in the Arab world had to confront the events in Libya, Egypt, and Syria by either engaging in them directly, or just 'succumbing' to the demands of their own societies, which suddenly emerged under the influence of these changes. However, the changes at the top or the concessions granted by the ruling powers did not make those who led to the overthrowing of the tyrants any better off. As the price of freedom seems incalculable, it is difficult to assess unequivocally all the costs of the Arab revolutions: the number of people killed and displaced, changes to the sizes of economies and standards of living, the impact on both immediate neighbours and the situation in the region. Interestingly, there is no agreement in the Arab world as to how the events should be designated; hence the terms coined vary, from the Arab Spring, the Arab revolt, the Arab uprisings, e-revolution, the Muslim revolution to the Islamic awakening (Osiewicz, 2014: 7–18).

Regardless of purely linguistic disputes, the scale of the achievements or concessions, the events in the Arab world have caused huge losses and destruction. In the four most violent uprisings in Libya, Egypt, Yemen and Syria, a total of nearly 200,000 people were killed, of which the conflict in Syria alone has left about 160,000 dead (according to UNHCR data) (*Tethered*, 2014). Yemen's gross domestic product (GDP) has decreased by several percent and Libya's has plummeted by one-third, while Egypt and Tunisia have recorded a slight increase (data for the period from 2010 to 2014). Data from Syria is not available, but estimates suggest a drop of about several-dozen percent. In the above-mentioned countries, GDP per capita has not changed since 2010, whereas in Libya it has dropped by a staggering sixty percent (in 2010 Libya had one of the highest GDP per capita in Africa) (*World*, 2014). In the 2014 edition of the annual *Fragile States*

Index developed by the magazine *Foreign Policy* and The Fund for Peace foundation, the ranking is spearheaded by Yemen (8th place) and Syria (15th place), which places them amongst the most unstable countries in the world. Similarly, Egypt, Libya and Tunisia have been unable to significantly improve their position in the ranking and are still amongst the countries considered high risk. One of the leading topics of FSI reports since 2012 has been the Arab Spring; however, the image portrayed by the authors is pessimistic, and the headings hitting the front pages of the global press, such as *Was the Arab Spring Worth It?* or *The Arab Spring. Has it failed?* speak for themselves (Ibish, 2012; *The Arab*, 2014).

Graph 1. GDP (ppp) of Arab countries in the years 2010–2013 (bln USD)

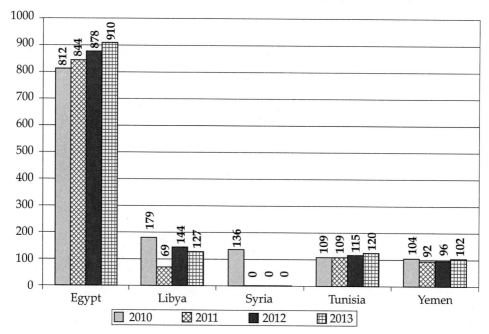

Source: *World Economic Outlook Database*, October 2014, http://www.imf.org/external/pubs/ft/weo/2014/02/weodata/index.aspx, 20.11.2014.

Each of the countries listed above has gone through changes in their own peculiar way. In Libya, it was mainly the devastating civil war and the defence strategy adopted by Muammar Gaddafi that claimed lives. In Egypt, growing political tensions and economic problems were far more distressing for the average inhabitant than the clashes between protesters and security forces. Prior to 2011, Yemen had one of the worst economic and social indicators in the world, a deteriorating economy and practically dysfunctional government agencies. Moreover, the benefits brought about by the protest movement have not yet materialised in any tangible way. Syria, in turn, is a completely different story. Here the revolution is not over yet, there are only growing costs: tens of thousands dead, hundreds of thousands of refugees, and the economy in tatters. In the meantime, several other issues have emerged, such as the use of chemical weapons, the political engagement of the global superpowers (the United States and Russia) and Islamic State (the Islamic State of Iraq and Sham, ISIS, formerly the Islamic State of Iraq and the Levant, ISIL). At this point, it is hard to foresee any potential benefits – if there are any, they will probably materialise in the very distant future, and only on condition that positive political changes take place (e.g. addressing the problem of Islamic State). However, despite months of chaos and violence, no one in Libya seriously regrets the absence of M. Gaddafi. The same can be said about Egypt where Hosni Mubarak is reminisced by very few. The situation in Yemen is much worse, where the crisis continues and it is hard to acknowledge that a change of power will put an end to it. Only the on-going civil war in Syria arouses ambivalent feelings. Not so long ago, the brutality and repressions towards the citizens led the society to believe that anyone would make a better ruler than Bashar Assad; however, the emergence of Islamic State in the Middle East forced a revaluation of these views. While it is difficult to settle unambiguously who could be a better ruler for Syria, there is one thing that is known for sure – namely, the enormous human and material costs that any prospective authorities are bound to face.

Graph 2. GDP per capita (ppp) of Arab countries in the years 2010–2014 (USD)

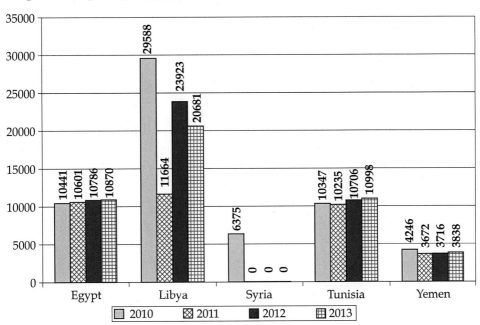

Source: *World Economic Outlook Database*, October 2014, http://www.imf.org/external/pubs/ft/weo/2014/02/weodata/index.aspx, 20.11.2014.

The aim of this study, however, is not to raise the issues flagged above. The subject of interest is selected external aspects and international implications of the Arab Spring. Therefore, the article will analyse the response of the international public to the transformations in the Arab world. At the stage of the revolutions themselves, countries reacted variously to the unfolding course of events: from astonishment at the actual fact of the outbreak of fighting (Tunisia), to favourable comments (Egypt) to military intervention (Libya) and indecisiveness and quarrels (Syria). Secondly, a brief overview of the positions of selected Arab states to the changes occurring in the region will be presented. Finally, as an example of the involvement of the Western world, the intervention of NATO in Libya will be discussed. Because of the limitations on length imposed on these types of studies, the considerations will be confined essentially to the immediate consequences and international implications of events in the Arab world; hence the author's interest focuses on the years 2011 and 2012. Where absolutely necessary, the author will refer to later events. In accordance with the assumptions presented above, the subject of the engagement of Russia and the United States in the inquiry into the use of chemical weapons in Syria and the activities of Islamic State will be excluded from this analysis. Naturally, the author treats these events as international implications of the Arab Spring; however, he believes that they were not their immediate effect.

THE RECEPTION OF THE REVOLUTIONS (MYTHS AND REALITY)

The events of the Arab Spring have reverberated widely, not only in the region, but also all over the world, disproving on this occasion several prevailing misconceptions about the Arab world. One of them is the statement that Arabs do not go out on the streets to protest. Before the protests erupted in Tunisia and Egypt, numerous experts had claimed that it had not been necessary to execute political reforms, as there had been no social need for them. This kind of logic indicated that Arab societies would not demand any changes, and that any suggestions for reforms would be perceived as a threat to the public interest. However, it transpired that such arguments misfired completely, as no one had envisaged the developments in Tunisia and Egypt. Therefore, it needs to be stated that no Arab state is immune to such events (see the case of Syria) (Bubnova, Salem, 2011). Governments do not have the luxury of waiting and should not abuse the myth of peace, in order to avoid instigating essential reform processes. Since the events in Tunisia, the states of the Middle East have allocated vast sums of money for various social programmes, mainly with the aim of appeasing the public mood. The largest financial support was declared by the Saudi Arabia authorities, who implemented a 15% salary increase in the public sector, with the final cost of the social programme reaching over USD 36 billion (Murphy, 2011; Gardner, 2011). Ideas about how to help varied among the countries: free food (Kuwait), an additional allowance for each family (Bahrain), tax reductions (Jordan) or minimum wage increase (Oman) (*Arab*, 2011). International institutions have also demonstrated some activity in providing economic aid for the Arab states. In May 2011, the G8 launched the *Deauville Partnership* programme, inviting collaboration from Gulf Arab states, Turkey, states of Northern Africa and international institutions (the International Monetary Fund and the World Bank). With a budget of approximately USD 40 billion, the aim of the programme is to provide the necessary financial support to states undergoing economic reforms. Other instruments devised to support Arab states are the Stand-by Arrangement (SBA) and flexible credit lines (Precautionary and Liquidity Line) implemented by the International Monetary Fund. Agreements with the IMF have been signed by Morocco, Jordan, Tunisia, and Egypt (*Deauville*, 2011).

Secondly, there was a prevailing conviction that liberalisation of the economy should precede political reforms. Arab governments and the representatives of the Western world alike had believed that liberalisation and economic reforms should take priority over political changes. The chief argument was that it is more important for people to satisfy their basic needs. It transpired, however, that the attempts to liberalise economies without a system of (democratic) control did not bring about an improvement in the economic well-being of the majority of society (Saif, 2011). Since the benefits of privatisation were enjoyed only by political and business elites, the Arabs had, in consequence, quite a negative disposition towards economic liberalism and globalisation. It seems quite obvious that economic reforms should occur in parallel to political changes, so that the institutional mechanisms of responsibility can function and economic benefits be more widely accessible (Mausher, 2011). Another statement was related to the necessity for the closed (authoritarian) systems to function in order to prevent Islamists from seizing power. The West feared that democracy would open the door for extremist political parties to legally come into power and institute radical changes to a country's foreign policy. The ruling elites in the Arab states exploited the situation, creating the impression that they are the only possible alternative to the complete domination of extreme political forces. It transpired, however, that in spite of constituting a crucial element of Arab communities and their political life (so far largely unrepresented), Islamists do not play such a significant role in Tunisia, Egypt or Libya. The claim that the only alternative to authoritarian regimes was Islamic extremists was also disproved. The protests of Arab communities in 2011 and 2012 seem to have repelled corrupt elements, pretence of justice and arbitrary treatment. The participation of Islamists in the post-revolutionary governments of Tunisia and Egypt shows that it is possible to create a pluralist system, since the majority of Arab states cannot allow themselves to be isolated on the international scene and burdened with economic troubles (the tourist industry is a crucial economic sector for Tunisia and Egypt in particular) (*Tunisian*, 2012; Hendrix, 2012).

17

Prior to the revolution, in order to maintain their domination Arab leaders had been proclaiming elections, but the parliaments (potential governments) created as a result of them were weak, unpopular and practically without social support. Elections in the region were used to create a facade of democracy and legitimise autocratic rulers in the eyes of the world. Arab public opinion is no longer capable of tolerating a situation like that. Instead of cosmetic remodelling of the manner of governing, society expects authentic changes that will lead to the enhancement of the economic situation on the one hand, and a greater participation in ruling (democracy) (Muasher, 2011). Last but not least, the final problem refers to the role the international community plays in relation to the Arab Spring. The United States and other remaining Western countries should support democratic reforms but not impose certain solutions. President Barack Obama has thrown aside many of President Georg W. Bush's methods, which were perceived by the Arab world as attempts to forcefully impose democracy. However, the silence surrounding the new shoots of young democracies may result in the fading of the reform process within the next several years. The West should enter into a discourse with the new leaders of Arab countries about the political and economic reforms that are being executed. In particular the increase of openness and separation of powers should not be sacrificed by Western leaders.

It is worth mentioning one other aspect of the Arab Spring that has been widely discussed all over the world – demography. It appears that it is impossible to explain the origins of the uprisings without pointing out the fact that Arab societies are very young: individuals less than 30 years old constitute approximately 65% of the population. In connection with the difficult economic situation (unemployment among young people in the region is the highest in the world, reaching 25%), this has caused growing dissatisfaction and frustration (Drine, 2012). In this case, new technologies like mobile phones and the Internet became the tools that accelerated the occurrence of certain events and facilitated communication. In addition, young Arabs are becoming increasingly better educated and knowledgeable about international events. They were noticing the wealth and freedom enjoyed by the elites of the Arab states, and felt angry and disenchanted that they were unable to participate in all that (Knickmeyer, 2011; Hoffman, Jamal, 2012: 166–188).

REACTION OF THE ARAB WORLD TO THE CHANGES

The sudden outburst of dissatisfaction in December 2010 (and its subsequent spreading to North African states) took most observers and Arab governments alike by surprise. Mohammed Bouazizi's seemingly unplanned act of self-immolation became a catalyst for change elicited by the socio-economic difficulties and political coercion of the Arab people. On one side stood a generation of young people who had been exposed to the influence of modernising powers (television, Internet, social media); and on the other – oppressive political regimes that were no longer capable of safeguarding a better life for that young generation in particular. New media and advanced communication technologies completely transformed the terms of the discussion between the ruling and the ruled, which in consequence led to an utter loss of control over the flow of information by the governments. Both in Tunisia and Egypt, mobile phones and Internet-enabled communication connected thousands of people with each other and provided a platform for the dissemination of information about upcoming protests and demonstrations. We need to remember that political tensions in the Arab world had already been growing prior to the uprising in Tunisia in the middle of 2010; in Bahrain and Kuwait, local authorities had marginalised the political activities of the opposition, narrowing the field of public discussion over the most important socio-economic issues. The first state of the Persian Gulf that experienced widespread protests against the Al-Khalifa royal family was Bahrain (spring 2011) (Bronner, Slackman, 2011: A1). Those protests, however, were stifled due to the intervention of the states belonging to the Gulf Cooperation Council (GCC), namely the forces of Saudi Arabia and the United Arab Emirates. Small-scale protests took place in Kuwait, Oman (where security forces opened fire on protesters in February 2011) and Saudi Arabia (Eastern provinces). Saudi Arabia's rulers arrested the founders of the first political party, whereas in the United Arab Emirates (UAE) intellectuals calling for political reforms in the emirate were arrested and sentenced (*Saudi*, 2011; Davidson, 2012).

Paradoxically, it was the GCC countries that became the supporters and inspirers of the intervention in Libya; Qatar and the United Arab Emirates, *ipso facto*, were the first countries to unequivocally declare support for the Libyan opposition. On the one hand, it was a sign of 'concern' for respecting the political rights of the opposition; on the other hand, more vitally, it was dictated by the willingness to play a more significant role in regional (or even international) policies. Another reason for the ambitious plans of both Qatar and UAE was diverting attention from their internal problems (the possibility for unrest to occur within these countries) as well as other, more prestige and image-related considerations (UAE forces had actively participated in suppressing riots in Bahrain). Thus, the fact of supporting the Libyan opposition was a clear signal that GCC regimes were not as conservative and repressive as they might have seemed and that they were capable of supporting opposition forces in the Arab states. Particular support for the concept of human rights protection and resolving the conflict in Libya in the fastest possible way was offered by Qatar. The Prime Minister of Qatar, Sheikh Hamad bin Jassim bin Jaber al Thani, played a leading role in persuading the GCC countries and the Arab League to establish a no-fly zone over Libya and to recognise the Libyan National Transitional Council. He also argued that "Qatar will participate in military action because we believe there must be Arab states undertaking this action, because the situation there is intolerable" (*Qatar*, 2011). In conjunction with the UAE, Qatar had provided military and financial aid, which became key for the international coalition forces and the success of the opposition in Libya. Qatari *Mirage 2000* jet fighters participated in the NATO operation in Libya, which at least partially dismissed voices about the intervention by the West (although their role was quite negligible) (Norton-Taylor, Rogers, Hopkins, 2011). In addition, Qatar supplied weapons and Qatari special forces provided the Libyan opposition with training and operational assistance, which to a large extent contributed to the ultimate victory of the opposition in Libya (Kerr, 2011; Black, 2011).

Qatar and the UAE alike provided substantial material and logistic support for the Libyan National Transitional Council. In May 2011, the UAE hosted a meeting attended by the representatives of the Libyan tribes and national groups, and in June 2011 a meeting of the International Contact Group (ICG). Qatar's non-military aid was estimated to exceed USD 400 million, comprising supplies of water, gas and basic necessities, as well as assistance with selling Libyan oil on the global markets. During the most intensive fights in Benghazi in June 2011, Qatar Petroleum covered most of the energy needs of the city and the neighbourhood area by supplying petrol and diesel oil. Furthermore, as mentioned above, Qatar was the first state to recognise the Libyan National Transitional Council as the legitimate representative of the Libyan nation, and also host of the first meeting of the ICG in April 2011 (Roberts, 2011). Amongst the remaining GCC states, it was Kuwait who had the greatest input in endorsing the Libyan revolution by donating USD 260 million to support the mechanism of financing the Libyan National Transitional Council and providing both medical and humanitarian aid. Even Saudi Arabia added Libya to the list of regimes (including Syria and Yemen) for which the country had withdrawn its political support (Colombo, 2012: 9–12). It is clear that the changes experienced by Arab states considerably affected the safety policy of the main players in the region, particularly of Saudi Arabia, for which the Arab Spring could have had grave consequences in the area of their internal policy. It has to be noted, however, that the events of 2011 provided a perfect opportunity for the GCC countries to change their image of being conservative regimes, although not all of the states took advantage of this in the same way Qatar did. Nevertheless, the actions undertaken by the GCC states showed that in spite of their intervention in Bahrain, they are capable of maintaining, at least temporarily, the pretence of control over their societies and reconciling their conservative internal policies with political and economic reforms.

Following the diplomatic success regarding Libya, the Qatari authorities intended to continue their engagement in resolving the conflict in Syria, the more so because Qatar held the rotating leadership of the Arab League in 2011–2012. However, attempts to find backing for solving regional problems ended in failure. Emir Sheikh Hamad became the first Arab leader who in the middle of January 2012 called for military intervention aimed at ending the bloodshed in Syria. His appeal, however, failed to produce any effect and attracted less attention than the Libyan case (*Syria*, 2012; Krause-Jackson, Gaouette, 2012). Even if the Arab states themselves saw the necessity of reaching agreement over the revolution in Syria, they did not succeed in the form of potential intervention itself (initially they had planned to send observer missions). Yet, the emir of Qatar was determined to perpetuate Qatar's role as the most responsible and actively engaged member of the Arab community. This turned out to be substantially more difficult than it had seemed, as the balance of power in Syria was considerably less attainable and the opposition more divided than in Libya. Because of that, diplomatic, political as well as economic and media pressure was increased. In February 2012 the Prime Minister, Hamad bin Jassim bin Jaber Al-Thani, publicly declared his support for changing the regime and appealed to the international community for arming the Syrian opposition and assistance in overthrowing al-Assad by all possible means (the fact of providing material support to the Syrian opposition by Qatar and Saudi Arabia was not without significance) (Worth, 2012: A1; Urlichsen, 2012). Due to its small population and vast oil and gas reserves, Qatar experiences neither socio-economic nor political pressure from its own citizens, as is happening in the other states of North Africa and the Middle East. It transpires that Qatar sees the events of the Arab Spring more in terms of new prospects that are opening up for itself, rather than a challenge. Perhaps it is about affirming its international reputation, even at the cost of good foreign relations with some of the Arab states.

One cannot help but notice the competition between Qatar and Saudi Arabia with regard to resolving the Syrian conflict, especially in the light of the fact that the call of Qatari authorities for arming the Syrian opposition occurred a few days after a similar offer had been put forward by Saudi Arabia's Prince Saud al-Faisal. It was also the Saudi Arabians who were the first to recognise the Syrian National Council as the legitimate representative of the Syrian nation, and at the non-state level are the biggest weapon supplier for the Syrian opposition (Sherlock, 2012). The behaviour of the GCC states towards Syria is, however, guided by entirely different and somewhat less noble motives. The protests of public opinion in Arab countries and positive reactions of Arab communities to the bloody events in Syria can hardly be applauded. On the other hand, it has to be noted that the vetoing of the UNSC draft resolution of 4 February by China and Russia (*Security*, 2012), sparked protests in the GCC countries (in Kuwait protesters even gathered in front of the Russian Embassy) (Mac Farquhar, Shadid, 2012: A1). The main motive behind the steps undertaken by Saudi Arabia is to weaken the position of Iran as the regional power and the desire to further isolate the regime. Apart from that, there is a reluctance from the Saudi Arabian rulers towards the Iraqi authorities, who are being accused of collaboration with Iran, and a concern that the potential cooperation of Iraq, Iran and Syria could lead to a shift in power in the Middle East and jeopardise the interests of the USA and Saudi Arabia. The support offered to the rebels in Syria averts such a possibility and strengthens the position of Saudi Arabia as the major regional power (Gordon, 2012: A1; Rahimi, 2012: 25–40).

While recapitulating the attitudes of selected Arab states towards the problem of Libya and Syria, it is impossible to avoid the issue of the double standards applied by some of them in their foreign and security policies. Such double standards are perfectly noticeable in the actions undertaken by Saudi Arabia. On 14 March 2011, over 1,000 soldiers of the Saudi Arabia National Guard, together with a United Arab Emirates police contingent marched into Bahrain. Even though they probably did not participate in the suppression of a pro-democratic opposition, their presence itself was enough to contribute to the collapse of the uprising (Bronner, Slackman, 2011: A1). Only a few days later, on 19 March, both Saudi Arabia and Qatar supported international intervention in Libya in order to protect civilians. After all, the Qatari authorities also found themselves in an awkward situation, especially given that the intervention in Bahrain was undertaken on behalf of the Gulf Cooperation Council (GCC). The manner in which the changes in the Arab world were commented live by Al-Jazeera television (broadcasting from Doha), where one could hear voices of unequivocal support for the uprisings in Libya and Syria, is also evidence of the degree of complexity of the international situation in the region. However, journalists of the station are very restrained and wary in expressing their opinions about the problems in Bahrain or the eastern provinces of Saudi Arabia (Ulrichsen, 2012).

WESTERN COUNTRIES AND THE ARAB SPRING: NATO INTERVENTION IN LIBYA

There are at least several reasons for the engagement of NATO troops in the protection of civilians in Libya. First of all, considering M. Gaddafi attitude, it was hard to rely on his voluntary resignation. The decided advantage of government forces was bound to result in the rebels' defeat and they could not have avoided this fate without external support. Second, the social structure itself, rooted in a tribal 'esprit de corps', created conditions in which the tribes that rebelled against M. Gaddafi were not inclined to cease their actions until they achieved their primary aim. Needless to say, the tribal revolt along with the government's reaction to it (the use of force against the rebels) led to the outbreak of the civil war. On 12 March 2011 the League of Arab States called for more radical actions with regard to the situation in Libya, whereas on 17 March 2011 the UN Security Council adopted resolution no. 1973 of 17 March 2011 (*Resolution*, 2011). In the resolution, Libya was denounced for not complying with a previous resolution of 26 February 2011. It was also condemned for attacks on civilians and breaching human rights. The resolution also stated that actions directed against the people in Libya could be classified as crimes against humanity. The UNSC's decision entitled member states to take all necessary measures to protect civilians (military occupation of Libya was, however, ruled out). The mechanisms leading to the accomplishment of these tasks were defined in the following way: firstly, by establishing a no-fly zone over the entire territory of Libya. Secondly, by introducing an embargo on all weapon supplies to Libya, including defining rules regarding cargo ship inspections. Thirdly, it opened the way to implementing a forcible solution, albeit limited to establishing a no-fly zone (and compelling observance of it) as well as protecting civilians. It is worth adding that the resolution did not give a mandate to support an offensive by the rebel forces from the air or engage land forces (Marcus, 2011).

The military intervention, under the code name *Odyssey Dawn*, began on 19 March 2011 and was initially led by a group of states under the leadership of France, Great Britain and the USA. Despite the fact that it was the Europeans that had mostly insisted on the armed intervention, it transpired that they did not have sufficient military potential and the greater engagement of the USA was required. However, the Americans announced from the very beginning that their participation in the mission would be gradually reduced and responsibility for it handed over to the Europeans. As a result of the talks, on 27 March 2011 it was decided that the North Atlantic Alliance would take over the leadership of the operation as a *Unified Protector* (the decision was put into effect on 31 March) (*Odyssey*, 2011). The primary aim of the operation was to force M. Gaddafi to fulfil the UN's demands. This turned out to be insufficient, as the rebels intended to topple M. Gaddafi regime, which received the endorsement of the Arab world in particular (*Libya*, 2011). Thus, the termination of intervention was in fact conditional upon the Libyan leader's stepping aside, which happened on 20 October 2011, and was sufficient reason for NATO to announce the end of its mission (*Statement*, 2011). The involvement of NATO troops came to an end on 1 November 2011 with the official termination of the *Unified Protector* operation. A few days earlier, on 27 October, the UNSC repealed the resolution of March 2011 (Gladstone, 2011: A10). The NATO military action can be considered a success not only because of the end of the civil war in Libya, but mainly due to the fact that it was non-US forces who played a decisive role in the military operations (with France, Great Britain and Italy in the lead). In addition, the following Arab countries participated in the operation: UAE, Qatar, Jordan and Morocco (Daalder, Stavridis, 2011).

Undoubtedly, the involvement of NATO troops in the conflict resolution in Libya ended in success, if one measures the successfulness of the mission by its effectiveness, i.e. regime change – even though this was not the primary justification of the UN resolution. Nevertheless, the following conclusions regarding relations between the West and the Arab world can be drawn on the basis of the operation in Libya. The legality of the intervention has to be considered in the first place. The intervention was possible because three basic conditions were met: legality (approval of the UNSC), legitimacy (endorsement of Arab states, including the Arab League) and providing effectual assistance (weakening of M. Gaddafi regime and existence of organised opposition). It is hard to believe that similar circumstances could occur in the future, which the conflict in Syria clearly shows; in addition, one has to take into account the interests of other international players, such as Russia and China. Second, the case of Libya will certainly not become a new war model (conflict resolution). Bombarding regime armies using NATO air forces in order to protect civilians undoubtedly brought about the desired effect. However, the toppling of the regime and taking power by the rebels was only possible thanks to the existence of strong and organised opposition forces. It appears that if an intervention of land forces (which obviously was not permitted) or special forces had been required, the conflict in Libya could have transformed into the 'Afghan' model. Third, it seems that the situation in Iraq, let alone Afghanistan, will not be repeated in Libya. Organised opposition against M. Gaddafi had been actively operating for the last few years, the extremist Islamic groups were relatively insignificant, the minor influence of the army (in comparison to Egypt, for instance), revenue yielded from exporting oil, relatively sparse population and fairly undamaged infrastructure – all these factors allow us to look to the future with optimism, perhaps even to venture the view that Libya has every chance to become one of the most developed African states. Four, the situation in the North Atlantic Alliance became complicated after Germany and Turkey raised a firm objection against the involvement of NATO in Libya. In fact, only a small number of European countries were engaged in military operations, which would not have been possible at all, had it not been for the support of the US troops present in the Mediterranean region. Last, it is worth considering the role and tasks the European Union and individual member states could play and perform in the 'new' Libya. On the one hand, one has to notice the essential role of this country in holding back a wave of international terrorism, issues related to immigration into the European continent, or the safety of supplies of energy resources to the south of Europe. On the other hand, any form of pressure exerted by European countries on the new government may result in it distancing itself from cooperation with Europe. From the onset, France and Italy have been expressing their interest in developing close cooperation regarding economic or energy joint ventures (Joshi, 2011: 16–19).

The power shift in Libya also undermined the foundations on which the former cooperation between the West and the Arab states rested on. Supporting political stability in North Africa was supposed to resolve the problem of terrorism or immigration to Europe. However, the belief that the endeavours to attain economic liberalisation will lead to moderating political regimes in North Africa proved to be an unsuccessful strategy which was challenged by the citizens of Tunisia, Libya and Egypt. The rationale behind the EU policy (or the policies of individual EU states) to support authoritarian but secular regimes (in the area of political and economic cooperation) was an attempt to prevent radical Islamic groups, which the regime – especially in Egypt – had kept in line, taking control. That assumption proved to be wrong as well, as the revolutions in Tunisia, Libya or Egypt had a more secular character, although Islamic groups did come to power in Egypt. Even though the European policy towards the North African states generally needs to be assessed negatively, elaborating a new vision of policy related to this region will require completely different rules, assumptions and goals. Therefore, both the European Union's policy and the instruments it uses with regard to the states of the region of the Middle East and North Africa (MENA) have to undergo a fundamental change. A step in the right direction will be to come up with and define new priorities for assistance based on four pillars: conditionality, differentiation among the states, support of democracy and emphasis on sustainable socio-economic development. The new policy is supposed to be forged under the banner: more money, more access to the market and more mobility, and its primary aim is to conclude the so-called Deep and Comprehensive Free Trade Agreement (DCFTA). Among the new EU initiatives, one can mention the SPRING programme (Support for Partnership, Reform and Inclusive Growth) where about EUR 350 million has been allocated for the states of the North African region, whereas in the years 2011–2013, within the framework of the European Neighbourhood Policy Instrument, Tunisia and Egypt have been allocated EUR 160 and EUR 450 million respectively. Curiously enough, the poor results yielded by previous programmes have definitely led to abandoning rigidly laid down conditions for providing assistance, and instead of putting forward a list of terms and conditions that the help-seeking countries should satisfy, the European Commission is suggesting a more lenient approach that involves a process of mutual listening ('listening mode'). The purpose of such behaviour is to draw the Arab countries into cooperation with the EU, whereas the relaxation of procedures for providing assistance is aimed at encouraging partners to not give up efforts in favour of political and economic reforms (Balfour, 2012: 27–37).

CONCLUSIONS

While attempting to perform an evaluation of the events in the Arab world initiated by Mohamed Bouazizi's self-immolation in December 2010, it is impossible to detach ourselves from the European perspective we adopt in order to assess political, social and economic changes. Certainly, it is difficult to be an impartial observer in a situation like that; however, it appears that the policy of the European countries regarding the Arab world was totally misguided. The supporting efforts provided by the European politicians to the regimes of Libya or Egypt proved myopic. The policy of Western partners was closely related to their belief that authoritarian regimes would secure certainty, stability and predictability, which would directly translate into good relations, both economic (supplies of energy resources from Libya) and political (the president of Egypt was perceived as a sufficient guarantee against Islamic extremism). It transpired, however, that the policy had weak foundations and Western European politicians misconstrued the intentions of the Arab communities. The overthrow of President Ben Ali left the Western world utterly perplexed, in the same manner as the course of the revolution in Egypt did. It was in Libya where the West finally intervened. Yet the situation in Syria has again surpassed the abilities of the leading global policy powers to collaborate.

It is difficult to unequivocally evaluate the behaviour of the outside world towards events in the Arab world. Initially, the Gulf Arab states were predominantly interested in maintaining the internal stability in their countries, which forced them to make primarily economic concessions and allocate additional funds for social programs. By contrast, the behaviour of the superpowers, especially towards Syria, was motivated by factors that were totally unrelated to the developments in this country. It seems that in this particular case the lack of agreement on military intervention and the overthrow of the Assad regime were the main reasons for the creation of Islamic State, although it is also reasonable to consider the turn of events in Iraq as a contributing factor to the success of this organisation. On the other hand, it is quite uncertain whether such an intervention would have stabilised the situation in Syria and prevented Islamic State from strengthening its position. Events in Libya clearly demonstrate that the overthrow of a dictator does not lead to stability and social peace.

BIBLIOGRAPHY

Arab economies. Throwing money at the street, "The Economist", 10.03.2011.

Balfour R. (2012), *Changes and Continuities in EU-Mediterranean Relations after the Arab Spring*, in: *An Arab Springboard for EU Foreign Policy*, eds. S. Biscop, R. Balfour, M. Emerson, Gent.

Black I. (2011), *Qatar admits sending hundreds of troops to support Libya rebels*, "The Guardian", 26.10.2011.

Bronner E., Slackman M. (2011), *Saudi Troops Enter Bahrain to Help Put Down Unrest*, "The New York Times", 14.03.2011.

Bubnova N., Salem P. (2011), *Arab Spring: View From Within the Region*, "Voenno-Promyshlennyi Kurier", 1.06.2011.

Colombo S. (2012), *The GCC Countries and the Arab Spring. Between Outreach, Patronage and Repression*, Istituto Affari Internazionali, "Working Paper", No. 12.

Daalder I., Stavridis J. (2011), *NATO's Success in Libya*, "The International Herald Tribune", 31.10.2011.

Davidson Ch. (2012), *Fear and Loathing in the Emirates*, http://www.carnegieendowment.org/ 2012/09/18/fear-and-loathing-in-emirates/dusw, 28.09.2012.

Deauville Partnership-IFIs (2011), IMF, Washington.

Drine I. (2012), *Youth Unemployment in the Arab World: What Do We Know? What is the Way Forward?*, http://www.wider.unu.edu/publications/newsletter/articles-2012/en_GB/06-07-2012-Drine, 24.08.2012.

Gardner D. (2011), *Citizens not serfs can save Saudi Arabia*, "Financial Times", 27.02.2011.

Gladstone R. (2011), *U.N. Votes to End Foreign Intervention in Libya*, " The New York Times", 27.10.2011.

Gordon M. (2012), *Iran's Master of Iraq Chaos Still Vexes U.S.*, "The New York Times", 02.10.2012.

Hendrix S. (2012), *For Egypt's new Islamist government, jobs is first priority*, "The Washington Post", 07.07.2012.

Hoffman M., Jamal A. (2012), *The Youth and the Arab Spring*, "Middle East Law and Governance", No. 4.

Ibish H. (2012), *Was the Arab Spring Worth It?*, "Foreign Policy", July/August 2012.

Joshi S. (2011), *Six lessons from Libya*, in: *The Arab Spring. Implications for British Policy*, Conservative Middle East Council, October 2011.

Kerr S. (2011), *Gamble on Libya pays off for Qatar*, "Financial Times", 28.08.2011.

Knickmeyer E. (2011), *The Arab World's Young Army*, "Foreign Policy", January 2011.

Security Council Fails to Adopt Draft Resolution on Syria as Russia and China veto text supporting Arab Leaude's proposed peace plan (2012), http://www.un.org/News/Press/docs/2012/sc10536.doc.htm, 15.10.2012.

Krause-Jackson F., Gaouette N. (2012), *Qatari Leader Calls for Arab-Led Intervention in Syria*, "Bloomberg Businessweek", 25.09.2012.

Libya: Gaddafi must step down, says 'contact group' (2011), http://www.bbc.com/news/world-africa-13058694, 24.11.2012.

Mac Farquhar N., Shadid A. (2012), *Russia and China Block U.N. Action on Crisis in Syria*, "The New York Times", 04.02.2012.

Marcus J. (2011), *Why China and Russia rebuffed the West on Syria*, http://www.bbc.co.uk/news/world-middle-east-15180732, 24.11.2012.

Mausher M. (2011), *Arab Myths and Realities*, http://www.project-syndicate.org/commentary/arab-myths-and-realities, 24.08.2012.

Muasher M. (2011), *How to Achieve Real Reform in the Arab World*, "The Washington Post", 02.02.2011.

Murphy C. (2011), *Saudi Arabia's King Abdullah promises $36 billion in benefits*, "The Christian Science Monitor", 23.02.2011.

Norton-Taylor R., Rogers S., Hopkins N. (2011), *Arab states play limited role in battle against Muammar Gaddafi's regime*, "The Guardian", 22.05.2011.

Odyssey Dawn, Unified Protector? Here's what it means... (2011), http://www.aco.nato.int/page76501852.aspx, 25.11.2012.

Osiewicz P. (2014), *Zmiany społeczno-polityczne w państwach arabskich po 2010 roku: krytyczna analiza stosowanych pojęć*, "Przegląd Politologiczny", No. 1.

Qatar to take part in military action over Libya (2011), "Reuters", 20.03.2011.

Rahimi B. (2012), *Iran's Declining Influence in Iraq*, "The Washington Quarterly", Winter 2012.

Resolution 1973 (2011), http://www.un.org/ga/search/view_doc.asp?symbol=S/RES/1973%282011%29, 23.11.2012.

Roberts D. (2011), *Behind Qatar's Intervention In Libya*, "Foreign Affairs", September 2011.

Saif I. (2011), *Economic Reform in Arab Countries and Escaping from the Trap of the 'Middle Income' Bracket*, "Al-Hayat", 25.10.2011.

Saudi Arabia: Free Political Activists. Secret Police Crackdown on Founders of First Political Party (2011), Human Rights Watch, 20.02.2011, http://www.hrw.org/news/2011/02/19/saudi-arabia-free-political-activists, 28.09.2012.

Sherlock R. (2012), *Saudi millions and special forces expertise turn Syria's rebels into a fighting force*, "The Telegraph", 21.09.2012.

Statement by the NATO Secretary General on Libya (2011), http://www.nato.int/cps/en/natolive/news_79742.htm, 25.11.2012.

Syria crisis: Qatar calls for Arabs to send in troops (2012), http://www.bbc.com/news/world-middle-east-16561493, 23.11.2012.

Tethered by history (2014), "The Economist", 05.07.2014.

The Arab Spring. Has it failed? (2013), "The Economist", 13.07.2013.

Tunisian Islamist in power. Doing well on parole (2012), "The Economist", 07.04.2012.

Ulrichsen K. (2012), *Small States with a Big Role: Qatar and the United Arab Emirates in the Wake of the Arab Spring*, http://www.dur.ac.uk/resources/alsabah/SmallStateswithaBigRole.pdf, 28.10.2012.

Urlichsen K. (2012), *Arab Solutions to Arab Problems? The Changing Regional Role of the Gulf States*, "Russia in Global Affairs", 25.03.2012.

World Economic Outlook Database (2014), http://www.imf.org/external/pubs/ft/weo/2014/02/weodata/index.aspx, 20.11.2014.

Worth R. (2012), *Citing U.S. Fears, Arab Allies Limit Syrian Rebel Aid*, "New York Times", 06.10.2012.

Przemysław OSIEWICZ
Adam Mickiewicz University, Poznań

SOCIAL AND POLITICAL CHANGES IN THE ARAB STATES AFTER 2010: A CRITICAL ANALYSIS OF TERMS APPLIED

INTRODUCTION

The process of social and political change in Arab states, initiated in Tunisia in late 2010, came as a surprise to a number of analysts and commentators. More or less turbulent changes could have been foreseen in one of the authoritarian states of North Africa or West Asia, but no one could have forecasted the domino effect caused by the success of the Tunisian opposition. Over the period of only a year, a majority of Arab states underwent a process of more or less profound political changes, ranging from relatively small changes in the political system (Bahrain and Morocco), to a change of government (Jordan), to the overthrow of authoritarian regimes (Egypt and Tunisia) and civil war (Syria, Yemen and Libya).

In several instances the protests were initially rooted in socio-economic factors (Tunisia and Egypt). A difficult economic situation and the consequent high unemployment rate, especially in the young population, coupled with the falling incomes of the majority of society created circumstances under which even a small spark would suffice to trigger violent social demonstrations. It was only after their brutal suppression by the security services that political postulates were voiced.

Rapid and extensive access to information made mutually exclusive news items appear in the media simultaneously. The events were commented on, not only by professional broadcasters but also by individual participants in the events, or their groups. By this token, popular press and electronic media were using different terms to refer to the processes of change in the Arab states. Some have been adopted, albeit sometimes indiscriminately, by political scientists, including researchers of modern international relations, and have come into use in academic publications.

Over a relatively short period, such notions as 'Arab Spring', 'Arab awakening', 'Arab revolution', 'Arab uprising' and 'e-revolution' spread in the West in particular. All the above notions emphasise the political and liberal character of the changes. Their colloquial rather than academic origin raises serious concerns, however. Have the Arab states really experienced a revolution? How to define the word 'awakening' or 'spring' and place it in theory of politics, and what is an 'e-revolution', after all?

It should be mentioned that the collection of concepts is even more extensive. For instance, Iranian authorities apply their own two terms – the 'Muslim revolution' and 'Islamic awakening', which, in contrast to the terms applied by European and American scholars, primarily stress the role of the religious factor in the changes in the Arab world. The Iranian attitude is therefore significantly different from the Western approach. Even in this case, however, there emerges a concern whether these terms are justified and are academic in nature. Can one speak about a Muslim revolution or Islamic awakening, when the postulates of the protesters in a majority of Arab states did not concern religious aspects? Can the processes of change in the Arab world be compared with the transformation initiated in Iran in 1979?

The objective of this chapter is to provide a critical analysis of the above terms and to attempt to select a notion that will be most appropriate as concerns the character of the changes that have taken place in the Arab states over recent years. The sources are provided by selected, acclaimed monographs and academic papers devoted to the changes in the Arab world after 2010.

THE 'ARAB SPRING'

While observing academic seriousness, it should be mentioned that the most significant events related to the process of political and social changes in the Arab states of North Africa and West Asia occurred in the fall of 2010, winter of 2011 and fall of 2011 rather than in the spring of 2011. By this token, the term 'Arab Spring' is at the very least not accurate when taking into consideration the chronology of events. That has to be said as far as the first associations of numerous people who are not involved in political science or international relations are concerned. It should also be emphasised, however, that this is the most widespread term in the literature on the subject of the changes in the Arab world after 2010.[1]

---

[1] For examples of the use of the term Arab Spring in the literature on the subject, see: J. Armbruster, *Arabska wiosna. Rewolucja w świecie islamskim*, Wrocław 2011; *Arab Spring Dreams: The Next Generation Speaks Out For Freedom and Justice From North Africa to Iran*, eds. N. Weddady, S. Ahmari, New York 2012; H. Dabashi, *The Arab Spring: the End of Postcolonialism*, London 2012; J. R. Bradley, *After the Arab Spring: How Islamists Hijacked the Middle East Revolts*, Basingstoke 2012; L. Noueihed, A. Warren, *The Battle for the Arab Spring: Revolution, Counter-revolution and the Making of a New Era*, London 2012; J. West, *Karama! Journeys Through the Arab Spring: Exhilarating Encounters With Those Who Sparked A Revolution*, London 2011; S. Abudayeh, *Początek wiosny arabskiej w Tunezji, Egipcie, Jemenie, Libii i Bahrajnie*, in: *Bliski Wschód coraz bliżej*, eds. J. Danecki, S. Sulowski, Warszawa 2011; M. A. J. Althani, *The Arab State and the Gulf States: Time to Embrace Change*, London 2012; *Now That We Have Tasted Hope: Voices From the Arab Spring*, ed. D. Abouali, San Francisco 2012; J. Avina, *The Evolution of Corporate Social Responsibility (CSR) in the Arab Spring*, "The Middle East Journal" 2013, Vol. 67, No. 1. This term is also applied in the reports and studies of numerous renowned research

Relatively few scholars have tried to justify the use of this, rather than another term.[2] For instance, Marc Lynch claims that he was the first to use the term 'Arab Spring' in an article published on his blog on 6 January, 2011, but fails to explain why he coined this particular phrase (Lynch, 2013: 9). It can also be noted that an even smaller group of scholars refer to the origins of this term. Some point to European historical sources. In the opinion of eminent Polish Arabist, Jerzy Zdanowski, the notion of an 'Arab Spring' is connected with the European Spring of Nations of 1848 (Zdanowski, 2011: 3). Hamid Dabashi is of the same opinion, as he compares the events in the Arab world in 2011 with the Spring of Nations in the 19th century (Dabashi, 2012: xv). Polish literature on the subject even features the term of 'Arab Spring of Nations', which should be deemed a substantial exaggeration, though (Sasnal, 2011). James L. Gelvin presents a similar outlook, as he additionally refers to the events of the Prague Spring of 1968 and the Arab Spring of 2005. Gelvin observes that this notion emerged in the context of events that occurred in the Middle East immediately following the US invasion of Iraq in 2003 and the announcement of the so-called 'freedom agenda' by George W. Bush (*Fact*, 2012). The 2005 spring was expressed by ousting Saddam Hussein in Iraq, the Cedar Revolution in Lebanon, the elections to local governments in Saudi Arabia, women's protests in Kuwait and the announcement of a democratic presidential election in Egypt (Gelvin, 2012: 32). The changes in Saudi Arabia, Lebanon and Egypt shortly turned out to be superficial and temporary. A question arises, though, whether such comparisons are justified and actually apply to the events in the Arab states after 2010.

The participants of the Spring of Nations not only fought for social or political causes, but mainly for national causes. The presence of the 'nation' in the name of this movement is more than a mere coincidence. Individual European nations were trying to ensure their sovereignty, or unification within new states. The protesters in the Arab countries were merely seeking better living conditions and political changes. Their protests were not national in character. What is more, the Spring of Nations failed, and its achievements gained importance only after many years, whereas the changes in the Arab world were in a large majority of cases successful and brought about permanent political changes. Nevertheless, the concept by Paul W. Schroeder should be borne in mind. He identified two trends within the Spring of Nations. The first one encompassed

---

institutions, such as the Middle East Institute in Washington (www.mei.edu) and International Crisis Group (www.crisisgroup.org).

2 Among others, the following authors use the term of Arab Spring while failing to justify their choice and never seeking its origin: J. R. Bradley, *After the Arab Spring: How Islamists Hijacked the Middle East Revolts*, op. cit.; L. Noueihed, A. Warren, *The Battle for the Arab Spring: Revolution, Counter-revolution and the Making of a New Era*, op. cit.; *Arab Spring Dreams: The Next Generation Speaks Out For Freedom and Justice From North Africa to Iran*, eds. N. Weddady, S. Ahmari, New York 2012.

"communities with a clearly developed national identity that having fallen under alien rule called for their national rights to be recognised in many ways" (Schroeder, 2011: 192). The second trend, on the other hand, included mainly the middle class and "sought to gain political rights and the abolition of restrictions imposed by the state hindering free social, economic and cultural development" (Schroeder, 2011: 192). There are no analogies whatsoever in the case of the first trend between the Spring of Nations and the Arab Spring, but they become pretty obvious in the case of the second one. As it was said, the middle class sought the recognition of their rights during the Spring of Nations, while during the Arab Spring the struggle for improved living conditions and political freedom was mainly fought by the young generation of the unemployed from the Middle East.

In spite of the above reservations, the notion of an 'Arab Spring' is admissible on account of at least three reasons. Firstly, due to how widely it was disseminated in the printed press, everyday language and academic literature. For instance, Mark L. Haas and David W. Lesch claim that the term 'Arab Spring' is highly controversial, especially in the Middle East. Yet, on account of its widespread use, they decided to use it in their publication all the same (Haas, Lesch, 2013: 2). Secondly, this spread of the term follows from its simplicity and symbolic meaning. The associations with the events of the 1848 Spring of Nations can be ignored. Spring, as a time of year, is commonly associated with a period of renewal in nature (Dabashi, 2012: xvii–xviii). In this context, the term 'Arab Spring' can be easily associated with renewal, profound changes in political life and changes of social standards in Arab states. From the opposition's point of view, the rule of President Hosni Mubarak in Egypt and Muammar Gaddafi in Libya can be considered as periods of stagnation, lack of progress, curbed civic freedoms and the ossification of the political arena. The people's revolt in the Middle East and North Africa has produced increased political self-awareness, and political as well as social changes. While this process has not been utterly successful everywhere, as in the case of Egypt, no one questions its importance. Thirdly, a certain analogy can be indicated between the events in Western and Central Europe in 1848 and those in the Middle East and North Africa in 2011. Both are characterised by turbulent social protests against authoritarian rulers who did not take into account social expectations and the need for systemic changes.

THE 'ARAB AWAKENING'

The word 'awakening' is undefinable in terms of political science. One can certainly seek a symbolic meaning of the 'Arab awakening' as a metaphor for the end of social lethargy and political stagnation in the Arab states. Nevertheless, the word 'awakening' is not present in the academic lexicon.

The term 'Arab awakening' was another one to emerge in journalese, to be consequently adopted by a number of scholars (Ramadan, 2012). Adeed Dawisha uses it to describe the process of changes in the Arab world after 2010, as well as the earlier wave of transformations initiated in the 1950s and '60s. For this purpose, he uses the term 'the first Arab awakening' and 'the second Arab awakening'. A. Dawisha takes this opportunity to emphasise the significant fact that some leaders of the first Arab awakening had become dictators who were ousted as a consequence of the second Arab awakening (Dawisha, 2013: 49). It should be noted, however, that the term 'awakening' has not become as widespread as that of 'Arab Spring'. In contrast to the latter, the origin of the 'Arab awakening' cannot be identified as referring to historical events, for instance.

THE 'ARAB REVOLUTIONS'/THE 'ARAB REVOLT'[3]

John R. Bradley can be considered one of the forerunners in using the term 'revolution' to refer to the socio-political events in Egypt. He can even be deemed to be a kind of a visionary, as he wrote about the country standing on the verge of a revolution long before the events of 2011 (Bradley, 2008). A number of other authors, such as Alaa Al Aswany, Jean Pierre Filiu, Lin Noueuihed and Alex Warren use the notion of 'Arab revolution' in their papers, but neither makes a single attempt to define it or at least explain why they have gone for this term (Al-Alswany, 2011).

In the opinion of the abovementioned Hamid Dabashi, "even the term of revolution calls for its redefinition" in the context of recent events in the Arab world (Dabashi, 2012: xvii). Can the events of 2011 be compared to the French or Bolshevik revolution, after all? The definition of the notion of 'revolution' needs to be examined in order to answer this question.

The definition of 'revolution' has clearly expanded over the last hundred years. A number of varieties can be distinguished, such as the industrial revolution, cultural, moral or sexual revolution.

Dabashi claims also that the process which "is developing in the region referred to as the Middle East and beyond determines the end of postcolonial ideological formations" (Dabashi, 2012: xvii). Can this claim be accepted, though? It is worthwhile noting that H. Mubarak, M. Gaddafi and even Zine El Abidine Ben Ali rose to the top echelons of power owing to the civic support they enjoyed, rather than thanks to any recommendation or interference from outside. None of the above rulers came to power due to the support of any foreign powers, as was the case of the Shah of Iran, Mohammad Reza Pahlavi, who

---

[3] For examples of the use of the term Arab revolution, see: J. P. Filiu, *The Arab Revolution: Ten Lessons From the Democratic Uprising*, London 2011; *The New Arab Revolt: What Happened, What It Means, and What Comes Next*, New York 2011.

returned to the throne in 1953 to stay there until 1979, on account of the support openly offered by the United States (Kinzer, 2008). What is more, the direct democracy based on people's committees, created by M. Gaddafi, under no circumstances can be considered to be postcolonial. On the contrary, the postulates in the *Green Book* confirmed a complete break with the colonial past (Al-Kaddafi, 1991). Since the ideological foundations have not changed, the notion of 'revolution' cannot be used. A change of the political elite that was not accompanied by observable, clear ideological and economic transformations, is by no means enough to justify the use of such a meaningful term.

THE 'ARAB UPRISINGS'

Some authors do not use the term 'Arab revolution', but substitute it with the more semantically moderate term 'Arab uprising' (Dalacoura, 2013). Marc Lynch is among those authors who simultaneously use two notions: the 'Arab uprising' and 'revolution'. The very title of his latest book is most meaningful: *The Arab Uprising: The Unfinished Revolutions of the New Middle East* (Lynch, 2013). The same term is also applied by Jerry M. Rosenberg (Rosenberg, 2012). A serious concern emerges here, however, whether the term 'Arab uprising' is universal and can be applied with reference to the events that took place in all Arab countries that witnessed changes after 2010.

The term 'uprising' is definitely too weak to render the nature of the internal conflict in Syria, and too strong to describe the protests in Bahrain and Tunisia. In many countries, including Poland, the word 'uprising' has positive connotations related to a national revolt against alien occupation. Yet in the changes in the Arab countries the factor of striving against an alien presence was absent. All the countries were sovereign. If an uprising is deemed to be an act of refusing allegiance to government, however, this would be the case of the Middle East after 2010. Yet people's protests did not meet one most important criteria of an uprising – that of having clear leadership and adhering to a defined agenda. Syria was the only exception to that. The notion of 'Arab uprising' can also be considered of having little spread and precision, as evidenced by the above mentioned concepts of the definition.

'E-REVOLUTION'

The opposition in the Arab states was clearly given an advantage by the development of modern technologies, especially the Internet and cellular telephones. It is obvious that, even fifteen years ago, organising mass opposition social movements in an authoritarian state in such a rapid manner would have been much more difficult, if at all possible. During the 2010 and 2011 protests, the young generation of Arabs, 'armed' with smartphones and computers, permanently connected with the social media, and communicators played the leading role. It was thanks to them that the whole world watched the protests live and received live coverage evidencing the repression and violence the security services applied against the demonstrators. The accounts and pictures from Tahrir Square in Cairo were posted to the Facebook profiles of demonstrators, there were comments on Twitter and films on YouTube. Social media played an equally important role when organising, for example, the venues and forms of successive demonstrations. By this token, first journalists, and then scholars have begun to use the terms 'e-revolution' or the 'media revolution' (Ghonin 2012). The question emerges, however, of whether mass demonstrations would have taken place anyway, even without modern technologies.

In the past, the lack of widespread and easy access to the means of communication posed no obstacle to those wishing to stage protests against the authorities. All around the world, including in the Middle East, mass demonstrations took place, not only before the Internet or cellular phones came into being, but even before analogue telephones were commonly available. The Iranian revolution of 1978–1979 is the best example here, where the demonstrations against Shah M. R. Pahlavi attracted hundreds of thousands of people (Buchan, 2012). The only difference in 2011 was that the electronic media facilitated immediate transmission of the news to recipients worldwide, making it more difficult for the authorities to deny, for instance, that peaceful demonstrations had been attacked by the security services. At the same time, there was increasing internal pressure on H. Mubarak and M. Gaddafi, but this was not the only factor that decided about the collapse of their regimes. The current situation in Syria is worth noting in this context, where the pressure exerted by the international community is to no avail, despite thousands of audiovisual items evidencing the instances of human rights being breached and documenting violence.

The authorities in the states covered by the wave of protests quickly realised the power of the Internet and the communication potential of cellular phones. In January 2011, the government in Egypt almost immediately limited access to modern media, which was criticised by President Barack Obama (Yafi, 2012: 39–42). The activity of the Egyptian opposition on the Internet had been monitored by the special services even before the protests, and bloggers or journalists criticising the socio-political system, or Hosni Mubarak personally, via the net were routinely arrested (El-Mahdi, Marfleet, 2009: 23–24). It can therefore be assumed that the influence of the electronic media on the dynamics of the 2011 events was significant, but not crucial.

Using the term 'e-revolution' to describe the process of changes in the Arab countries may sound good, but is of no academic value. It is a typical journalistic term that has been indiscriminately adopted by a part of academic circles. One can argue that without the first posts published on Facebook profiles in Tunisia or Egypt there would have been no demonstrations, and the authorities would have concealed, for instance, the fact of self-immolation by Mohamed Bouazizi in the Tunisian town of Sidi Bouzid (Haszczyński, 2012: 5–6). It is true, though, that individual activities were not the actual sparks for the outbursts of social discontent, but they coincided with extremely poor economic, political and social circumstances in the countries flooded by the protests. Modern media clearly influenced the dynamics of the processes of change, but their role should not be exaggerated. Therefore, naming the entire exceptionally complex process of socio-political change in the Arab countries as an 'e-revolution' or 'revolution 2.0' seems wrong. It is a very spectacular, yet misleading, oversimplification.

IRANIAN TERMINOLOGY: THE 'MUSLIM REVOLUTION' AND 'ISLAMIC AWAKENING'

In the case of the term 'Muslim revolution', comparisons with the 1979 revolution in Iran are unavoidable. When referring to the overthrow of the Shah and the introduction of the theocratic system, the Iranian authorities officially use the term of the 'Islamic revolution'. Comparing the events in Iran to those in other Arab countries can, or even should, raise serious doubts. The outcome of the protests and strife in the Arab states after 2010 is not even remotely related to the assumptions and outcomes of the Iranian revolution, rooted in the complex ideology of Ayatollah Ruhollah Khomeini, which was based on the fundamentals of Shia Islam (Khomeini, 2000). The Arab states were not dominated by any ideology to set the direction and scale for the changes, the way Khomeinism did for the political and social changes in Iran (Ożarowski, 2006: 42–49).

The events in Iran in 1979 and those in the Arab states in 2011 certainly share one feature. In both cases the protests resulted in authoritarian rulers being ousted. In Iran, this concerned Shah M. R. Pahlavi, whereas in Egypt – H. Mubarak, in Libya – M. Gaddafi, in Yemen – Ali Abdullah Saleh, and in Tunisia – Z. A. Ben Ali. In contrast to the Iranian scenario, however, the new authorities in the Arab states did not manage to stabilise the political situation, or even to take full control over the entire country (Egypt, Libya and Yemen). What is more, the 2011 protesters accuse their new authorities of having satisfied themselves with changing the political elite, while failing to transform internal politics. This is particularly notable in Egypt, which continues to be shaken by successive waves of protests and riots practically every couple of months.

Another difference between the Iranian Islamic revolution and the transformation in the Arab states concerns the scale of changes. In revolutionary Iran the change involved more than the political elite, and encompassed also the economic elite and intellectual circles. A profound, radical, political change took place, as confirmed by the stipulations of the 1979 *Constitution of the Islamic Republic of Iran*. By virtue of the *Constitution*, Iran was transformed into a theocratic state, or into an Islamic democracy, as Iranian authorities and scholars name it.

Iranian authorities, including the Supreme Leader Ali Chamenei, among others, use the official term of an 'Islamic awakening'. In contrast to the terms used in Western literature, the 'Islamic awakening' clearly emphasises the religious rather than political nature of the changes in the Arab states. Yet in the vast majority of the Arab states, the protesters did not call for freedom of religion, or equal rights for any religious groups. The only exception was Syria and Bahrain, where an element of competition between Shia and Sunni Muslims (in the latter) and between many different religious groups (in the former) could be observed. It should also be clearly stressed that no Arab state witnessed a strong desire to be transformed into a religious state, as was the case of Iran in 1979.

The main reason for this can be sought in the predominant religion. With the exception of Bahrain, the process of change in the Middle East and North Africa mainly involved countries dominated by Sunnis. In contrast to Shia Muslims, Sunnis are in favour of a clear separation between political and spiritual authorities. The utterly different concepts of the authority and role of religious leaders in political life draw a dividing line across the Muslim world. Whereas the Shia, who clearly predominated in Iran, were inclined to accept a theocratic system and the consequent rule of the Ayatollahs, the Sunni in Egypt and Libya never made such demands, for doctrinal reasons.

Another aspect of the transformation in the Arab states was the role of religious law in the socio-political system. Demands for an increased role of religious law in social life were voiced in Egypt, Libya and Tunisia, among others, but nowhere did they aim to transform republics into theocracies. The demands made by a part of the opposition circles mainly concerned the needs for moral renewal and the introduction of some restrictions, such as the absolute ban on the consumption of alcohol, or a strict dress code for women.

As evidenced by the above arguments, the term 'Islamic awakening' in relation to the changes in the Arab states seems unjustified. It brings erroneous associations with the Islamic revolution in Iran, whereas the Arab states are not copying Iran but following their own path of change. The only common denominator for both processes is that authoritarian leaders were ousted. The religious aspect plays a secondary role in these Arab states, unlike in Iran, where it was of supreme importance.

CONCLUSIONS

The literature on the subject reveals the absence of in-depth considerations on the terms applied with reference to the political and social changes in the Arab world after 2010. It has been evidenced that scholars apply a variety of terms but, unfortunately, do not attempt to define them or even justify their choice of the notion. By this token, journalistic terms have uninhibitedly seeped into academic publications. While they certainly simplify the message and are understood by a majority of recipients, they make no contribution to the theory of politics or to the theory of international relations. They are merely descriptive notions the literature on the subject abounds in.

The authors' selection of the term they would apply in the analysis or description of the process of socio-political changes in the Middle East and North Africa is in practical terms decisive for what aspects will be stressed by them. For instance, use of the term 'Arab revolution' or 'Arab Spring' imposes certain obligations. The former stresses the violence and forceful aspect of the political turning point, which actually corresponds to the events in Syria and Libya. The latter term can suggest the positive aspect of political transformation. It is free of violence, and in contrast to 'revolution' it brings evolutionary associations.

The term 'Islamic awakening', officially applied by Iranian authorities, raises considerable concerns. The reference to the Islamic revolution in Iran is as explicit as it is unjustified. In contrast to the events in Iran, the changes in the Arab states did not and do not have a religious aspect. The Arab states are following their own paths of change, and are not following Iran in any way other than that they have also ousted their authoritarian leaders. For the same reasons, the justification of the term 'Muslim revolution' should be challenged. What is more, the social, political and economic changes in the Arab states were neither as violent nor as radical as those in Iran at the end of the 1970s.

It is practically impossible to define any of the above presented terms. All of them are symbolical and indefinable in nature. The terms incorporating such words as 'spring', 'awakening' and 'revolution' do have defined meanings which get lost, though, when combined with the adjective 'Arab'. What is more, their application in academic literature may sometimes result in unintended distortions or oversimplifications, as in the case of the term 'Arab revolution'. The events of 2010–2012 cannot be compared to the French or Bolshevik revolutions. Political and social changes in the Arab states have not been as complex and have not brought about profound systemic changes, yet. They have only been about the rapid change of the ruling elite.

It should be noted that the term 'Arab Spring' is the most widespread one. While imperfect, of all the other notions analysed in this paper, this term is the best expression for the socio-political changes in the Arab states. It is also free from any evaluative approach, in contrast to the terms 'Arab revolution', or 'Arab uprising'.

BIBLIOGRAPHY

Althani M. A. J. (2012), *The Arab State and the Gulf States: Time to Embrace Change*, London.

Al-Aswany A. (2011), *On the State of Egypt: What Caused the Revolution*, Edinburgh.

Al-Kaddafi M. (1991), *Zielona Książka*, Trypolis.

Armbruster J. (2011), *Arabska wiosna. Rewolucja w świecie islamskim*, Wrocław.

Avina J. (2013), *The Evolution of Corporate Social Responsibility (CSR) in the Arab Spring*, "The Middle East Journal", Vol. 67, No. 1.

Bradley J. R. (2008), *Inside Egypt: The Land of the Pharaohs on the Brink of a Revolution*, Basingstoke.

Bradley J. R. (2012), *After the Arab Spring: How Islamists Hijacked the Middle East Revolts*, Basingstoke.

Buchan J. (2012), *Days of God: The Revolution in Iran and Its Consequences*, London.

Dabashi H. (2012), *The Arab Spring: the End of Postcolonialism*, London.

Dalacoura K. (2013), *The Arab Uprisings Two Years On: Ideology, Sectarianism and the Changing Balance of Power in the Middle East*, "Insight Turkey", Vol. 15, No. 1.

Dawisha A. (2013), *The Second Arab Awakening: Revolution, Democracy, and the Islamist Challenge from Tunis to Damascus*, New York.

Fact Sheet: President Bush's Freedom Agenda Helped Protect the American People (2012), http://georgewbush-whitehouse.archives.gov/infocus/freedomagenda/, 12.02.2012.

Filiu J. P. (2011), *The Arab Revolution: Ten Lessons From the Democratic Uprising*, London.

Fundamentals of the Islamic Revolution: Selections from the Thoughts and Opinions of Imam Khomeini (2000), Tehran.

Gelvin J. L. (2012), *The Arab Uprisings: What Everyone Needs to Know*, Oxford.

Ghonim W. (2012), *Revolution 2.0*, New York.

Haas M. L., Lesch D. W. (2013), *Introduction*, in: *The Arab Spring: Change and Resistance in the Middle East*, eds. M. L. Haas, D. W. Lesch, Boulder.

Haszczyński J. (2012), *Mój brat obalił dyktatora*, Wołowiec.

Kinzer S. (2008), *All the Shah's Men: An American Coup and the Roots of Middle East Terror*, Hoboken.

Lynch M. (2013), *The Arab Uprising: The Unfinished Revolutions of the New Middle East*, New York.

Marfleet P., El-Mahdi R. (2009), *Introduction*, in: *Egypt: The Moment of Change*, eds. R. El-Mahdi, P. Marfleet, London and New York.

Noueihed L., Warren A. (2012), *The Battle for the Arab Spring: Revolution, Counter-revolution and the Making of a New Era*, London.

Ożarowski R. (2006), *Ideologia na Bliskim Wschodzie*, Gdańsk.

Ramadan T. (2012), *The Arab Awakening: Islam and the New Middle East*, London.

Rosenberg J. M. (2012), *Aftermath of the Arab Uprisings: The Rebirth of the Middle East*, Lanham.

Sasnal P. (2011), *Bliski Wschód bliższy niż Wschód. Polska wobec arabskiej wiosny ludów*, "Polski Przegląd Dyplomatyczny", No. 1.

Schroeder P. W. (2011), *Polityka międzynarodowa, pokój i wojna 1815–1914*, in: *Dziewiętnasty wiek*, ed. T. C. W. Blanning, Warszawa.

Supreme Leader Meets with Participants of International Conference on Islamic Awakening, http://www.leader.ir/langs/en/?p=contentShow&id=10215, 15.03.2013.

West J. (2011), *Karama! Journeys Through the Arab Spring: Exhilarating Encounters With Those Who Sparked A Revolution*, London.

Yafi W. S. (2012), *Inevitable Democracy In the Arab World: New Realities in An Ancient World*, New York.

Zdanowski J. (2011), *Bliski Wschód 2011: bunt czy rewolucja?*, Kraków.

Sebastian WOJCIECHOWSKI
Adam Mickiewicz University, Poznań

WHAT ARE THE CURRENT IMPEDIMENTS AND THREATS TO DEMOCRATISATION IN EGYPT?

The current transformation Egypt is experiencing can be analysed in terms of many different research concepts. They provide a more or less exhaustive picture of the individual processes, determinants and events. Whereas many research concepts focus on the issues related to the Arab Spring, democratisation and the transformations the Middle East is undergoing, much less attention is paid to presenting different factors that pose a threat or impede democratisation in Egypt. This paper aims to illustrate them briefly and attempts to systemise these factors.

The first point of reference is provided by the considerations Samuel Huntington presented in his study *The Third Wave. Democratization in the Late Twentieth Century* (Huntington, 1991). Discussing the factors that are conducive to anti-democratic tendencies, Huntington points to seven fundamental ones, namely:
1) poor identification of the elite, or society with democratic values;
2) an economic crisis or breakdown;
3) social and political polarisation;
4) conservative groups attempting to exclude populist and left-wing movements, as well as the parties of lower classes, from power;
5) the collapse of law and order under the influence of terrorism or armed uprisings;
6) intervention and occupation by a non-democratic state;
7) the avalanche effect of successive states adopting non-democratic solutions.

The following questions can be asked here: to what extent have the above-mentioned factors occurred in Egypt? Do they pose a threat to Egyptian democracy? Can they contribute to diluting the democratic tendencies in Egypt further in the future?

The first element to be examined concerns the poor sense of identification of the elite, or society with democratic values. In the case of Egypt, this is a consequence of a multitude of factors, for instance the dearth of democratic traditions, related to the long predominance of a powerful authoritarian system in Egypt. This is evidenced by a number of premises, such as the persecution of the opposition or the less than democratic legal solutions (such as the constitutional provisions from 1971 and their subsequent modifications) (Kienle, 2000; Ruthendorf, 2008). They provided for a state of emergency to continue starting in 1981, and for Hosni Mubarak to be the only presidential candidate from 1981 to 2000, who enjoyed the official "universal support" of the society (Lipa, 2013). Similar practices occurred before (for instance at the time of Anwar Sadat) and later, as evidenced by the bloody 'crackdown' by President Abdel Fattah el-Sisi against the *Muslim Brotherhood*, or the decrees issued by President Mohamad Morsi in November 2012. They stipulated that no official body, including the Supreme Court, could reverse a decision taken by the Head of State until a new Constitution was drafted. This was also connected with the ousting of a number of high-ranking officers, including the Attorney General, which triggered a wave of social protests and harsh criticism. The winner of the Nobel Peace Prize, Mohamed El-Baradei wrote on *Twitter*, that M. Morsi was a "new pharaoh", while the spokesman of the UN *High Commissioner for Human Rights* expressed his concern that the above-mentioned decrees would "adversely impact on the status of human rights and rule of law in Egypt." Replying to that, President M. Morsi declared: "I fulfil obligations to God and the people, and before making decisions I consult them with everybody" (*Prezydent*, 2012).

The poor sense of identification of a large part of Egypt's society with democratic principles is also the result of other factors, such as the economic situation, cultural and religious circumstances, strong position of the army, low levels of education and the influence of radical circles.

Another significant factor indicated by Huntington involves the economic crisis, which in the case of Egypt was the outcome of internal difficulties and the global crunch that started in 2007. This has influenced broad sectors of Egypt's economy, including tourism, the energy industry and agriculture (for instance the cotton harvest). This is also reflected in the fluctuations of Egypt's GDP.

Table 1. Fluctuations of GDP in Egypt and other selected countries covered by the Arab Revolution

Country	2008	2010	2012	2014*
Egypt	7.2	5.1	2.2	2.3
Yemen	3.6	7.7	2.4	5.1
Libya	2.7	5.0	104.5	–7.8
Syria	4.5	3.4	...	...
Tunisia	4.5	2.9	3.6	3.0

... no data available;
* estimated data.

Source: *World Economic Outlook. Recovery Strengthens, Remains Uneven* (2014), International Monetary Fund, Washington, p. 185, http://www.imf.org/external/pubs/ft/weo/2010/01/pdf. Quoted after: *Rocznik Strategiczny. Przegląd sytuacji politycznej, gospodarczej i wojskowej w środowisku międzynarodowym Polski* (2014), Warszawa, p. 267.

The gravity of the economic problems in Egypt is also evidenced by the fact that nearly half of Egyptians live on the brink of poverty, accompanied by high inflation and a very low income in part of society (53% live on under 2 dollars a day). A report prepared in 2014 by banking analysts showed that Egypt requires an immediate loan of USD 2 bln in order to cover its energy costs, among other things. Over the next six months this amount will increase to USD 9 bln.

Another symptom of economic difficulties is famine and malnutrition. A report by the UN *World Food Programme* (WFP) indicates that malnutrition in Egypt may stunt the growth of 31% of children between six months and five years of age, one of the highest rates in the world. The WFP also found in 2009 that malnutrition reduced Egypt's GDP by about 2%. One in five Egyptians faces food insecurity and 5% of the population suffers from it and "a growing number of people can't afford to purchase enough nutritious food" (Pipes, 2014). This is a result of different factors, for instance flawed government policies of consistently favouring urban over rural areas, leading to a lack of financial support, cock-eyed subsidies, corruption, and black markets. Another reason is imports of food, which is rather surprising, given the fact that Egypt was self-sufficient in this respect for years. At present, however, it has to import around 60% of its food.

Graph 1. The double burden of malnutrition: adult obesity and child stunting in selected countries

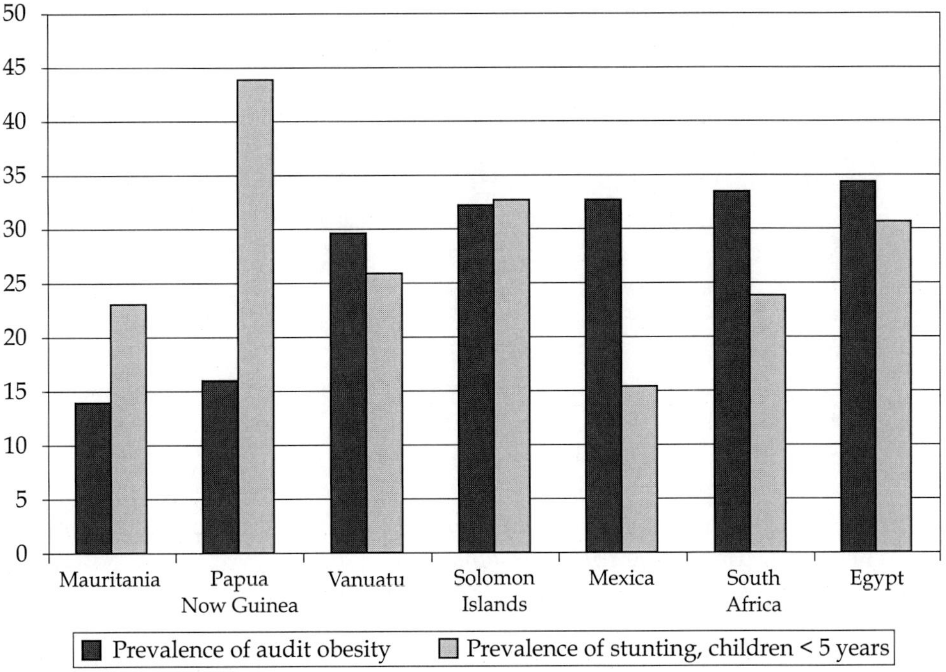

Source: D. Pipes (2014), *Hunger Growls in Egypt*, "The Washington Times", 6.10.2014.

On the one hand, economic difficulties exacerbate social frustration and dissatisfaction, on the other, they significantly contribute to growing authoritarian or fundamentalist tendencies. This translates into increasing unemployment, declining foreign investment and income from the tourist sector aggravating socio-economic problems even further.

The third factor concerns the increasing polarisation of society in political, social, financial and religious terms. Its most expressive illustration is the difference between the group of reformers and that of conservatives. Some experts are justified to observe that the "transformations in Egypt have shown first and foremost the presence of profound ideological differences in society and the lack of agreement on the future direction of transformations. Power has been taken by the military despite the guise of civil political institutions" (*Rocznik,* 2014). This is a return to the situation from 1952–2012, when the army played a very important (albeit covert) role. The strong position of the army does not result solely from its political and social influence, but also from its prestige, as well as its economic influence, related to the fact that the army oversees considerable assets, such as businesses and farms.

A number of other important questions arise here. How long will the dominant role of the army continue to be approved of by society? Will not the future bring more mass protests? How will army officers respond to them? Are the present authorities able to tackle the highly complex economic and social issues? Will they opt for political reforms? It is beyond the scope of this study to answer these questions, and it would be both highly complex and fraught with a large margin of forecasting error. Nevertheless, the above-mentioned issues are strictly related to the fourth of S. Huntington's factors, that is the attempt to exclude certain groups and circles from ruling. This mainly concerns fundamentalist, left-wing and populist movements. In Egypt, they were marginalised as a result of legal processes, as well as by forceful measures (such as the ousting of President M. Morsi). This sparked numerous protests staged by the *Muslim Brotherhood*, and resulted in brutal clashes with law enforcement forces and mass arrests. For instance, the outcome of just one demonstration in Cairo on 14 August, 2013, was 638 fatalities and 4,000 injured participants (according to official statistics).

The marginalisation of parts of society is also evidenced by the persecution of Christians, mainly Copts, in Egypt. The 10–12 million-strong Christian community has suffered different forms of oppression, ranging from people being set on fire, to damage to property, to kidnapping, to coercing people to leave the country (in recent years this was the case for over 200,000 persons), to wrecking churches. According to the 2015 *World Index of Religious Persecution*, Egypt ranks 23rd in this respect (it ranked 22nd in 2014) (*Open*, 2015).

There is also a considerable risk that the removal from power of President M. Morsi and the breakdown of the *Muslim Brotherhood*, accompanied by intensifying socio-economic problems, may boost the support for and the activities of fundamentalist circles, resulting in further destabilisation of the internal situation (element five).

The sixth factor that is conducive to anti-democratic tendencies, namely intervention or occupation by a non-democratic state, did not occur in Egypt. This is not to mean that no attempts were made to influence the political stage of Egypt by external entities, such as the US, the European Union, Muslim countries and radical Islamist movements of a transnational range.

The final factor S. Huntington mentions is the avalanche effect of a destabilised internal situation and escalating religious fundamentalism in successive states of the Middle East. In S. Huntington's opinion, the avalanche effect means that anti-democratic trends that emerge in one country can inspire or enhance similar changes in other states in the region. This is the mechanism of 'reproduction' we are currently facing in Syria, Iraq, Somalia, Libya and Egypt, among others (Huntington, 1991).

The avalanche effect in Egypt can also be examined in the context of the rapidly escalating violence and successive waves of political transformations following one another. Daniel Pipes estimates that toppling H. Mubarak in 2011 took 18 days and involved the death of around 850 persons, whereas it took four days to overthrow M. Morsi and caused the death of around 40 persons (Pipes, 2013). Is the present situation the end of the tumultuous transformations in Egypt and the end of the avalanche effect? It is difficult to answer this question unanimously, yet a lot seems to suggest that further violent changes in Egypt are likely.

Examining the events in Egypt vis-à-vis the overall situation in the Middle East, the essential role of Egypt in this region should be stressed. This concerns the geopolitical, geo-economic and geo-strategic dimensions, as well as Egypt's ambition to act as a leader in this part of the world. The internal weakening of Egypt is therefore taken advantage of by other countries that compete against Egypt for influence in the region (for instance Iran or Israel). It is also beneficial to some of Egypt's neighbours, who can accomplish their own interests more easily. This is illustrated by Egypt-Ethiopia relations, and the dispute over their use of the Nile's water. This competition illustrates the conflict over water, where one country seeks to acquire the greatest resources of potable water at the expense of other countries. In the case of Egypt and Ethiopia, the conflict concerns the water supplied by the Nile, and the decision made by the Ethiopian authorities to erect a dam across the Blue Nile, which may result in diminished water flow to Egypt from 55 to 40 billion cubic meters.

The German sociologist and economist Gunnar Heinsohn has come up with a very interesting theory of the reasons for anti-democratic trends, including wars, revolutions and terror. In his opinion, the fundamental source of the above-mentioned phenomena is provided by a disproportionate number of young men (*youth bulge*) without prospects for the future. Although frequently qualified, with a permanent residence and means to live, they do not have access to "a sufficient number of respectable social positions" (Heinsohn, 2003). Therefore, their attitudes are the outcome of overpopulation, shortage of resources and land, as well as of the dearth of long-term prospects. This is also the case of Egypt, where there is an acute sense of the lack of prospects for the youth bulge. This is evidenced by the fact that 28% of young people live in poverty there, and a further 24% live just above the poverty line. At present, Egypt ranks 15th in the world in terms of population, and it is forecasted to rank 14th in 2050, when its population will amount to around 114 mln. The importance of the youth bulge is therefore sure to be even greater.

Egyptian political writer, Hany Ghoraba, a businessman and freelance journalist, in the book entitled *Egypt's Arab Spring. The long and winding road to democracy* (Ghoraba, 2013) points to the following numerous and diverse factors that influence the transformations in Egypt, including the anti-democratic processes there:

– the balance of power among Islamists, liberals and revolutionaries, the silent majority and the Egyptian army;
– the end of the peaceful nature of the revolution;
– the role of the Supreme Council of the Armed Forces (SCAF);
– the chaos in Egypt during the Arab Spring: armed robberies, organised crime, assaults on banks and money transports, murders, kidnappings, ransoms, arson, vandalism, etc.;
– the presidential system;
– weak Egyptian liberalism, for example: lack of unified leadership, lack of proper political and social representatives, lack of common goals, Islamist apologists and pseudo-Liberals, divisive media outlets and lack of a clear message;
– Egyptian Leftists' dilemma;
– Islamists' religious exploitation of Egypt;
– the Egyptian media as a culprit;
– the USA, the *Muslim Brotherhood* and the Qatari connection;
– Egyptian Israeli relations;
– challenges faced by Egyptian youth and wars in general;
– the problems of minorities.

Due to the highly limited scope of this study, it concentrates solely on selected factors that pose a threat to Egyptian democracy. These considerations are only the starting point for further studies into these highly interesting, yet extremely complex issues. Their exploration will surely facilitate better recognition of the threats to modern democracy, and better understanding of the situation of Egypt and the Middle East.

Further academic considerations have to encompass a broad spectrum of various factors operating in Egypt, ranging from political, social and religious ones to matters of culture, economy, history, mentality and geopolitics, accounting for their various and numerous interrelations.

BIBLIOGRAPHY

Bunt czy rewolucja? Przemiany na Bliskim Wschodzie po 2010 roku (2012), eds. K. Górak-Sosnowska, K. Pachniak, Łódź.

Coppedge M. (2012), *Democratization and Research Methods*, New York.

Ghoraba H. (2013), *Egypt's Arab Spring. The long and winding road to democracy*, Pau.

Heinsohn G. (2003), *Söhne und Weltmacht. Terror im Aufstieg und Fall der Nationen*, Zürich.

Huntington S. (1991), *The Third Wave. Democratization in the Late Twentieth Century*, Oklahoma.

Kienle E. (2000), *A Grand Delusion. Democracy and Economic Reform in Egypt*, London–New York.

Lipa M. (2013), *Autorytaryzm na arabskim Bliskim Wschodzie, Egipt w latach 1981–2010*, Warszawa.

Open Doors: Egypt (2015), http://www.opendoors.org.au, 13.03.2015.

Pipes D. (2014), *Hunger Growls in Egypt*, "The Washington Times", 6.10.2014.

Prezydent Egiptu sam zwiększył swoją władzę (2012), "Głos Wielkopolski," 24–25.11.2012.

Rocznik Strategiczny. Przegląd sytuacji politycznej, gospodarczej i wojskowej w środowisku międzynarodowym Polski (2014), Warszawa.

Ruthendorf B. (2008), *Egypt after Mubarak. Liberalism, Islam and Democracy in the Arab World*, New Jersey.

Tilly C. (2007), *Democracy*, New York.

World Economic Outliook. Recovery, Strengthens, Remains Uneven (2014), International Monetary Fund, Washington.

Przemysław OSIEWICZ

Adam Mickiewicz University, Poznań

THE CAUSES AND COURSE OF THE POLITICAL TRANSFORMATIONS IN EGYPT IN 2011–2014

INTRODUCTION

The political crises in Egypt in 2011 and 2013 constituted an essential element in the entire process of politico-social transformations in the Arab states of North Africa and the Middle East. The ousting of the influential President Hosni Mubarak in February 2011 had a special and symbolic meaning for both Egyptians and the citizens of other Arab states. Therefore, the victory of the demonstrators in Tahrir Square was significant in both its domestic and regional dimensions. The Egyptian success provided a clear incentive for the societies of other authoritarian Arab states, such as Syria, Libya and Yemen.

In this context, it is crucial to answer the question of what social, political and economic factors brought about such a rapid political change in Egypt. From the point of view of 2015, is it really true that the ruling elite was replaced, or were the 2011 events largely inspired by the circles close to President H. Mubarak, thereby being only the manifestation of internal competition inside the army and the National Democratic Party (NDP) belonging to the regime?

The purpose of this paper is to answer the above question on the basis of a thorough analysis of the causes and the course of the political changes in Egypt in 2011–2014. The starting point is marked by the protests that commenced in Tahrir Square in January 2011, while the ending – by Abd al-Fattah al-Sisi being elected Egypt's president. In this context, the analysis of the political crisis in July 2013 is especially significant, which resulted in the deposition of the representatives of the Muslim Brotherhood, including President Muhammad Morsi. The object of this research encompasses political, economic and social causes.

OUTLINE OF THE SOCIO-POLITICAL SITUATION IN EGYPT RULED BY HOSNI MUBARAK

The events that took place in Tahrir Square at the turn of January 2011 stemmed, among other things, from the events that had occurred nearly fifty years earlier. In 1952, a group of Free Officers coerced the King of Egypt, Farouk, to abdicate and leave the country. Farouk abdicated in favour of his son – Fuad II. One year later, a republic was proclaimed in Egypt, the Regency Council was dissolved and President Muhammad Nagib took power. These events radically changed

49

the political system in Egypt. Afaf Lufti as-Sajjid Marsot was right to observe that "for the first time in over two thousand years, since the time of the pharaohs, Egypt came to be ruled by the Egyptian. The Turkish-Circassian monarchy, upheld and strengthened by the British military, passed away" (Marsot, 2009: 147). The Egyptian gaining influence on state policies did not automatically mean the end of problems, however. On the contrary, it was to turn out that the activities of successive rulers resulted in a profound division of Egyptian society. Members of state elites had connections and accumulated capital which ensured their political and financial advantage over other citizens. President Gamal Nasser was an honourable exception in this respect, whose banking account amounted to merely 610 Egyptian pounds at the time of his death (Stępniewska-Holzer, Holzer, 2006: 116).

The above-mentioned state elites were dominated by the military whose contribution to the toppling of the monarchy ensured them the gratitude and exceptional favour of the majority of citizens. This was the case as early as during the administration of President G. Nasser who advocated the presence of the army in the government in order to limit the Muslim Brotherhood's potential assuming power. This issue was one of the reasons for the political confrontation between G. Nasser and M. Nagib – a proponent of the democratisation of political life in Egypt. It was G. Nasser who emerged victorious from this trial of strength and replaced M. Nagib as president of Egypt in 1954.

Gilbert Achcar is justified to note that the army became the foundation for power in Egypt then (Achcar, 2013: 149). The military gained a direct influence on the policy of the state and on its economic development. The Egyptian army gained in importance during G. Nasser's presidency and reinforced its position during the administrations of successive presidents – Anwar Sadat and H. Mubarak. In the political system that emerged, staying in power was guaranteed either by good relations with the army or by allowing the military to direct participation in the executive. Additionally, at the time of A. Nasser, new political elites were introducing elements of socialism to the system and followed the policy of rapprochement with the Soviet Union (Ginat, 1997: 195). The reforms in the field of economy did not help solve the most urgent issues thereby forcing Egypt's authorities to alter their policies in the mid-1970s.

President A. Sadat opened Egyptian market to foreign investments. The reform package was named *infitah* – 'the Opening' (El-Naggar, 2009: 34). After the assassination of A. Sadat in October 1981, however, the economic situation began to deteriorate. "During the 1980s, Mubarak blocked the process of economic liberalization launched by his predecessor and restored a degree of the 'economic planning' that had been common under Nasser" (Soliman, 2012: 45). Consequently, in the first half of the 1980s, Egypt struggled with complex economic problems, including the instable economic growth. A high unemployment level, accompanied by a rapid decline in budget revenue, brought about the necessity to curb expenditure, particularly in the social sector, and reduce state subsidies. Michał Lipa rightly notes that it "was a blow to the unwritten social contract under which the Egyptian, in return for the relatively good living conditions they could not afford otherwise, did not protest against authoritarian political relations. When this contract was breached, the primary factor that legitimised the undemocratic rule of Mubarak and his regime began to disappear, thereby forcing them to resort to violence more often" (Lipa, 2014: 9). Bruce K. Rutherford expresses a similar outlook saying that "since the 1960s, the regime had made a commitment to provide citizens with a wide range of services including jobs in the public sector and the civil service as well as substantial subsidies on food, electricity, gasoline, public transportation, education, and medical care. The regime's legitimacy was grounded in providing these benefits. However, the economy simply did not generate sufficient wealth or state revenue to sustain these services, particularly as Egypt's population grew dramatically in the 1980s and 1990s" (Rutherford, 2008: 1).

In the early 21st century the movement of Kefaya – 'Enough' played a highly important role in Egyptian politics. This and other collaborating movements were referred to as *Harakat al-Tag'eer* – 'Movements for Change'. For the first time in years Egyptians took part in anti-government protests. While they were not as massive as those in 2011, they attracted the attention of domestic circles as well as numerous commentators abroad. Members of the Kefaya movement staged street protests in December 2004, when President H. Mubarak implied that he would like to stay in office for the fifth term. Additionally, the circles close to the government were releasing the news that H. Mubarak was planning a family succession of presidential power and he was gradually preparing his younger son, Gamal, for the office. Kefaya's protests were soon supported by some influential professional circles, such as academics, writers, journalists, artists and students. They were all in favour of political changes in Egypt, forming the Egyptian Movement for Change (Al-Sayyid, 2009: 45). Kefaya's members made two fundamental demands. One was H. Mubarak's resignation from running in the next presidential elections and the second – the guarantees that his son, Gamal, would not run either (Tadros, 2014: 149).

It should be clearly remarked here, however, that in the opinion of some authors, the idea of passing the office on to Gamal Mubarak did not come from the President or his son, but from his closest political advisors trying to ensure their own future in case H. Mubarak retired or died (Amin, 2011: 149). President's adherents probably feared that the lack of agreement over the succession and of a successor that had clearly been indicated by H. Mubarak himself, would result in an uncontrollable competition within the ruling NDP – *al-Hizb al-Watani al-Dimuqrati*.

Kefaya lost in significance after the 2005 presidential elections. Its weaknesses involved internal divisions and lacking political experience of a majority of activists (El-Mahdi, 2009: 88). H. Mubarak learned his lesson from the conflict with Kefaya and strengthened the repression apparatus and control over the media. Simultaneously, political and social influence of the Muslim Brotherhood was growing as the Brotherhood succeeded in the 2005 elections and began cooperation with the Kefaya movement's leaders (Zahid, 2012: 125).

The Brotherhood was an attractive political alternative for people from outside the establishment circles, and in particular for the opponents to secularisation, for everybody interested in curbing the army's influence in the country as well as for young unemployed Egyptians. For years, the Egyptian authorities had been trying to eliminate the Brotherhood or at least seriously limit its influence, but their efforts were soon to have turned out largely inefficient. Still, it is worth noting that in the first decade of its presidency, H. Mubarak tried to involve the Muslim Brotherhood in a broader political coalition, primarily aiming at the elimination of fundamentalist groups, such as *Tandheem al-Jihad* and *Gamaah al-Islamiyah* (Bokhari, Senzai, 2013: 51). Andrzej Purat notes that "during Hosni Mubarak's rule, the Muslim Brothers led charitable and educational activities which had the official approval. At the same time, they were trying to register a political party affiliated to their association. The authorities declined, however, because Egyptian law on political parties did not allow an organisation with religious connotations to be registered" (Purat, 2014: 223).

H. Mubarak first realised that the Muslim Brotherhood was reviving in Egypt seeing the results of the parliamentary elections in November 2005. Despite various restrictions and limitations imposed on the Brotherhood, such as limiting the number of their eligible candidates to 150 persons, the movement succeeded in ensuring as many as 88 mandates, accounting for approximately 20% of seats in the parliament. Members of so-called secular political groups won only 14 mandates, accounting for 3% of all seats (Naguib, 2009: 155156).

Walid Kazziha claims that before January 2011, Egyptian opposition could be divided into two groups. One group included political powers that rejected the political system operating during H. Mubarak's presidency or refused to observe its rules. The latter included the National Front Party, Kefaya and Mohamed el-Baradei, among others. The former group encompassed those who were trying to take advantage of the weaknesses of the political system and sought to destabilise it on purpose, for instance the Muslim Brotherhood, the Wafd Party and Tegammu Party (Kazziha, 2013: 30). The opposition was divided, different groups had different goals and it was difficult to imagine any organised force capable of ousting H. Mubarak and his adherents after thirty years in power. The more so as internal security services were exceptionally well-organised and the President was additionally supported by the army, which in Egypt enjoys great respect and extensive politico-economic influence. It was about to turn out, however, that it was not an organised political force that posed the greatest challenge to the regime, but a mass of individuals who were dissatisfied with the situation in the country. The core of this spontaneous group were young people who decided to follow their peers in Tunisia and replace the ruling elite.

THE COURSE OF THE 2011 REVOLUTION

On 25 January, 2011, thousands of people took to the streets of Cairo, Alexandria and many other cities in Egypt. The day was spontaneously named the 'Day of Anger'. Crowds of demonstrators gathered in Tahrir Square, chanting a slogan that expressed the core of social demands and expectations: "'*aish, hurriyya, karama insaniyya*' – bread, freedom, human dignity" (Clarke, 2013: 197). The unexpectedly brutal response of the police and security services only added to the strength of the protests and their further expansion. According to Bahgat Korany and Rabab El-Mahdi, the protest "was strengthened by police brutality and heavy-handedness, which increased the volume of protesters to such an extent that police forces were overpowered and routed. It was bolstered again by the hesitation and division within the political elite, even at the highest levels" (Korany, El-Mahdi, 2012: 11).

These spontaneous protests gained in strength, primarily thanks to the widespread access to social media. Young Egyptians followed the example of Tunisians and posted all kinds of information about the course of the protests and organised themselves via YouTube and Facebook, among other things. Wael Ghonim became the most recognised Internet activist. He set up a Facebook account devoted to Khaled Saeed (Ghonim, 2012: 58), an Egyptian student who was brutally murdered by two police officers after he had been arrested in one of the Internet cafes in Alexandria in June 2010. His case became famous after his family posted the pictures of his mutilated body on the Internet. This is what inspired Wael Ghonim. The account he set up was titled "We are all Khaled Saeed" – *Kullena Khaled Said*. It received nearly 336,000 likes from registered users by December 2014.

Tahrir Square in Cairo became the symbol of the protests, which were carefully observed by foreign journalists. "Tahrir Square was named by President Gamal Abdel Nasser to commemorate the 1952 liberation of Egypt from monarchy that was propped up by Great Britain. [...] Tahrir thus narrates a multilayered history of renewal and triumph at the same time that it embodies the oppressive script of the Mubarak regime" (Schwedler, King, 2014: 169170).

The protests that lasted over two weeks brought victory to the demonstrators. On 11 February, President H. Mubarak resigned and the Supreme Council of Armed Forces, headed by Field Marshal Hussein Tantawi, took power in the country. Preparations for constitutional reforms commenced at the same time. Several months later, H. Mubarak, his son Gamal and a few of his closest collaborators stood trial.

POLITICAL CAUSES

Michał Lipa claims that the political system in Egypt could be named "semi-authoritarian as the definite prevalence of executive power was accompanied by such elements of democracy as parliamentary elections and, after 2005, also presidential elections. The presence of efficient repression apparatus, strict legislation, the institution of emergency rule, the subsystem of special judiciary as well as the organisations and institutions to support the regime left no doubts as to the true nature of the system" (Lipa, 2013: 101).

Among the political causes of the outbreak of social discontent in January 2011, are the results of the parliamentary elections in the autumn of 2010. The NDP won over 90% of the seats. The extent of the electoral victory of the ruling party aroused the doubts of opposition and independent observers alike. It suffices to remember that the Muslim Brotherhood managed to get only one seat and its representative took part in the elections as an independent candidate (Sharp, 2011: 19).

In the opinion of numerous analysts, the outbreak of violent social protests in Egypt was triggered by the success of the Tunisians, who managed to oust the influential President Zine El Abidine Ben Ali. For many years, his position had seemed unquestionable, in particular on account of his personal supervision of the key sectors in the economy and security services. Nevertheless, spontaneous protests organised with the help of modern social media led to him losing control over the army, and forced him to resign and leave Tunisia (Achcar, 2013: 145–147). It was a warning signal for other autocratic leaders in the region of North Africa and the Middle East, including the President of Egypt. The Tunisian case also set the example for other societies, such as Egyptian society, who were tired of the arrogance of power, curbing fundamental rights and freedoms and political repressions (Sharp, 2012: 48). Samuel Tadros takes a slightly different stance, though. In his opinion, the Egyptians did not carefully follow the events in Tunisia from the very beginning. Although Arabic, Maghreb does not attract the attention of Egyptians and is not interesting for them, unlike the Arab countries of the Levant. The change was brought by Z. A. Ben Ali fleeing Tunisia on 13 January, 2011. The unexpected success of the Tunisian opposition became the source of inspiration for the Egyptians. This was when W. Ghonim called for a mass protest against H. Mubarak, the Day of Anger, on 25 January (Tadros, 2014: 334).

Another cause was the lack of political plurality, and in particular the elimination of influential religious organisations, such as the Muslim Brotherhood, from the competition for power. In the opinion of Ali Abi Issa, "the elite, educated in line with the Western ideas of the Orient, constituted the main circle and offered fundamental support of non-democratic systems ruling Muslim countries in the post-colonial period. This elite supported them in their fight to maintain the separation of power from religion, in excluding pan-Islamists regardless of their doctrine and in generally treating religion like a source of civilisational backwardness pestering the Muslim world" (Issa, 2011: 14).

One of the reasons for deposing H. Mubarak was the internal competition among the members of the ruling elite, in particular within the NDP. Several months after the victorious revolution of January 2011, the NDP was officially dissolved and its entire assets were handed over to the state treasury. This does not change the fact that its former members retained considerable private assets and extensive economic influence. Apart from that, the changes in the top echelons of the army were insignificant. The protesters tried not to provoke the military because the army did not act against them in January. It could even be said that the army took another opportunity to guard public order and, by this token, take actual control over the political life of the country. It was H. Mubarak and the security service he supervised that were blamed for the deaths of demonstrators, and the attempts at the violent suppression of the protests. Owing to that, the army could take the side of the winners and safeguard their own interests, such as retaining control over numerous hotels in resorts, and the enormous fortunes of higher-ranking officers.

It is difficult to argue with the opinion of Joshua Stacher that "in a mere eighteen days, Egypt went from a model of authoritarian durability under Mubarak to experiencing a historic political revolution. Yet, the revolution remains unfinished, as the rigid class structure that underpins Egypt remains intact. In some cases, many of the revolutionaries themselves have unconsciously participated in the replication of the class hierarchies" (Stacher, 2012: 159). The years of NDP rule had limited the access of opposition politicians to power, consequently the vast majority of them had no experience whatsoever. The West put a lot of hope in Muhammad el-Baradei, ex-Director General of the International Atomic Energy Agency and winner of the Nobel Peace Prize. He could only count on the support of the liberal and progressive part of society, though. Allegedly, he was to become the Prime Minister of Egypt after the military coup in July 2013, but he did not take up office on account of the protests voiced by the Salafi al-Noor party (Sen, 2013). He was appointed Vice President instead, but it turned out to be for one month only.

The counter-revolution of July 2013, the removal of the Muslim Brotherhood from power and the further election of General Abdel Fattah el-Sisi as the President of Egypt seem to confirm Joshua Stacher's observations. Now that over four years have passed since the revolution of January 2011, it can even be concluded that Egypt did not witness the replacement of the ruling elite, but only a reconfiguration within the elite connected with the NDP and the army. The incumbent President of Egypt, A. F. as-Sisi, in the final period of H. Mubarak's rule, assumed the office of the head of Egypt's intelligence, which he held until July 2012, when he became Minister of Defence and the chief of the Egyptian Armed Forces. The result may be that, in the long term, his presidency will further strengthen the influence of the army both in politics and the economy.

ECONOMIC AND SOCIAL CAUSES

The economic reforms launched at the time of Sadat's presidency did not bring the expected results. The problems of the country became even more acute during H. Mubarak's rule. What needs to be especially emphasised is the extremely excessive bureaucracy. At the end of 2010 there were 5.5 mln Egyptians working in the central administration, while state-owned businesses employed only 600,000 workers (Kandil, 2012: 203). No new jobs were created in the private sector at that time, which exacerbated the problem of unemployment, especially among university graduates. Their situation had been difficult since 1995, when the International Monetary Fund coerced the Egyptian authorities to go back on their guarantees to provide employment to university graduates. This was one element of the remedial programme. Additionally, Egypt's government reduced the level of subsidies by over 75% when compared to that in the 1980s (Kandil, 2012: 205). According to Nadia Ramsis Farah, "contrary to the developmental experience of the newly industrialized countries, Egypt's experiment in economic liberalization has resulted in what can be called a predatory state, that is, a state dominated by narrow special interests" (Farah, 2009: 52).

As concerns the causes of the Arab Spring, Gilbert Achcar stressed the growing problem of unemployment and, strictly related to that, increasing group of the excluded in modern Arab societies. In his opinion, in Egypt and elsewhere, the following three groups suffering from the lack of permanent employment can be distinguished:
– young people,
– women,
– university graduates (Achcar, 2013: 22–37).

In the opinion of Galal Amin, the Egyptian authorities tried to counter unemployment among the youth, "pretending to be working to solve the problem by setting up a Ministry of Youth, for example, or by releasing statistics that showed a reduction in unemployment, but it was growing worse day after day. So the officials must have counted the employed and the unemployed in a way that included the lost youth among the ranks of the employed" (Amin, 2013: 20). Therefore, one has to accept the view that "the state's withdrawal from an actively participatory role in the economy was not compensated for by the building of an efficient capacity to enhance economic development" (Farah, 2009: 52).

The opportunities for Egypt to develop economically were also limited, due to the global economic downturn that followed the financial crunch of 2008. In the opinion of Jerzy Zdanowski, "the impact of the crisis increased in 2009 not only on account of barriers in investment and crediting, but mainly due to the falling oil prices, decreased tourist traffic and smaller amounts of money sent to Egypt by its citizens working abroad" (Zdanowski, 2011: 73).

Discussing the social causes of the revolution in Egypt, a broader cultural context needs to be considered, which is characteristic of Egypt as well as other Middle East countries, not only Arab ones. Jerzy Zdanowski rightfully notes that "the reality of the Middle East is a meaningful example of the influence culture exerts on social relations. The relations between employer and employee, landowner and tenant, schoolmaster and parents, the leader of a party and its members are highly personalised" (Zdanowski, 2013: 38). Therefore, a number of young Egyptians whose parents did not have broader connections were doomed to marginalisation. It is worth adding that this problem was not only a consequence of the way in which H. Mubarak and his people wielded power, although members of the former regime clearly contributed to the strengthening and advancing clientelism in modern Egypt. Nothing seems to show that the situation improved in the wake of the revolution, though. The large groups of the excluded who do not stand a chance of a career in the central administration or the army continue to exist. Since 2013, one such group has encompassed the members and adherents of the Muslim Brotherhood.

THE 2013 COUNTERREVOLUTION: THE CAUSES, COURSE AND CONSEQUENCES

As early as 2011, some commentators claimed that the Muslim Brotherhood movement in Egypt was ready to compete for power by means of legal instruments, and exercise that power for the benefit of the entire society, although its leaders were more divided than ever before. One of these commentators, Carrie Rosefsky Wickham wrote in *Foreign Affairs* that "over the last 30 years, Brotherhood leaders have become habituated to electoral competition and representation, developed new professional competencies and skills, and forged closer ties with Egyptian activists, researchers, journalists, and politicians outside the Islamist camp. Calls for self-critique and self-reform have opened heated debates on policy matters that were once left to the discretion of the General Guide and his close advisers. [...] With a track record of nearly 30 years of responsible behavior if not rhetoric and a strong base of support, the Muslim Brotherhood has earned a place at the table in the post-Mubarak era. No democratic transition can succeed without it" (Wickham, 2014). This and similar opinions were confirmed by the parliamentary elections at the turn of 2011. The Freedom and Justice Party affiliated to the Brotherhood won a sweeping success, gaining over 37.5% votes, more than the Salafi Islamist party, Al Nour, with 20% votes and the liberals with 15% votes (Sedky, 2013: V–VI). If we add the success of M. Morsi in the presidential elections, the victory of the Muslim Brotherhood seems absolute. Even a few years earlier, any participation of Brotherhood members in the central authorities would have seemed out of the question. In 2012, however, the Brotherhood gained influence on legislative as well as executive powers.

The main task of the newly elected parliament was to appoint one hundred members of the Egyptian Constituent Assembly, which was to draft a new constitution. After the Assembly was established, a legal campaign commenced involving the Supreme Constitutional Court, which sought to block work on the document on account of the excessive influence of the Muslim Brotherhood and the Salafi. On 14 June, the Court found the elections unconstitutional and invalid. Interestingly, the Court passed another judgment invalidating a decree that banned the members of the dissolved party of H. Mubarak from running in elections (*Egypt Supreme*, 2012). Consequently, under pressure from the Court and public opinion, the composition of the Assembly was extended to include representatives of various political parties and institutions. There emerged a problem of a number of opposition members boycotting the sessions of the Assembly, though. Nevertheless, the Constituent Assembly approved the new constitution on 29 November, 2012.

A part of Egypt's society was concerned about the declarations by some members of the Brotherhood and the al-Nour party in favour of increased state involvement in matters of world-view. Religious groups that were particularly affected by the changes after 2011 included the Copt in Egypt.

Soon, the representatives of the Brotherhood were forced to give up office and to withdraw from legal political activities altogether. In the opinion of Bruno Drwęski, "the legal Islamic government in Egypt was not able to effectively mobilise the society to defend its government, even though the nation had shown its revolutionary fervour before" (Drwęski, 2014: 9). The weakness and lack of political experience of the Muslim Brotherhood's politicians encouraged the army to intervene under the slogan of defending public order.

The Egyptian counterrevolution is believed to have started on 30 June 2013. President M. Morsi was arrested on that day. He was accused of encouraging the use of violence and, which aroused serious controversy, of spying and conspiring with Hezbollah and Hamas in order to destabilise the situation in Egypt (Abdallah, 2013). For a period of several weeks prior to these events, the opponents of the Brotherhood's government and of the President were calling for Egyptian society to openly act against the state authorities. Many analysts believe that Brotherhood members did not seize their opportunity while controlling Egypt. Over a short time, they fell into disfavour with security officers, the police, the army and judges, who had long had a decisive influence on Egypt's political life. Many politicians connected with H. Mubarak's regime were also against them, backed by a considerable part of Egyptian society, which turned out to be a critical factor. The Brotherhood was also unable to uncover and prevent the attempt at their removal from power in June 2013. The main reason was their lack of political experience and of full control over the police and security services (Al-Banna, 2014: 951). Soon after the removal of M. Morsi from the office, thousands of his adherents took to the streets. Raba'a Square became a symbolic venue for the protests of the Brotherhood's supporters. By this token, Egyptian society was symbolically divided again, into those who were against the Brotherhood's government, and who gathered in Tahrir Square or supported those protesting there, and those from Raba'a Square in favour of the continuation of the Brotherhood's government. The confrontation between these two groups was soon to turn out to be exceptionally bloody, and the number of casualties was to exceed by far that of the 2011 revolution.

The adherents of the overthrown President M. Morsi were consistent in re-ferring to the political transition of July 2013 as a coup d'état, whereas his oppo-nents named it the Egyptian revolution of 2013. Before the new president was elected and sworn in, in June 2014, the duties of the head of state were assumed by the head of Egypt's Constitutional Court, Adly Mansour. There were no doubts, however, that the main figure in the July overthrow was Field Marshal A. F. el-Sisi, Egypt's Minister of Defence and the chief of the Egyptian Armed Forces between August 2012 and March 2014, and Vice President of Egypt be-tween July 2013 and March 2014.

RULE OF PRESIDENT ABDEL FATTAH EL-SISI: A CHANCE FOR STABILISATION?

In May 2014, a court in Cairo banned members of the NDP, which was dis-solved in 2011, from running in elections. Presidential elections were held soon after that, bringing victory to A. F. el-Sisi. Although he clearly won over Hamdeen Sabahi with 96.91% votes, commentators emphasised the very low turnout at 47.5% (*El-Sisi*, 2014). This was not prevented even by announcing a holiday on the election day and extending the elections by one day. To a large extent, this was influenced by the supporters of the Muslim Brothers boycott-ing the elections. It could therefore be stated that another chapter in the post-revolutionary history of Egypt had ended. President A. F. el-Sisi prom-ised the stabilisation of the political situation in Egypt, economic reforms and also, or probably first and foremost, the ultimate elimination of the Muslim Brotherhood from politics.

While he did manage to exclude the Brotherhood from the legitimate fight for power and considerably limit its influence, neither the state of security nor the economy has improved. Analysts from *The Economist* forecast economic growth in Egypt for 2015 at a level of 3.3% (*The World*, 2014: 100). At a time of countering the aftermath of the global economic crisis this seems like a good forecast, but it should be noted that in the case of Egypt, this growth level is much too low to provide a tangible improvement of the financial status of the majority of citizens. At the same time, the attempts at the Muslim Brotherhood's marginalisation may bring about the radicalisation of its members, as happened in the past. They are most likely to undertake activities against the system, mak-ing use of all available measures, including violence and terror. The events of 2013 led to deepening divisions among Egyptians, including the representa-tives of young people, who jointly made H. Mubarak resign in February 2011. The issue is a much more serious and complex one, though. Artur Wejkszner is right to observe that "Islamism, or Jihadism, on the one hand and pro-demo-cratic movements of Islamic youth in North African countries on the other stand in opposition to one another. This is because Jihadists *a priori* reject Western culture and political tradition, which Egyptian youth unequivocally refers to" (Wejkszner, 2014: 198).

CONCLUSIONS

The replacement of the ruling elites of Egypt, including the removal of President H. Mubarak from power, stemmed from various political, economic and social factors. As concerns the counterrevolution of July 2013, however, political and religious factors were decisive.

The most important political causes of the 2011 revolution included the lack of plurality and repressions against members of opposition groups. The policy of excluding the members of the Muslim Brotherhood and the opposition concentrated around the Kefaya movement brought about the gradual alienation of the ruling elite. The deposition of President H. Mubarak was also a consequence of internal competition within the ruling NDP and the commanding circles of the Egyptian army. The repression and ruthlessness of the regime were symbolised by the death of K. Saeed. W. Ghonim used social media to publicise this event, thereby giving the revolutionary process a new kind of dynamics never experienced in Egypt before. In 2005, the leaders of the Kefaya movement did not have such efficient media at their disposal. The events at the turn of January 2011 united a majority of Egyptian society and opposition politicians, regardless of differences in their world-view. They had a common goal of removing H. Mubarak and the members of the ruling NDP from power. Once this goal was attained, there emerged problems with creating a common political platform that would ensure stable and efficient governance in Egypt. Significant differences between the liberal and conservative parts of society emerged almost immediately, reaching their peak when the coup d'état and bloody fights in the streets of Cairo occurred in summer 2012.

Paradoxically, the good macroeconomic results of Egypt in the final year of H. Mubarak's rule did not translate into an improved economic situation for the majority of Egyptian society. It was just the opposite. Egyptians continued to experience the aftermath of the international financial crunch of 2008. The situation of young people was particularly difficult, including university graduates. High unemployment levels and relatively low salaries prevented further development. Another, equally important issue was the increasing social stratification and clientelism. The regime rewarded obedient and loyal citizens, for instance, by means of its personnel policy in the army or central administration. The events of 2011 were therefore perceived not only as a great opportunity for political transition, but also as an opportunity for profound economic and social transformations that were supposed to translate into improved living standards.

The outburst of social discontent in Egypt was also related to the success of the Tunisian opposition, as indicated, among others, by Jeremy M. Sharp. Samuel Tadros showed, however, that the Tunisian case became a source of inspiration for Egyptians only after President Z. A. Ben Ali fled from Tunisia. The former events, including the self-immolation and death of Mohamed Bouazizi did not attract any special interest of Egypt's public opinion.

BIBLIOGRAPHY

Abdallah A. H. (2013), *Prosecutor general orders Morsi tried for espionage along with Brotherhood leaders*, http://www.dailynewsegypt.com/2013/12/18/prosecutor-general-orders--morsi-tried-for-espionage-along-with-brotherhood-leaders/, 30.12.2014.

Achcar G. (2013), *The People Want: A Radical Exploration of the Arab Uprising*, Berkeley–Los Angeles.

Al-Banna I. M. (2014), *Egypt and Revolution*, Cairo.

Al-Sayyid M. K. (2009), *Kefaya at a Turning Point*, in: *Political and Social Protest in Egypt*, ed. N. S. Hopkins, Cairo.

Amin G. (2011), *Egypt in the Era of Hosni Mubarak 1981–2011*, Cairo.

Bokhari K., Senzai F. (2013), *Political Islam in the Age of Democratization*, Basingstoke.

Clarke K. (2013), *Aish, huriyya, karama insaniyya: Framing and the 2011 Egyptian Uprising*, "European Political Science", No. 12.

Drwęski B. (2014), *Islam, laickość – islamizm, laicyzm. Kwestia postępu w polityce muzułmańskiej*, "As-Salam", No. 2.

Egypt supreme court calls for parliament to be dissolved, http://www.bbc.com/news/world-middle-east-18439530, 24.12.2014.

El-Mahdi R. (2009), *The Democracy Movement: Cycles of Protest*, in: *Egypt: The Moment of Change*, eds. R. El-Mahdi, P. Marfleet, London.

El-Naggar A. El-Sayed (2009), *Economic Policy: From State Control to Decay and Corruption*, in: *Egypt: The Moment of Change*, eds. R. El-Mahdi, P. Marfleet, London.

El-Sisi wins Egypt's presidential race with 96.91%, http://english.ahram.org.eg/NewsContent/1/64/102841/Egypt/Politics-/BREAKING-PEC-officially-announces-AbdelFattah--ElSi.aspx, 23.12.2014.

Farah N. R. (2009), *Egypt's Political Economy: Power Relations in Development*, Cairo.

Ghonim W. (2012), *Revolution 2.0. The Power of the People is Greater Than the People in Power: A Memoir*, New York.

Ginat R. (1997), *Egypt's Incomplete Revolution: Lufti al-Khuli and Nasser's Socialism in the 1960s*, London.

Issa A. A. (2011), *Doktryna Braci Muzułmanów a sytuacja doktrynalno-prawna świata muzułmańskiego*, "As-Salam", No. 1.

Kandil H. (2012), *Soldiers, Spies and Statesmen: Egypt's Road to Revolt*, New York.

Kazziha W. (2013), *Egypt Under Mubarak: A Family Affair*, in: *Egypt's Tahrir Revolution*, eds. D. Tschirgi, W. Kazziha, S. F. McMahon, London.

Korany B., El-Mahdi R. (2012), *The Protesting Middle East*, in: *Arab Spring in Egypt: Revolution and Beyond*, eds. B. Korany, R. El-Mahdi, Cairo.

Lipa M. (2013), *Autorytaryzm na arabskim Bliskim Wschodzie. Egipt w latach 1981–2010*, Warszawa.

Lipa M. (2014), *Polityczne aspekty Arabskiej Wiosny w Egipcie*, in: *Porewolucyjny Egipt. Wybrane aspekty społeczne i polityczne*, eds. P. Niziński, M. Lipa, Kraków.

Marsot A. L. S. (2009), *Historia Egiptu. Od podboju arabskiego do czasów współczesnych*, Warszawa.

Naguib S. (2009), *The Muslim Brotherhood. Contradictions and Transformations*, in: *Political and Social Protest in Egypt*, ed. N. S. Hopkins, Cairo.

Purat A. (2014), *Znaczenie Bractwa Muzułmańskiego w polityce Egiptu oraz w wydarzeniach Arabskiej Wiosny 2011 roku*, "Przegląd Politologiczny", Vol. 19, No. 1.

Rutherford B. K. (2008), *Egypt After Mubarak: Liberalism, Islam, and Democracy in the Arab World*, Princeton.

Schwedler J., King R. (2014), *Political Geography*, in: *The Arab Uprisings Explained: New Contentious Politics in the Middle East*, ed. M. Lynch, New York.

Sedky A. R. (2013), *Cairo Rewind: The First Two Years of Egypt's Revolution 2011–2013*, Victoria.

Sen A. K. (2013), *Egypt's interim president names leadership, Salafists approve*, "The Washington Post", 9.07.2013.

Sharp J. M. (2011), *Egypt: the 25 January Revolution and Implications for U.S. Foreign Policy*, Washington D.C.

Sharp J. M. (2012), *Egypt: The January 25 Revolution and Implications for US Foreign Policy*, in: *Tunisia and Egypt: Unrest and Revolution*, ed. J. C. De Leon, C. R. Jones, New York.

Soliman S. (2012), *The Political Economy of Mubarak's Fall*, in: *Arab Spring in Egypt: Revolution and Beyond*, eds. B. Korany, R. El-Mahdi, Cairo.

Stacher J. (2012), *Adaptable Autocrats: Regime Power in Egypt and Syria*, Cairo.

Stępniewska-Holzer B., Holzer J. (2006), *Egipt. Stulecie przemian*, Warszawa.

Tadros S. (2014), *Reflections on the Revolution in Egypt*, Stanford.

The World in 2015 (2014), "The Economist".

Wejkszner A. (2014), *Ewolucja zagrożenia dżihadystycznego a przemiany demokratyczne w państwach Maghrebu*, "Przegląd Politologiczny", Vol. 19, No. 1.

Wickham C. R. (2014), *The Muslim Brotherhood After Mubarak. What the Brotherhood Is and How It Will Shape the Future*, http://www.foreignaffairs.com/articles/67348/carrie--rosefsky-wickham/the-muslim-brotherhood-after-mubarak, 10.10.2014.

Zahid M. (2012), *The Muslim Brotherhood and Egypt's Succession Crisis: The Politics of Liberalisation and Reform in the Middle East*, London.

Zdanowski J. (2011), *Bliski Wschód 2011: bunt czy rewolucja?*, Kraków.

Zdanowski J. (2013), *Klasy, elity i klientelizm na muzułmańskim Bliskim Wschodzie*, in: *Władza na muzułmańskim Bliskim Wschodzie. Wybrane aspekty*, ed. J. Zdanowski, Warszawa.

Radosław FIEDLER
Adam Mickiewicz University, Poznań

ROLE OF THE NEW MEDIA IN THE ARAB SPRING IN EGYPT: NEW AND TRADITIONAL MEDIA

The mass media are the product of industrialisation and technological revolution. They developed dynamically over the 19th and 20th centuries. They encompass newspapers and periodicals, radio, movies and television, which are currently named traditional or mainstream media. The emergence of a new medium turned out not to eliminate the old ones. The traditional media convey their message from top to bottom, that is from the author of the message to its recipient.

The term 'new media' has been around for several decades. Technological advances and traditional media using the Internet to communicate with their recipients have blurred the borderline between the traditional and new media (Castells, 2003: 28). The new media are characterised by such properties as mutual links, or the access of individual users, who can act both as senders and recipients, blurring the borderline between authors and readers. Users can post content and comment on what other authors post (McQuail, 2007: 57). The accessibility of the content published via the new media, also named social media, is much broader, which is the result of practically everybody having free access to them and the rapid and permanent supply of information, which is in contrast to the traditional media, where publications are one-off. Another difference between traditional and new media is the presence of a certain type of censorship. Whereas in the former, the decision on what news will be included in the news bulletin is made in the newsroom, in the latter, the users typically decide which content is going to be read, altered or simply copied from other news services, social websites and Internet blogs. Even if moderation only means censoring, it is difficult to conduct due to the scale of publications, and it could make users less determined to express their opinions.

Table 1. Division of the new media

Discussion forums	Based on a mechanism facilitating dialogue. Typically divided into different issues and topics. Users enjoy considerable opinion-forming potential.
Blogs	Include chronological posts that can be commented on. Highly varied topics.
Microblogs	Multimedia platforms to exchange thoughts and opinions where every user is an author, reader and commentator at the same time, and comments are most often limited by the number of characters they are allowed to use.

Content sharing websites	Videos (youtube.com) and photos (Flickr.com) as well as knowledge (wikipedia.org).
Social websites	The most advanced platforms, facilitating communication within the community of a given website of users admitted to the group of a user's friends.

Source: Developed on the basis of: Manovich, 2006: 32–37.

The digitalisation process has erased the borders separating the traditional and new media. This is named convergence, that is the merging of different platforms: printed media (newspapers and periodicals), telecommunication media (TV, radio, cable and satellite TV broadcasters) and the Internet (Jenkins, 2007: 23; Goban-Klas, 2006: 18; Kopiecka-Piech, 2011: 11–26).

The new media have provided users with completely new opportunities, but they have primarily strengthened their political influence.

TRADITIONAL AND NEW MEDIA IN EGYPT

Egypt has a population of about 83 million, with a young median age of just 24 year. Before the Arab Spring, the media system in Egypt was dominated by state-owned media, encompassing press, radio and television. On the basis of a 2011 assessment by Freedom House, Egypt was downgraded from 'partly free' to 'not free' in terms of the freedom of the media.[1]

Printed press continues to be a highly popular medium in Egypt. Egyptians turn to the press, mainly seeking political news and reports on current local events. Newspaper readership is high in Egypt, with approximately 45% of the population reading a newspaper every day.[2] Although the number of newspapers, magazines and periodicals amounts to around 500 in Egypt, they are all managed by state institutions. The three erstwhile leading national newspaper houses – *Al-Ahram* (The Pyramids), *Al-Akhbar* (The News) and *Dar Al-Tahrir* (The Liberation House) – are all owned by the government and operate under

---

[1] This downgrading followed from the restrictions the authorities imposed on the media during parliamentary elections in November 2010. The Freedom House report stressed that the "restrictions included legal harassment, spurious arrests, and violations of due process against journalists and bloggers. The pre-election period also saw satellite television outlets and text-message based news services banned; both are key outlets for disseminating independent views," quotation Freedom House Egypt; https://freedomhouse.org/report/freedom-press/2011/egypt#.VRbIveGKKGm.

[2] In comparison to Saudi Arabia, where newspaper readership is 41%, Egypt fares better, yet it is lower than that of the UAE at 56%. Newspaper subscriptions are also low, with close to 98% of the population not subscribing to newspapers, suggesting potentially high free circulation; more in: *Report Arab Media Outlook 2011–2015. Arab Media: exposure and transition*, Dubai Press Club 2012, p. 139.

Graph 1. Freedom of press in Egypt, 1993–2013 (countries are scored on a 100-point scale. The lower the numeric score, the greater the press freedom)

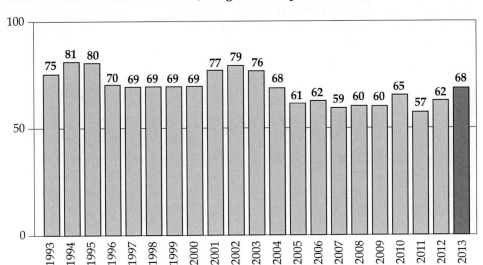

Source: *Press Freedom by Country, 1993–2013,* https://freedomhouse.org/report/freedom-press-2014/press-freedom-numbers#.VRkihOEl-Gk.

significant government control. The Editors-in-Chief of all these three main newspapers are appointed by the President.[3]

Another traditional medium alongside the press is radio, whose role consistently grows on account of news bulletins. There are twelve radio stations broadcasting in Egypt, only two of which (*Nile FM* and *Nugoom FM*) are private, which causes certain limitations, related among other things to broadcasting news services.[4]

Terrestrial television and satellite television are the most important traditional media in Egypt. Analogue terrestrial television is still received by 41% of households. The state owns 17 television channels. Forty percent of Egyptians watch television four hours per day, and only a small proportion of the population (0.5%) does not watch television at all.[5] Before the Arab Spring, the official

---

[3] "Each newspaper house publishes a large number of different titles (18, 12 and 12, respectively). There are four other State newspaper houses, as well as the Middle East News Agency, and collectively the State sector comprises some 54 newspapers, employing 27,500 individuals;" quotation from: Assessment of Media Development in Egypt based on UNESCO's Media Development Indicators Published in 2013 by the United Nations Educational, Scientific and Cultural Organization; http://unesdoc.unesco.org/images/0022/002207/220742E.pdf.

[4] The private radio station Nugoom FM ranks the highest in the country in terms of popularity with its audience, being particularly strong in the youth segment (15–24), ibid.

[5] It is notable that in 2012 news has overtaken sports amongst the most viewed genres of TV programs; ibid. p. 142.

monopoly for information in Egypt, and in the entire region, was broken by the 'Al-Jazeera effect.' As Faisal Al Kasim observed: "for the first time, Arab viewers could watch a group of politicians and journalists discussing a political issue live on the air" (Kasim, 2005: 93).

Compared to other regions, the development of the Internet in Egypt and other Arab states was delayed. In 2003, there were 18 computers per 1,000 inhabitants on average in the Arab world, while the global average amounted to 78 at that time. In late 2007, 21% of inhabitants of the Middle East and North Africa had access (often through shared access) to the Internet, compared to 48% in Europe and 71% in the US (Seib, 2008: 11–17).

Table 2. Egypt: Internet Usage and Population Growth

Year	Users	Population	Percentage
2000	450,000	66,303,000	0.7%
2006	5,100,000	71,236,631	7.0%
2008	10,532,400	81,713,517	12.9%
2009	12,568,900	78,866,635	15.9%
2009	12,568,900	78,866,635	15.9%
2012	29,809,724	83,688,164	35.6%

Source: *Egypt Internet Usage and Telecommunications Reports*, http://www.internetworld-stats.com/af/eg.htm.

Almost the entire communication infrastructure in Egypt belongs to the state-owned company Telecom Egypt, which gives the regime the opportunity to cancel access to the Internet or to limit its speed. The dynamic increase in the number of Egyptians with access to the Internet resulted in the development of new media (Stepanova, 2011). In 2010, there were four million Facebook users and 16,000 bloggers in Egypt.[6] New media provided the opposition with an effective tool for social mobilisation and informing about abuses by the authorities. In spite of repressions and restrictions the authorities have not managed to significantly curb this field of activities. There were attempts at threatening bloggers and supervising the Internet. The authorities suffered a symbolic defeat in December 2007, when the Administrative Court rejected its motion to

[6] As the Egyptian blogosphere continues to grow, so does the government's crackdown on bloggers and Internet users. For example, blogger Abdel Kareem Nabil Suleiman Amer ("Kareem Amer") was sentenced in February 2007 to four years in prison for "incitement to hatred of Islam" on his blog and for insulting the president; UN Experts conclude blogger Kareem Amer is being arbitrarily detained, a violation of international human rights standards," March 24, 2009, http://www.ifex.org/egypt/2009/03/25/un_experts_conclude_blogger_kareem/, 29.04.2015; Meghan Michael, *Blogging on the rise in Egypt despite security risks, threats, says report*, "Daily Gulf News," July 31, 2008, http://www.thedaily-newsegypt.com/article.aspx?ArticleID=15427, 29.04.2015.

block access to 49 websites. The court emphasised the support for freedom of expression, as long as such websites do not harm beliefs or public order.[7]

The new media have increased the range of influence of opposition movements. For instance, when Esraa Abdel Fattah set up the "April 6 Strike" group (calling on people to support the struggle of the Mahalla workers) on Facebook in 2008, she did not expect that it would soon be joined by over 73,000 users of this social website (Lim, 2012: 234–236). The watershed was marked by the "We are All Khaled Said" group set up in November 2010 by Wael Ghonim (a regional executive at Google) to commemorate the death of blogger Khaled Said from Alexandria, murdered by the police on 6 June 2010. This brutal crime has catalysed an unprecedented increase in Internet activities (Howard, Hussain, 2013: 50–57).

NEW MEDIA AND THE ARAB SPRING IN EGYPT

Numerous publications have stressed the role of the new media, which facilitated the toppling of President Hosni Mubarak. The names of the 'Internet, Twitter or Facebook revolution' have emerged in publications (Górak-Sosnowska, Pachniak, 2012; Zdanowski, 2012; Herrera, 2014). Although the new media did play a significant role from 25 January to 11 February 2011, other social, political and economic reasons should not be downplayed, additionally coupled with the exhaustion and crisis of power of H. Mubarak and his son, Gamal, who was weakened by the conflict with a part of the command of the Egyptian army (Abul-Magd, 2012; Amin, 2012: 132–145). In the period from 25 January to 11 February, 2011, the authorities and President H. Mubarak turned out to be unable to efficiently oppose the young Egyptians becoming increasingly active on social websites, which translated into even greater demonstrations in Tahrir square (Sehata, 2012: 105–114)[8].

New media played a significant role when earlier protests before the Arab Spring and the "Day of Anger" on 28 January 2011 were staged. Social websites, such as the "We are All Khaled Said" group on Facebook, had 300,000 users in the first days of the Arab Spring, facilitating the mobilisation, coordination of protests and conveying information (Zawrotna, 2012: 177). The authorities tried to stop this mobilisation, disabling the Internet almost entirely on 27 January 2011. The blackout lasted until 2 February. Not only did they fail to curb the demonstrations, but the people who had been cut off from the Internet joined the protests even more willingly (Cohen, 2011). The Internet blackout had significant outcomes for the Egyptian economy (Olson, 2011).

---

[7] *Internet Filtering in Egypt*, OpenNet Initiative; https://opennet.nct/sites/opennet.net/files/ONI_Egypt_2009.pdf, 29.04.2015.

[8] As Genevieve Barrons observed: "prior to and during the first protests there was a massive surge (increase of 68%) in Internet use [...] while traffic to Al Jazeera and Google also increased, the biggest surge was in the use of Facebook;" a quotation from: Barrons 2013: 13.

Traditional media, supervised by the authorities, initially ignored the protests. For instance, *Al-Jumhirya* published the information that the number of protesters in Tahrir square did not exceed 100, similarly in Cairo, Alexandria and Suez. Only shortly before H. Mubarak stepped down, traditional media began to glorify the protesters and the transformations they initiated (Owais, 2011).

Three types of new media that played a significant role in mobilising, coordinating and covering the events of the Arab Spring in Egypt can be distinguished. The most important news sources but also, in a way, command staff of the demonstrations were provided by Facebook, Twitter and YouTube (Khondker, 2011: 675–679).

- **Facebook**: Egypt, with around 4.7 million Facebook users, constituted, by the end of 2010, 22% of total users in the Arab region. In May 2011, there were 7 mln FB users in Egypt. The most popular FB groups were: "April 6 Youth Movement," created in 2008; by January 2010 the group had over 100,000 members. The other group "We Are All Khaled Said" had almost 1 mln users by January 2011. These FB groups, influenced attitudes prior to the Arab Spring (Giglio, 2011: 15).
- **Twitter**: While having only 130,000 users, its range exceeds that of Facebook and provides contact with the outside world. This website is an Internet microblog, in a way, allowing users to post short messages ('tweets') of up to 140 characters. The tweets can be categorised by using hashtags (for instance #jan25) allowing the service to identify a tweet as related to a given topic. Categorised tweets can all be found in a joint stream, which can later be followed by surfers all over the world. Over the course of a week before H. Mubarak's resignation, the total rate of tweets from Egypt – and around the world – about political change in that country ballooned from 2,300 a day to 230,000 a day (Eltahawy, 2011). As one activist tweeted: "We use Facebook to schedule the protests, Twitter to coordinate, and YouTube to tell the world" (Howard, 2011).
- **YouTube**: Its primary function was to cover the course of the Arab revolution in Egypt. Four types of films can be distinguished: 1. coverage of society's mobilisation and protests; 2. comments by citizens and protesters; 3. expert opinions; and 4. music intended to motivate and inspire others to take part in the revolution (Rybak, 2014).

Table 3. Viral Video Content from Egyptians, By Upload Date and Number of Viewers

Title	Channel	Views	Date
1	2	3	4
Protest in Egypt – Jan 25, 2011	lukasjakubicka	676,701	25-Jan-11
Day of Anger in Egypt	ReutersVideo	217,518	25-Jan-11
Egypt's Protests Day of Anger Riots 25 Jan 2011	AusNetwork	110,162	25-Jan-11

1	2	3	4
The Most AMAZING video on the Internet #Egypt #jan25	hadi15	2,127,384	27-Jan-11
Man Shot in Egypt	NeroAlex1988	154,823	27-Jan-11
Egypt Unrest: Video of police killing teen protester, riots aftermath	RussiaToday	397,099	28-Jan-11
28th Jan. 2011 – Storyful – Egypt Cairo uprising protest video – Mohamed Ibrahim Elmasry	Storyful	285,628	28-Jan-11
Demanding change in Egypt	AlJazeeraEnglish	111,908	28-Jan-11
Egyptians renew protests after curfew	AlJazeeraEnglish	106,191	28-Jan-11
Juju's message to Mubarak	oneholysinner	275,302	29-Jan-11
Video of Egypt's bloody clashes as protesters defy curfew in Cairo	RussiaToday	204,736	30-Jan-11
Video of fighter jets & choppers over Cairo as military tries to take control	RussiaToday	167,422	30-Jan-11
Egyptian Revolution 2011 COMPLETE. World MUST watch this. Freedom for All!	eyeinsidefilm	484,043	01-Feb-11
'March of Millions' in Cairo as Egypt riots death toll reaches 300	RussiaToday	123,965	01-Feb-11
Video of fierce Egypt clashes as pro-gov crowds attack anti-Mubarak protesters	RussiaToday	322,708	02-Feb-11
Fourth Horseman (death) Egyptian riots. Full Original Video	PunkersTV	1,551,796	03-Feb-11
The fourth horseman (of Death) at the Egypt protests	FooledToaster	150,532	03-Feb-11
Hosni Mubarak, a citizen of the people of Egypt at the end of wisdom	Shaghelhom	139,526	04-Feb-11
Riz Khan - Tariq Ramadan and Slavoj Zizek on the future of Egyptian politics	AlJazeeraEnglish	107,769	04-Feb-11
US Intervention: Pentagon sends warships to Egypt	otraverdad1	281,201	07-Feb-11

Source: (Horwad, Freelon, Hussain, 2011).

The video material from Egypt, however, would not have had such a great range without the traditional media, such as Al-Jazeera and Russia Today, which both retransmitted them and posted them to their own websites.[9] As

---

[9] As Manuel Castells remarked: "Al Jazeera has collected the information disseminated on the Internet by the people using them as sources and organized groups on Facebook, then retransmitting free news on mobile phones. Thus was born a new system of mass communi-

Genevieve Barrons observed, "[a]ll the videos posted on YouTube became a digital record of the events of the revolution. They allowed the protestors to share their side of the story, which quickly became the dominant narrative. YouTube, and all-user-generated videos, were undoubtedly important tools of communication between the protestors and those watching what was going on from home, in Egypt, the Middle East and abroad" (Barrons, 2013: 246).

POSSIBILITIES AND LIMITATIONS. ASSESSMENT OF THE ROLE OF NEW MEDIA IN THE ARAB SPRING IN EGYPT

Scholars have presented different assessments of the role of the new media before and during the Arab Spring in Tunisia and Egypt. Critical towards the role of the new media during the Arab Spring being overrated, Malcolm Gladwell stressed two aspects:

1) social media create weak ties, thereby limiting social participation in higher risk activities. Social media can increase participation, but in reality people are much more likely to sign a petition if they do it from a computer, but are still not taking active part in demonstrations (Gladwell, 2010);

2) social media create networks rather than hierarchy. A single authority cannot control the new media (Gladwell, 2010).

Clay Shirky presented the opposite opinion: "mass media alone do not change people's minds; instead, there is a two-step process. Opinions are first transmitted by the media, and then they get echoed by friends, family members, and colleagues. It is in this second, social step that political opinions are formed. This is the step in which the Internet in general, and social media in particular, can make a difference. As with the printing press, the Internet spreads not just media consumption, but media production as well – it allows people to privately and publicly articulate and debate a welter of conflicting views" (Shirky, 2011: 38). This was the debate started in Egypt by bloggers who criticised H. Mubarak's regime in Internet cafes, on social websites, but also outside of the Internet, during heated discussions about the content posted in the Internet held among family members and friends. In the opinion of Larry Diamond and Shirky, this continuous exchange of opinions contributes to the emergence of a 'shared awareness,' which creates a kind of an 'imagined community' allowing more extensive activities. In the opinion of these scholars, in contrast to Gladwell's 'weak ties,' the network-like and non-hierarchical connections make it difficult for authoritarian governments to combat opposition effectively.

cation built like a mix between an interactive television, internet, radio and mobile communication systems. The communication of the future is already used by the revolutions of the present;" a quotation from: *The Sociology Elders on The Social Movements in Tunisia and Egypt*, http://globalsociology.com/2011/02/07/the-sociology-elders-on-the-social-movements-in--tunisia-and-egypt/, 29.04.2015.

L. Diamond and C. Shirky stress that co-ordinating this loose, network-like and non-hierarchical structure via social media is relatively simple, it is more spontaneous and, importantly, cost-efficient (Diamond, 2010: 69–83; Shirky, 2011: 28–41). This enthusiastic opinion is not shared by Evgeny Morozov, however, who points out that new media can and have been used to track and arrest dissidents who are networked together. E. Morozov believes that the authorities can use these media to spread propaganda or even misinform. He emphasises that both authoritarian regimes and oppositions are in a constant technological race, with both sides enjoying certain advantages, as well as suffering weaknesses that can significantly hamper opposition activities (Morozov, 2012).

What is the most adequate assessment of the role of new media in Egypt, both during and after the Arab Spring? The democratic parliamentary and presidential elections raised hopes that the demands made by the protesters – who initiated the process of transformation backed by the power of the Internet – would be achieved. The situation turned out to have been much more complicated, though. Disappointment with the government of President Mohamad Morsi and the Muslim Brotherhood instigated another wave of opposition activities on social media, which facilitated the organisation of mass demonstrations once more. The Supreme Council of the Armed Forces took advantage of the intensifying crisis and carried out a military coup d'état. Military dictatorship was reinstated, this time headed by President Abdel Fattah el-Sisi. Democratisation processes came to a complete halt after 2013. The army used the dissatisfaction of part of society to depose President M. Morsi. The new Egyptian authorities are considerably more experienced in countering and combating opposition, which continues to be active on the Internet. It seems that E. Morozov was right, claiming that the authorities can easily turn to the Internet when fighting their opponents, to demonstrate their anti-government activities, also in the past. Nevertheless, the repressive activities of the authorities have not eliminated opposition from the new media altogether.

The authorities grew increasingly provocative in their activities, for instance the courts dismissed the charges against H. Mubarak in connection with shooting demonstrators, which deprived even some of A. F. el-Sisi's advocates of their illusions. The non-hierarchical structures, stressed by L. Diamond and C. Shirky, and the involvement of hundreds of thousands of Internet activists may trigger another Arab Spring if the democratisation process is not resumed. In this context, E. Morozov's scepticism would seem justified, only provided that the activists using the new media limit their activities, which seems unlikely even in the face of repression.

BIBLIOGRAPHY

Abul-Magd Z. (2012), *Understanding SCAF,* "The Cairo Review of Global Affairs", http://www.auc-egypt.edu/GAPP/CairoReview/Pages/articleDetails.aspx?aid=216, 29.04.2015.

Amin G. (2012), *Egypt in the Era of Hosni Mubarak*, Cairo–New York.

Barrons G. (2013), *Suleiman: Mubarak decided to step down #gypt#jan25 OH MY GOD: examining the use of social media in the 2011 Egyptian revolution*, in: *The Arab Spring. Critical Analyses*, ed. Khair El-Din Haseeb, New York.

Castells M. (2003), *Galaktyka Internetu*, Poznań.

Cohen N. (2011), *Egyptians Were Unplugged, and Uncowed*, http://www.nytimes.com/2011/02/21/business/media/21link.html, 29.04.2015.

Diamond L. (2010), *Liberation technology*, "Journal of Democracy", Vol. 21, Issue 3.

Eltahawy M. (2011), *Twitter*, https://twitter.com/monaeltahawy, 29.04.2015.

Giglio M. (2011), *The Facebook freedom fighters*, "Newsweek", 21.02.2011.

Goban-Klas T. (2006), *Radiomorfoza w kontekście ewolucji, adaptacji i konwergencji mediów*, "Studia Medioznawcze", No. 3 (26).

Herrera L. (2014), *Revolution in the Age of Social Media: The Egyptian Popular Insurrection and the Internet*, London–New York.

Howard P. N. (2011), *The Arab Spring's Cascading Effects*, http://www.psmag.com/politics/the-cascading-effects-of-the-arab-spring-28575, 29.04.2015.

Howard P. N., Duffy A., Freelon D., Hussain M. (2011), *Opening Closed Regimes What Was the Role of Social Media During the Arab Spring? Working Paper 2011*, http://pitpi.org/wp-content/uploads/2013/02/2011_Howard-Duffy-Freelon-Hussain-Mari-Mazaid_pITPI.pdf, 29.04.2015.

Howard P. N., Hussain M. M. (2013), *Democracy's Fourth Wave?: Digital Media and the Arab Spring*, Oxford.

Jenkins H. (2007), *Kultura konwergencji. Zderzenie starych i nowych mediów*, Warszawa.

Kasim F. (2005), *The Opposite Direction: A Program which Changed the Face of Arab Television*, in: *The Al Jazeera Phenomenon Critical Perspectives on New Arab Media*, ed. M. Zayani, London.

Khondker H. (2011), *Role of the New Media in the Arab Spring*, "Globalizations", Vol. 8, Issue 5.

Kopiecka-Piech K. (2011), *Koncepcje konwergencji mediów*, "Studia Medioznawcze", No. 3 (46).

Lim M. (2012), *Clicks, Cabs, and Coffee Houses: Social Media and Oppositional Movements in Egypt, 2004–2011*, "Journal of Communication", Vol. 62.

Manovich L. (2006), *Język nowych mediów*, Warszawa.

McQuail D. (2007), *Teoria komunikowania masowego*, Warszawa.

Morozov E. (2012), *Facebook and Twitter are just places revolutionaries go*, http://www.guardian.co.uk/commentisfree/2011/mar/07/facebook-twitter-revolutionaries-cyber-utopians, 29.04.2015.

Olson P. (2011), *Egypt's Internet Blackout Cost More Than OECD Estimates*, http://www.forbes.com/sites/parmyolson/2011/02/03/how-much-did-five-days-of-no-internet-cost-egypt/, 29.04.2015.

Owais R. (2011), *Arab Media during the Arab Spring in Egypt and Tunisia: Time for Change*, http://ro.uow.edu.au/cgi/viewcontent.cgi?article=1001&context=meme, 29.04.2015.

Rybak M. (2014), *Rola nowych mediów w Arabskiej Wiośnie na przykładzie Egiptu*, https://apd.amu.edu.pl/diplomas/88860/, 29.04.2015.

Sehata D. (2012), *Youth Movements and the 25 January Revolution*, in: *Arab Spring in Egypt. Revolution and Beyond*, eds. B. Korany, R. El-Mahdi, Cairo–New York.

Seib P. (2008), *The Al Jazeera Effect: How the New Global Media Are Reshaping World Politics*, Washington.

Shirky C. (2011), *The Political Power of Social Media*, "Foreign Affairs", Vol. 90, Issue 1.

Stepanova E. (2011), *The Role of Information Communication Technologies in the "Arab Spring" Implications Beyond the Region*, http://pircenter.org/kosdata/page_doc/p2594_2.pdf, 29.04.2015.

Zawrotna M. (2012), *Państwo Facebooka. Rola internetowych portali społecznościowych w Rewolucji 25 Stycznia w Egipcie*, in: *Bunt czy Rewolucja? Przemiany na Bliskim Wschodzie po 2010*, eds. K. Górak-Sosnowska, K. Pachniak, Łódź.

Zdanowski J. (2011), *Bliski Wschód 2011: bunt czy rewolucja?*, Kraków.

Robert CZULDA
University of Lodz

THE IMPACT OF THE ARAB SPRING ON THE MILITARY SECURITY POLICY OF EGYPT

Even now, after only a few years, we can say without any exaggeration that the Arab Spring has been one of the most significant political and social events in recent years and decades, not only for the Middle East but for the whole world. When discussing and analysing this phenomenon the natural question arises – what internal (for individual states), regional and global impact has the Arab Spring had? Due to its wide geographical range, as well as its scale and causes (not only political, but also social, economic and military) it is most likely to have a long-term, strategic impact. The consequences of the Arab Spring will only be seen and understood in more detail in the future. Many decisions and events will bear consequences only after a few years or even decades have passed. However, even now it is tempting to look for an initial and limited answer about the impact of the "Arab Tsunami" (Lev, 2013) on the military security policy of the most important and the strongest Arab state – Egypt. This paper seeks to answer that question by evaluating four dimensions of the potential impact: on the Egyptian Armed Forces, on the internal security environment, and – last but not least – the external dimension, which for clarity of analysis will be divided into two parts: relations with Israel and with the United States.

EGYPTIAN ARMED FORCES AND THE ARAB SPRING

To analyse the impact of the Arab Spring on Egypt's military security policy, it is important to start by presenting the main executor, and also the creator of this policy in the Egyptian decision making process: the Egyptian Armed Forces. This actor can be analysed in two dimensions: internal and external. While the latter is not the subject of this paper, from the perspective of this paper it is more understandable to focus on the internal position of the Egyptian military. In democratic systems there is usually a form of civilian control which can be defined, in the words of S. Huntington, as "governmental control of military" (Welch, 1976: 2). Very clear boundaries between the civilian and military worlds exist, and the influence of serving officers on politics is usually very limited. Civilian institutions control the military entity, whose role is usually limited to an executive and consultation role, but does not involve decision making. However, in the case of many authoritarian states, the military has a significant influence – in some cases a state does not have an army, but an army has a state. In the Middle East, this applies particularly to Algeria and Egypt.

Without any doubt, it can be said that in Egypt there is a visible lack of an equilibrium between the historically powerful military and civilian society. In other words, the armed forces are a key player in Egypt, which is an "officers' republic" (Sayigh, 2013). The military entity is powerful and influential enough to either install or remove a president, who usually comes from the armed forces and thus is not interested in antagonising them. In fact, it is rather the opposite – although Mubarak expanded the internal security forces to weaken the regular military, Egypt's leader needs support from the armed forces, because "building a strong, capable security apparatus is key for repressing internal dissent, preventing regime overthrow, and sustaining authoritarian rule" (Makara, 2013: 335). As a consequence, "while Egypt is not a military dictatorship in technical terms (since the president is officially a civilian now), it is a military-backed authoritarian system" (Repucci, Valker, 2005: 212). Surprisingly, heavy military defeats (1956, 1967 and 1973) did not hamper the armed forces' internal strength.

To present the potential impact of the Arab Spring on the role and position of Egypt's Armed Forces, the internal strength they had before 2011 must briefly be illustrated. Apart from their classic, military functions, as well as the strong influence on the political sphere in Egypt, the armed forces are also present in the social and economic dimension, however the extent of the military's holdings and influence is unknown. Paul Sullivan claims that the military accounts for some 10% to 15% of the Egyptian economy, while Mohamed Kadry Said estimates 8% of GDP (Mayton, 2012). Estimates vary because, as Khaled Fahmy noted, this is a "grey economy, in the sense that we know very little of them, they are not subject to any Parliamentary scrutiny, the Egyptian government auditing office has no control or knowledge of them" (Tadros, 2012). No matter which estimates are true, the Egyptian army is an "uncontested economic power" (Hauslohner, 2014).

The Egyptian military has forged an industrial empire over decades and become one of the biggest employers in a relatively poor country. It has dozens of factories and companies which produce almost everything: from olive milk, bottled water, clothes to televisions and cars. The Egyptian military owns sports grounds, restaurants, farms, resorts and hotels. The best evidence of its role and power within the Egyptian economy is the bread crisis of 2008, when President Hosni Mubarak ordered the army to bake it. In February 2014, the Egyptian military took over parts of the bus system in Cairo, as a response to mass strikes which hampered public transport in the city. Perhaps the best evidence of the unusual role of the military in Egypt is the loan worth USD 1 bn that was given by the armed forces to the central bank in December 2011.

The potential impact of the Arab Spring on the Egyptian military can be analysed in two dimensions – political and economic. Since 1952, Egyptian officers have maintained extraordinary political powers, the scale of which depends on many factors, including the charisma and personal strength of the president. Mohamed Elmenshawy calls the Egyptian military a "deposer, kingmaker, and powerful political and commercial entity" (Elmenshawy, 2014). From a more academic point of view, the Egyptian model can be seen as armed institutional racketeering. In this model "the army neither created the state, nor gave it its identity. However, it is an intact institution that believes in its superiority compared to any other state institution, including elected bodies as well as civilian judicial ones" (Ashour, 2013).

Evidence of this unusual and extraordinary position appeared, for instance, in December 2011, when Minister of Defence el-Sisi invited (sic!) President Mohamed Morsi and all political parties and forces to hold a "social dialogue" (El Gundy, 2011). The military's strong political position can be seen not only in the fact that the National Defence Council is controlled by military leaders and not civilian politicians, but also when the background of Egyptian leaders is taken into account. The presidency of M. Morsi, the only civilian, was just a brief exception to the rule and not a new standard. Even during the Arab Spring in Cairo, the military did not lose its power.

Despite the popular uprising in Cairo, during the Arab Spring the military establishment showed its wisdom and strength – both in terms of its capability to remove and install new "civilian" leaders. First of all, it was strong and confident enough not to defend H. Mubarak and his regime (the opposite happened in Iran in 1979, when the Iranian military was unable to protect the Shah). The then president's power collapsed, not only due to public pressure but also due to the deliberate lack of support from the military, whose role and strength H. Mubarak had been trying to decrease. The military knew that it was strong enough to survive without H. Mubarak, which cannot be said – for example – in the case of the Syrian military establishment which is closely connected to the regime of Assad on sectarian grounds.

At the same time, the military was smart enough to understand that they were not untouchable, and supporting H. Mubarak, especially by shedding blood in the streets (like in Libya and Syria) would harm its position – rather than being a puppet of the regime, the military decided to play the role of a "people's army". Therefore, the military put "significant pressure on Mubarak to abdicate" (El Fegiery, 2012). Officers were also strong enough to neutralise H. Mubarak as a possible successor to his father. During the interregnum period in Cairo, the armed forces – via the Supreme Council of the Armed Forces chaired by Field Marshal Mohamed Hussein Tantawi – remained a key political player without facing much substantial risk of losing power.

After the parliamentary elections in January 2012, the struggle for political control intensified. The civilian president was strong enough just once – in August 2012, when he dismissed Field Marshal M. H. Tantawi (from his posts of

Commander-in-Chief and Minister of Defence) and Lieutenant General Sami Hafez Anan (Chief of Staff). However, in the end it was the military and not the president who were victorious again and saved their supremacy over all elected bodies. M. Morsi, who failed to secure full control over the military, was overthrown in July 2013. The Muslim Brotherhood's leadership was either jailed or killed. In January 2014, a new constitution for Egypt was passed in a referendum. The military retained its right, which does not exist in virtually any democratic state – to appoint the Minister of Defence.

In terms of the economy, the Arab Spring had a negative influence, not only on the Egyptian military, but also the Egyptian economy. While during the last period of H. Mubarak's presidency, the Egyptian economy was growing (albeit with a parallel increase in economic inequality), the Arab Spring stopped this progress. This applied mainly to one of the most important sectors, which is tourism. The political turmoil in Egypt scared away hundreds of thousands of foreigners, which also negatively influenced the Egyptian military which – as mentioned above – has very strong connections to the tourism sector. However, this seems to be a short-term problem. According to forecasts, while in 2011 GDP growth was at 1.8%, 2.2% in 2012, 2.1% in 2013 and 2.2% in 2014, in 2015 it could even reach 3.5% (MacBride, 2013). Although such a forecast looks very optimistic, Egypt could recover if it attracts tourists once again and eliminates some of the uncertainty which scares away potential foreign investors. The first step in that process is to provide a level of stability and personal security which did not exist during M. Morsi's presidency.

The recovering economy means that in the longer term the Egyptian military's position will not be negatively impacted. It could even be the opposite – both H. Mubarak and M. Morsi have been eliminated, so the Egyptian generals can expand their business activities. There is no political force that can stop them. Since 2011 the armed forces have increasingly taken on the biggest infrastructure projects. As Joshua Stacher put it, "we're dealing with a brand-new economy that's now run by 'Military Inc.'" (Hauslohner, 2014). The claim that the Egyptian military's role in economy is likely to be even bigger in the future is supported by recent developments. The overthrow of M. Morsi torpedoed the Muslim Brotherhood's plan – by using Qatar's financial aid – to develop the Suez Canal, which is also in the military's hands. This project was introduced by the Muslim Brotherhood in 2012, during the presidential elections, and then explored by the Prime Minister Hesham Qandil. However, this project was finally 'hijacked' by the military – in August 2014, President Abdel Fattah el-Sisi officially launched the Suez Canal Corridor Area Project with the participation of the military. This multi-billion dollar project was announced just a few months after the Egyptian president signed a deal for a housing programme with an Emirati company worth USD 40 bn. This shows the growing strength of military circles.

IMPACT ON EGYPT-ISRAEL SECURITY RELATIONS

For many decades Israel was the arch-enemy of Egypt. After a heavy defeat in the Yom Kippur War of 1973, Egyptian President Anwar Sadat decided to change his policy, and in 1979 he signed a peace agreement with Israeli Prime Minister Menachem Begin. Violent and conflictual relations were replaced not with a stable and lasting peace, but by a state of a lack of war, which from the perspective of Middle Eastern relations was still a great achievement and progress. Both sides ceased major hostilities, but Egypt decided to leave its forces deployed mainly between Cairo and the Suez Canal. While one of the reasons for this decision was economic in its nature (the high cost of repositioning troops) the other was military – the still existing perception of threat. Israel, similarly, has never fully trusted Egypt.

A visible sign of good relations appeared in 2007, when H. Mubarak closed the Rafah crossing between Egypt and the Gaza Strip as a reaction to Hamas's takeover of power in that Palestinian territory. Two years later Egypt started building a wall along the Gaza border which was criticised both by Hamas and Hezbollah. As the Israeli daily "*Haaretz*" put it, "Mubarak's last years in power were marked by suspicion bordering on outright hostility towards Hamas" (*Egypt's*, 2012). H. Mubarak was afraid that if Rafah was opened, then radical armed groups would spill over and relations with Israel would be damaged. Thus, until the Arab Spring, Rafah was closed (apart from humanitarian aid) which caused a deterioration in relations between Egypt and Hamas. This policy was welcomed by Israel. In January 2011, the former Israeli minister of defence Binyamin Ben-Eliezer stated openly that "Egypt is not only our closest friend in the region, the co-operation between us goes beyond the strategic" (Kershner, 2011).

The Arab Spring, and especially the election of M. Morsi, was greeted in Israel with great anxiety – more as a threat than as an opportunity. Despite the new president's close ties to Hamas, Prime Minister Benyamin Netanyahu sent a message of congratulation and expressed hope that bilateral relations would remain cooperative, but in reality he expected problems (Ignatius, 2012). However, the impact of the Arab Spring on Egypt-Israel relations very soon became visible. Bilateral communication at the operational level, mainly through security and intelligence channels, stopped. In September 2011, the Israeli embassy in Cairo was evacuated after protesters destroyed a security wall and then vandalised buildings. This was a mob reaction to the killing of Egyptian soldiers by the Israeli army, who were engaging Palestinian militants near the border. The best proof that during that time bilateral relations hit a low, is the fact that Israel lost direct communication with Egypt and had to rely on information provided by the United States. However, at the same time it was confirmed by the Israeli press that Prime Minister B. Netanyahu talked once every few weeks with the head of Egyptian intelligence or with the head of the Supreme Council, M. H. Tantawi (Ravid, 2011).

In January 2012 – during the peak of its political power – the Muslim Brotherhood's deputy leader Rashad Bayoumi not only warned that Egypt would not recognise Israel, but also that it would "take legal actions against the peace treaty with the Zionist entity" (*Muslim...*, 2012). To some degree this policy found support in Egyptian society, of which – according to a poll conducted by the Menachem Begin Heritage Centre – whilst 90% did not want the peace treaty to be cancelled, at the same time 85% opposed any form of normalisation with Israel and were keen to see a worsening of relations, even to levels of "hatred" (Siryoti, 2012). In March 2012, the Egyptian parliament, already dominated by the Muslim Brotherhood, called for the cutting of ties with Israel, including stopping exporting gas, as well as "re-examining" the Camp David peace accords of 1978 between "revolutionary Egypt" and the "Zionist regime" which was labelled the "primary enemy of Egypt and its Arab people" (Miller, 2012). The Egyptian reaction to the armed insurgency uprising in Sinai, i.e., sending in heavy armour, upset Israel because this violated the peace treaty (Kershner, 2012).

No wonder that Israel from the beginning passively sought a restoration of the *status quo*. If the Muslim Brotherhood, without a doubt a "re-born child" of the Arab Spring, stayed in power longer, it could in the long term damage the relatively positive relations between Egypt and Israel. This would result in a negative impact not only on bilateral relations, but also on the whole regional security architecture, which is already highly unstable. If the Muslim Brotherhood had strengthened its power, it would have not been impossible to rule out a scenario in which Egypt acted like Iran after the Islamic Revolution in 1979 and re-orientated its foreign policy, which would have meant a break-up of the political and military cooperation with the United States and the beginning of a hostility campaign against Israel.

While the Muslim Brotherhood having political power meant there was a risk of a negative impact on relations between Egypt and Israel, and thus also with the United States, M. Morsi's overthrow and the seizure of power by the biggest beneficiary of cooperation with Washington, i.e., the military, meant a return to the desired *status quo* – the situation before the Arab Spring. The short period of very cold relations between Egypt and Israel was just a brief exception before it transformed into a new trend. What is more, the ousting of M. Morsi restored the previous relations between Egypt and Hamas, which has strong links to the Muslim Brotherhood. The pro-Hamas policy of Egypt under M. Morsi was decisively stopped by President A. F. el-Sisi, who actively brokered a cease fire between Hamas and Israel during a military crisis in July 2014.

Egypt banned Hamas (now considered as an enemy) from operating inside the country, shut off the Rafah border crossing, destroyed all known tunnels going from Egypt to the Gaza Strip and demolished homes along the border, to establish a planned buffer zone to prevent smuggling. This was a very conscious, but at the same time very provocative and hostile act A. F. by el-Sisi. The rationale for such a move was not only international in its nature (i.e., strengthening relations with Israel and as a consequence with the United States), it also had a very strong internal reason. By halting the flow of goods into the Gaza Strip from Egypt, A. F. el-Sisi as well as military circles, weakened not only the Muslim Brotherhood, but at the same time reduced the likelihood of their resurgence and secured their own economic profits. Daniel Nisman explained in his interview on "*Al Jazeera*" that Egypt's current political and military decision-makers have "a very, very big Suez Canal expansion project, and they don't want Hamas to have any demands like expanding a seaport, building a seaport which could allow weapons to flow from Gaza into the Sinai peninsula" (Xenaxis, 2014). In other words, "an alliance" between Israel and Egypt is based not only on political and military grounds but also economic grounds.

RELATIONS WITH THE UNITED STATES

When in the late 1970s President A. Sadat made a sudden about turn and decided to halt close cooperation with the Soviet Union and sign a peace accord with Israel, Egypt became a cornerstone of Washington's regional policy and a major political, economic and military ally. Despite a poor record of human rights and personal freedoms, the United States decided to invest heavily in Egypt in order to keep Cairo in the pro-Western and pro-Israeli camp. Between 1975 and 1990 Washington provided approximately USD 10–12 bn in military assistance in the form of waived payments and concessional credits (Mott, 2002: 158).

The best example of trust in Egypt and its role in the security policy of the United States is the scale and range of arms transfers. Thanks to the generosity of Washington, H. Mubarak's regime was able to phase out some of its ageing systems of Soviet origin. Now the Egyptian armed forces are equipped with American hardware: among others, there are more than 1,000 M1A1 *Abrams* tanks and a similar number of older M60A1/A3 *Patton* tanks; approximately 2,000 tracked vehicles of the M11A2 family, almost 400–500 M109A2/A5 self-propelled howitzers. What is more, it has factories co-producing M1A1s. Cairo has received more than 220 F-16C/D *Fighting Falcon* multirole jets and 35 AH-64A *Apache* assault helicopters. What is more, every year Egypt receives USD 1.3–1.5 bn of American aid. The United States is also involved in training, mentoring and assisting in order to boost Egyptian capabilities. One of these elements is the "*Bright Star*" joint training exercises held every two years in Egypt. In other words – the United States is the most generous supplier of highly advanced military equipment to the Egyptian military.

Some of those arms transfers were conducted despite Israel's opposition, which shows how high Egypt's position in Washington's security policy is.

However, despite close relations the United States still considers Israel as a top priority partner and its alliance with Egypt as secondary. Washington, despite Cairo's request, decided not to sell it modern, active-homing AIM-120 AMRAAM missiles, which has forced Egypt to use the older and less effective AIM-7P *Sparrow* and AIM-9F/L/P *Sidewinder* missiles. Another example of this limited will to enhance Egypt's war capabilities is the decision to upgrade AH-64A *Apache* helicopters to D standard, but without the *Longbow* fire-control radar which is essential in engaging armoured threats (it can identify and track 256 targets simultaneously). The United States makes sure that the Egyptian armed forces will be equipped with relatively modern, yet inferior weapons compared to Israel (which has received the *Longbow* radar and AIM-120 AMRAAMs). This shows which state is the priority for the White House. It seems that no matter how pro-American Egyptian leaders are, the United States will always prefer, despite some minor crises, Israel as a main regional ally.

H. Mubarak was an ally of the United States, but Washington decided not to risk its own reputation and did not support him. His surprise removal from power did not significantly damage relations between the United States and Egypt. The only consequence then was a cancellation of *"Bright Star"* in 2011, due to "ongoing transition events and the military leadership serving in an interim executive role" (*Egypt*, 2011). What exerted a negative impact on bilateral relations, and thus on Egypt's security policy as well – at least in the short term – was not H. Mubarak's removal, or the temporary reign of the interim military council or the election of M. Morsi, but the military's pacification, which occurred after the president from the Muslim Brotherhood was ousted. While during the first phase of the Arab Spring the army decided not to become an active player by using force (except the Maspero incident in October 2011), as mentioned above, it did that later – when M. Morsi was replaced by A. F. el-Sisi. The total number of victims is unknown but the exact figure is irrelevant in this context – the Egyptian streets were flooded with the blood of the protestors and the United States had no choice but was forced, at least temporarily, to freeze military cooperation with the country.

Just hours after M. Morsi lost power in July 2013, President Barack Obama ordered a review of aid to Egypt and called for a "return of democracy" and to "return full authority to a democratically elected civilian government as soon as possible" (Klein, 2013). In August, after a brutal crackdown, when 500 deaths were reported, Washington cancelled *"Bright Star,"* scheduled for the following month. White House officials did not hide the fact that this was a reaction to the brutal pacifications. This move was supported by the opposition from the Capitol. Republican Senator John McCain urged suspending aid to the Egyptian military, "because the military has overturned the vote of the people. We cannot repeat the same mistakes that we made in other times of our history by supporting removal of freely elected governments" (*McCain*, 2013).

Since the beginning of the Arab Spring, the United States has been trying not to cool its relations with Egypt too much. Washington's wrath was only temporary and little more than symbolic. The United States did not even create convincing semblances of outrage. In late June, the Senate, by a vote of 83–13 rejected a bill to block USD 1.5 bn worth of aid to Egypt because of the military coup. In mid-2013 the White House halted deliveries – not only of kits for the local production of M1A1 *Abrams* tanks, but also AH-64 *Apache* helicopters, RGM-84L *Harpoon* Block II anti-ship missiles and remaining F-16 jets – but the training of the Egyptian military went ahead.

At the same time, the White House did everything possible to convince the public and itself that M. Morsi's removal was not a coup, and thus did not merit a harsh reaction. This should not be greeted with surprise – this is not the first time that the United States chose *Realpolitik* instead of human rights and liberal values. It is worth remembering that in 2006, the White House blocked attempts by Congress to make aid to Egypt conditional on its progress on human rights and democracy. The same hypocritical approach applies to the "jet issue" – in early July 2013, the United States approved the delivery of four F-16C/D Block 50/52 *Fighting Falcon* fighters but later that month – due to public pressure – they decided to delay it. This did not mean either the cancellation of the project or the withdrawal of financial military aid. A few months ago it was announced that Egypt would buy patrol boats in the United States. In April 2014, it was announced that the United States would continue with the sale of 10 AH-64D helicopters.

This tells us two things. First of all, Barack Obama's foreign policy remains inconsistent, ambiguous and contradictory. Secondly, Washington's weak protest is not a result of actions conducted by Egyptian leaders, including President A. F. el-Sisi, but it comes from American interests and the role of Egypt which is too important for the United States to stop military cooperation – especially now, when many armed Islamist groups are active in the Middle East and North Africa, and when Israel is engaged in the Gaza Strip. Frank Wiser, former Ambassador of the United States in Egypt, put it bluntly: "Egypt is the largest and most influential country in the Middle East. Egypt is central to peace with Israel. Egypt's fate will influence the course of politics elsewhere in the region" (*Former*, 2013). In March 2014, General Lloyd J. Austin III (Commander of US Central Command) called Egypt an "anchor state" (*Statement*, 2014: 25). In other words – Egypt is too important to let go, no matter what happens inside it. The best proof of this statement is in the numbers: in 2012 more than 2,000 US military aircraft flew in Egyptian airspace. Up to 45 US 5th Fleet naval ships pass through the Suez Canal annually.

Cutting aid would push Egypt into the hands of anti-Western groups, and neither the United States nor Israel can afford that. There is also a geostrategic reason. Keeping arms deliveries flowing reduces the risk that Egypt will establish close ties with Russia. A. F. el-Sisi is not going to stand by idly, and he used the first opportunity possible to show that he was independent and would not beg the United States for military assistance. He met Russian President Vladimir Putin in Moscow in August 2014. During that meeting, it was reported by Alexander Fomin, the head of Russia's Federal Service for Military-Technical Cooperation, that Egypt had reached a preliminary deal with Russia for arms worth approximately USD 3.5 bn (according to other sources Egypt has already signed two deals worth USD 6.5 bn) (Mustafa, 2014). This move might be an attempt to provoke the United States to re-launch arms deliveries before it is too late.

It is reported that Egypt is interested in procuring MiG-35 jet fighters, air defence systems (probably S-300PMU2s or/and S-300VMs) and Mi-35M assault helicopters. It is also believed that Egypt is interested in mobile coastal defence missiles and submarines, as well as the opening of a Russian helicopter maintenance centre. For Russia, a contract with Egypt would bring not only success in terms of prestige, but also economic and political benefits. This is very important to Moscow not only because of economic sanctions against the Russian economy but also because Russia has been pushed away from the Middle Eastern arms market (including from Libya), and now the Russian defence industry is present significantly only in Syria and Algeria. What is more, in 2014 Russia lost its dominant position in India – it was replaced by the United States. Thus, military relations between Egypt and the United States must be considered from a wider perspective, i.e., relations between the United States and Russia.

INTERNAL DIMENSION

Since Egypt signed a peace accord with Israel in 1979, Cairo has not had any strategic enemies in the region. However, this does not mean that Egypt does not face any threats at all. The major, re-emerging security challenge is the radical Islamist movements – not only domestic groups, but also international fighters pouring into Egypt from outside (including neighbouring, war-torn Libya). The main arena of struggle is the partially demilitarised Sinai Peninsula, which includes the strategic Suez Canal. Both A. Sadat and H. Mubarak fought the Islamic underground, including the Muslim Brotherhood, al-Gamaa al-Islamiya and the Egyptian Islamic Jihad, which despite governmental efforts remained dangerous. Members of radical groups conducted many attacks on tourists, members of parliament, ministers, prime ministers, judges, officers and even H. Mubarak himself.

Despite the activities of the Egyptian security forces, even before the Arab Spring, Sinai, remote, unpopulated, politically alienated and undeveloped, was a region known for smuggling weapons, transnational crime, human trafficking, the activities of armed groups and thousands of refugees. Islamist groups targeted Egyptian policemen, soldiers and even tourists, not to mention the three bomb attacks in October 2004 on tourist hotels in the Gulf of Aqaba in which 34 people were killed and 171 were injured. In July 2005, the resort of Sharm el-Sheikh became a target, and 88 people died. In April 2006, three bombs exploded in a popular resort in Dahab. Islamist terrorists killed 23 people and wounded 80. Approximately 1,200 people died between 2004 and 2006.

After the Arab Spring and the toppling of H. Mubarak, Sinai became the scene of highly dramatic events. Especially after the military removed M. Morsi (who allowed radical elements to enter Sinai, and who made a speech in which he announced opening the door to jihad in Syria, and as a consequence furthering the radicalisation of Egyptian youth), insurgent attacks in Sinai have surged. Three reasons for that change can be found. First of all, for many citizens that was the straw that broke the camel's back, so they decided to fight the military regime. Their rage was also fuelled not only by the fact that M. Morsi was from the Muslim Brotherhood (religious factor), but also because he had promised a new opening in relations between Cairo and Sinai (political and economic factors). Their hopes were left unfulfilled. Secondly, after the Arab Spring, a political and military vacuum was created in Sinai. The Egyptian security forces were withdrawn from Sinai and deployed in the Nile Valley. Some were sent to Cairo, which allowed the radical Islamists to exploit this situation. These two factors created an inflammatory mix which was ignited by a third factor – an influx of weapons from Libya.

The list of attacks is too long to be presented here. It is enough to mention that in August 2011, Egypt launched a campaign code-named operation *"Eagle"* to confront the Sinai insurgency. In August 2012, 16 soldiers were killed near the Rafah border crossing and insurgents assaulted Israel which triggered an armed response from the IDF. After this spectacular attack, the Egyptian security forces launched another crack-down operation, code-named *"Sinai"*. In May 2013, seven soldiers were kidnapped. Since M. Morsi's removal in July there has been an increase in violence. The Egyptian army answered with operation *"Desert Storm,"* but without success – in August at least seven soldiers were killed near El-Arish. Four days later, militants killed 25 policemen in an attack on two busses heading to Rafah. In September, Ansar Beit al-Maqdis tried to assassinate the Minister of the Interior, Mohamed Ibrahim in Cairo, and in November they succeeded in killing Lieutenant Colonel Mohamed Mabrouk, a senior intelligence officer. In October, four soldiers and policemen were killed in a suicide attack, while in November, 10 soldiers died (35 others were wounded). On just one day in October 2014, at least 31 security forces members were killed in two attacks in Sinai. The current war in Sinai has resulted in at least 1,100 fatalities.

Islamist insurgents became very active – they started using not only machine guns, but also RPGs, and staging multi-stage, terror suicide bomb attacks. Armed groups attacked soldiers, policemen, civilians, ships passing through the Suez Canal and infrastructure – including the Arab Gas Pipeline, which exports gas to Jordan, Lebanon and Syria, and even stormed the facilities of the MFO. The security threat forced Israel to temporarily close an airport in Eilat. The concern is even greater when taking into account that local groups receive aid from outside and are affiliated with global jihad.

CONCLUSIONS

Without any exaggeration, it can be said that the Arab Spring has had a massive impact on the Middle East and its political, economic, social and military dimensions. The scale and nature of this impact will be fully recognised and understood only after many years. The Arab Spring brought many changes to the environment around Egypt – some regional leaders were removed, Islamic radicals gained the strength to rise and fight and people in Tunisia, Libya or Syria acquired the courage to demand their rights. Egypt alone was also affected in many ways by the Arab Spring, but surprisingly not too much in its military security dimension. The main reason for that is the fact that the real power was preserved by the military, who did not lose it even for one day. The military keeping its position meant that the direction of Egypt's military security policy remained the same.

With regard to the armed forces, it is impossible to claim that the Arab Spring had any significant impact. The only visible change was a change of leadership – H. Mubarak was replaced at the end of the day by A. F. el-Sisi. The position, influence and tasks of the military did not decrease. The military kept its influence by concentrating on several factors: pressure from the United States, who supports, finances and arms them, but who at the same time has limits to its tolerance; and street pressure. It was rather the reverse – the Arab Spring, particularly the period during protests against H. Mubarak, demonstrated the wide general support on the part of Egyptians for the military. It is true, however, that during the revolution there were voices in Egypt calling for an end to the military's control over entire economic sectors, but the final failure of the Arab Spring allowed the military to survive any attempts aimed at limiting its freedom and imposing civilian control over the armed forces. Of course, this victory is a success for the officer corps and not for the lower ranks, who after finishing their conscription period will become civilians again and will be affected, just like every average Egyptian, by the poor economy.

Preserving the *status quo* will have negative economic and thus social and political consequences in the longer term, but from the short-term perspective it serves Egypt's stability and the interests of many actors who did not want any deep changes. This applies first of all to the United States who, despite the removal of its ally, H. Mubarak, and the bloody crackdowns, decided not to limit its cooperation with Egypt or to increase the pressure for democratisation. The same applies to Israel, who wants to keep the current *status quo*, i.e., a rational, stable and predictable military government. Stability is also in the interest of states like Saudi Arabia, the United Arab Emirates and Kuwait, which have invested billions of dollars in Egypt in recent years. Egypt under military reign, of whether A. F. el-Sisi or other officers, is in their best interests, and thus they will not seek any deep changes.

The Arab Spring did not bring an increase in threats to Egypt from neighbouring states. With regard to internal security, however, the consequences are different. The Arab Spring, particularly the overthrow of M. Morsi, led to a revival of the armed resistance of radical Islamists, strengthened from the Gaza Strip and Libya. This violent struggle occurred not only in the Sinai Peninsula, historically unstable and socially, politically and economically undeveloped, but also in Cairo. The rise of violence since 2011, therefore also during the reign of the pro-Islamic M. Morsi, was a surprise, and occurred for many reasons, including the appearance of a political and military vacuum as well as the frustration that had been growing for years. This is without any doubt the biggest challenge for the Egyptian security forces, and it is highly likely that Egypt will face more security problems in the Sinai and other parts of the country in the coming period.

Only a proper combination of military instruments, international cooperation and the removal of the roots of popular discontent can bring a change in the long term. However, is the Egyptian military capable of delivering this? It is highly unlikely. What is more probable is that the problem of radical Islamist militants, as well as the geostrategic and economic meaning of the Suez Canal (eight percent of global trade passes through the canal, including three percent of oil) will keep the United States and Israel engaged in Egypt, no matter who runs the country, as long as they are not anti-Western. If the Egyptian leaders decide not to change their current course (which is highly likely – they have no reason to change as they are the main beneficiary of the current relations) both the United States and Israel will not change their policy towards Egypt either. Neither of them can afford for Egypt to sink into a civil war, like Syria since 2011, or for it to be captured by radical, anti-Western, hostile Islamists, as happened to Iran in 1979.

However, although the Arab Spring has not had a significant impact on Egypt's military security policy so far, it does not mean that it will not do so in the future, and that we will not witness deep changes. Even deep-rooted foundations can be replaced by other strategic assumptions, which is obvious when the Iranian example of 1979 is taken into account. If the Muslim Brotherhood had remained in power longer, it would have likely led to some (possibly deep) changes – including in relations with the United States and the "Zionist regime". The army stopped this process, and even imposed a more repressive policy than in the past (*Egypt*, 2014). However, even the position of the armed forces could then deteriorate. The Egyptian military saved the situation, but for how long? Even such a powerful institution can be defeated and lose power.

As mentioned above, preserving the *status quo* will not bring positive economic, and thus social and political changes in Egypt in the longer term. In other words, saving the *status quo* in the security dimension means also maintaining the petrification in the Egyptian economy. This means that the Egyptian revolution will start again one day – it was interrupted when M. Morsi was overthrown, but the potential for a fresh wave of public anger still exists – promises of reforms remain unfulfilled. The economy is in a poor condition and the military have no idea how to change that. What is more, they see no reason to change it significantly, as they profit from the current situation. Social peace in Egypt requires more jobs and higher salaries, but this is impossible without more freedom and liberalism. However, in such a system there is no space for the military and their economic privileges, including tax exemptions, the best salaries, healthcare and the comfort to offer prices far below private-sector companies.

Military rule means stability, but also stagnation, and the Egyptian society still expects changes. What is more, after the revolution in 2011, it seems to be more open, more opinionated and daring, more aware of its power and rights. The Egyptian army might win another round of internal struggles, but at some point it will lose – every regime has its end someday. This change might arrive sooner than we expect, because we do not fully know the morale of the Egyptian troops (especially the lower ranks) and the current strength and cohesion of the military. Furthermore, the Islamists are far from being marginalised or defeated. Many people in Egypt are pro-Islamist, as they see religion as the only possible remedy to the current poor economic and political situation, the only constant and trustworthy element in their lives. The military, based on conscription, are a reflection of Egyptian society. At some point, Islamic movements could infiltrate the army's "hearts and minds" so deeply that soldiers will commit mutiny. Of course, one could oppose such a claim by answering that thousands of Egyptian military personnel have been trained by the Americans, so they will not oppose good relations with the United States and Israel, but the same was said about Iran in 1979.

BIBLIOGRAPHY

Ashour O. (2013), *Ballots versus Bullets: The Crisis of Civil-Military Relations in Egypt*, http://www.brookings.edu/research/articles/2013/09/03-civil-military-relations--egypt-ashour, 29.04.2015.

El Fegiery M. (2012), *Crunch Time for Egypt's Civil-Military Relations*, "Policy Brief – Fride", No. 134/2012.

El Gundy Z. (2011), *Egypt's Defence Minister Calls for 'Dialogue Meeting' Wednesday*, http://english.ahram.org.eg/NewsContent/1/64/60316/Egypt/Politics-/Egypts-defence-minister-calls-for-dialogue-meeting.aspx, 29.04.2015.

Egypt's Rulers Resist Muslim Brotherhood's Push to Open Gaza Border (2012), http://www.haaretz.com/news/middle-east/egypt-s-rulers-resist-muslim-brotherhood-s-push-to-open-gaza-border-1.420035, 29.04.2015.

Egypt: Unprecedented Expansion of Military Courts (2014), http://www.hrw.org/news/2014/11/17/egypt-unprecedented-expansion-military-courts, 29.04.2015.

Egypt, U.S. Delay 'Bright Star' Exercise (2011), archive.defensenews.com/article/20110817/DEFSECT04/108170301/Egypt-U-S-Delay-Bright-Star-Exercise, 29.04.2015.

Elmenshawy M. (2014), *Revisiting Egypt's Civil-Military Relations*, http://www.aljazeera.com/indepth/opinion/2014/05/revisiting-egypt-civil-militar-2014528115444200894.html, 29.04.2015.

Former US Ambassador to Egypt Says Morsi Ouster Not a Coup (2013), http://www.newsmax.com/Newsfront/wisner-ambassador-egypt-morsi/2013/07/05/id/513572/, 29.04.2015.

Hauslohner A. (2014), *Egypt's Military Expands its Control of the Country's Economy*, http://www.washingtonpost.com/world/middle_east/egyptian-military-expands--its-economic-control/2014/03/16/39508b52-a554-11e3-b865-38b254d92063_story.html, 29.04.2015.

Ignatius D. (2012), *Israel's Arab Spring Problem*, http://www.washingtonpost.com/opinions/david-ignatius-israels-arab-spring-problem/2012/07/05/gJQAV5JrRW_story.html, 29.04.2015.

Kershner I. (2012), *Israel Asks Egypt to Remove Tanks from Sinai*, http://www.nytimes.com/2012/08/22/world/middleeast/israel-asks-egypt-to-remove-tanks-from-sinai.html?_r=0, 29.04.2015.

Kershner I. (2011), *Warily Eyeing Egypt, Israelis Feel Like Spectators*, http://www.nytimes.com/2011/01/27/world/middleeast/27israel.html, 29.04.2015.

Klein K. (2013), *Obama Orders Review of US Aid to Egypt*, http://www.voanews.com/content/obama-orders-review-of-us-aid-to-egypt-after-morsi-ousted/1694817.html, 29.04.2015.

Lev D. (2013), *Farkash: It's Not an 'Arab Spring,' But an 'Arab Tsunami'*, http://www.israelnationalnews.com/News/News.aspx/171694#.VUDZ6iHtmko, 29.04.2015.

McCain Urges US to Suspend Military Aid (2013), http://www.aljazeera.com/news/americas/2013/07/2013766819603784.html, 29.04.2015.

Makara M. (2013), *CoupProofing, Military Defection, and the Arab Spring*, "Democracy and Security", 2013.

MacBride E. (2014), *While We Weren't Looking, an Arab Economy Took Off*, http://www.cnbc.com/id/102141210, 29.04.2015.

Mayton J. (2012), *The Egyptian Army's Invisible Hand*, http://www.jpost.com/Middle-East/The-Egyptian-armys-invisible-hand, 29.04.2015.

Miller E. (2012), *Egyptian Parliament Demands to Cut Ties with Israel Over Gaza*, http://www.timesofisrael.com/egyptian-parliament-demands-to-cut-ties-with-israel--over-gaza/, 29.04.2015.

Mott W. H. (2002), *United States Military Assistance: An Empirical Perspective*, Westport 2002.

Muslim Brotherhood Vows Not to Recognize Israel (2012), http://www.jpost.com/Middle-East/Muslim-Brotherhood-vows-not-to-recognize-Israel, 29.04.2015.

Mustafa A. (2014), *Russia Making Major Push Into Mideast Market*, "DefenseNews", 18.10.2014.

Ravid B. (2011), *Israel's Diplomatic Ties with Egypt Down to Bare Minimum*, http://www.haaretz.com/print-edition/news/israel-s-diplomatic-ties-with-egypt-down-to-bare-minimum-1.383848, 29.04.2015.

Sayigh Y. (2013), *Morsi and Egypt's Military*, http://www.al-monitor.com/pulse/originals/2013/01/morsi-army-egypt-revolution.html, 29.04.2015.

Siryoti D. (2012), *Poll: Most Egyptians Hate Israel, But Don't Want War with It*, http://www.israelhayom.com/site/newsletter_article.php?id=4428, 29.04.2015.

Statement of General Lloyd J. Austin III Before the House Appropriations Committee Defense Subcommittee (2014), http://docs.house.gov/meetings/AP/AP02/20140314/101863/HHRG-113-AP02-Wstate-AustinL-20140314.pdf, 29.04.2015.

Sullivan D. (2005), *Egypt*, in: *Countries at the Crossroads: A Survey of Democratic Governance*, eds. S. Repucci, C. Valker, Lanham.

Tadros S. (2012), *Egypt Military's Economic Empire*, http://www.aljazeera.com/indepth/features/2012/02/2012215195912519142.html, 29.04.2015.

Welch C. E. (1976), *Civilian Control of the Military: Myth and Reality*, in: *Civilian Control of the Military: Theory and Cases from Developing Countries*, ed. C. E. Welch, New York.

Xenaxis J. J. (2014), *World View: Hamas is at War with Egypt More Than Israel*, http://www.breitbart.com/national-security/2014/08/09/9-aug-14-world-view-hamas-is-at-war-with-egypt-more-than-israel/, 29.04.2015.

Marcin STYSZYŃSKI

Adam Mickiewicz University, Poznań

POLITICAL REACTIONS OF EGYPTIAN ISLAMISTS DURING AL-SISI'S PRESIDENCY

INTRODUCTION

After three years of the Arab Spring, local societies have changed their attitude to the crucial values of the revolution such as democracy, freedom, liberalism or the struggle against authoritarianism. Egyptian, Tunisian or Libyan
societies started to compare those ideas to chaos, destabilisation, terrorism
and economic crisis. Public opinion in the Arab world invented a new definition: *kharif arabi* (Arab autumn), which has replaced the positive meanings of
the Arab Spring.

The overthrow of President Mohammad Morsi and the Muslim Brotherhood
authorities in Egypt, as well as General Abd al-Fattah al-Sisi's takeover in 2013,
provoked concerns among Islamists who accepted the post-revolutionary authorities, or were involved in radical activities like terrorist attacks, kidnappings
and guerrilla fights.

POSITIVE REACTIONS OF ISLAMIST REPRESENTATIVES

Some Salafi movements reinterpreted loyalty to the government, basing their
opinions on the philosophy of conservative Muslim scholars like Abu Hanifa
(d. 767), Ahmad Ibn Hanbal (d. 855) or Ibn Taymiyya (d. 1328) and Abd
al-Wahhab (d. 1792), who ordered allegiance to the caliphs and emirs representing the *Umma* (Muslim Nation) (Al-Khazraji, 2011: 277–286). Disobedience of
the ruler was allowed in case of sinful and corrupt behavior or policies. However, negative opinions about the Caliph were elaborated carefully by different
theologians who issued a common *fatwa* (legal judgments) to accuse and im-
peach the Ruler. The following examples show the implementation of the philosophy by particular Islamist leaders.

President A. F. al-Sisi encouraged some Islamists to attend his symbolic conference on July 3, 2013, declaring the defeat of the Muslim Brotherhood's power
in Egypt. A positive response was declared by the *Nour* (Light) party and its representatives, such as Nader Bakkar or Jalal al-Mura. The party follows a Salafi
ideology and a preaching activity called *Dawa salafiyya* (Salafi Call). *Nour*
played an important role after the collapse of Hosni Mubarak's regime, and it
became the second political power after the Freedom and Justice party affiliated

with the Muslim Brotherhood. In addition, Salafi theologians like Yasser Borhami supported A. F. Al-Sisi's presidential campaign by issuing theological manifestos and a *fatwa* justifying the policy of the army and glorifying the candidate for the presidency. *Nour's* key figures stated that A. F. Al-Sisi guaranties security, stability and a peaceful transition process in the country. In their opinions the new leader also preserves the Muslim identity of the society and the moral values of Islam (Cunningham, 2014).

The secular and military authorities strengthened the state surveillance of political and social life. They arrested the core leaders of the Muslim Brotherhood and sentenced many of them to death or exile. In addition, Islamist communication sources, such as newspapers, TV channels and public offices were closed.

Moreover, religious institutions, such as Al-Azhar (one of the oldest theological universities in the Muslim world) or the Ministry of Religious Affairs were forced to control mosques, Muslim scholars and *khutba* (sermon). In fact, the state tried to avoid conflict between religious and political debate in the country. Muslim theologians often combined the religious structure and messages of a sermon with political slogans and supported particular parties or organisations. In fact, a sermon in Islam can be delivered not only by accredited theologians, but also by persons called a *sheikh*. This is usually an old man, respected in the local community, who can recite the Quran and has some experience in public speaking. Political leaders took advantage of the idea, called themselves *sheikhs* and delivered ideological or political manifestos based on the structure and stylistic devices of *khutba* (Lewis, 1988).

In this regard, religious institutions forbade radical scholars from delivering public speeches. This concerns Sheikh Mohammad Hasan Yaqub, Sheikh Mohammad Hassan and Ishaq al-Huwayni in particular, who supported the Islamist movements and some radical candidates in the parliamentary and presidential elections in 2012. The Ministry of Religious Affairs also appointed 20,000 new scholars who were loyal to the new government. The restoration of the basic structures and stylistic devices of the discourse played an important role as well. Muslim scholars presented certain norms and advice regarding the narration, subjects and style of a sermon, as well as the attributes of the orator (Rashdi, 2014).

Muslim scholars state that sermons should be delivered by accredited persons who hold religious education, skills, common sense, responsibility and experience. A sermon shall be presented from a podium in the mosque at high noon. The speaker wears liturgical clothes and always stands up during the first part of the speech. After a short prayer he can sit down and start his speech. In addition, chaotic gestures, uncontrolled behavior or a very loud voice should be avoided (Jones, 2012; Qutbuddin, 2008: 176–274).

Apart from personal skills, religious institutions stress that orators must obey the liturgical narration of *khutba* regarding religious invocations, appropriate quotations from the Quran and *hadiths* (stories and statements attributed to the Prophet Mohammad) as well as phrases indicating particular sections of the sermon.

Theologians also criticise the political context of the sermons and they recommend a conciliatory and moderate character in the discourse. They advise imams to reinforce the theological, existential and social message of the sermon. In their opinions, orators should focus on religious and moral values, such as piety, honesty, dignity, patience, justice as well as generosity, forgiveness or *huda* (the right way in life). The words are confronted with negative meanings in order to prevent believers from a sinful life and bad behavior (Maher, 2014). Apart from religious questions, a sermon has to refer to current social needs and expectations, such as poverty, unemployment, hunger, or drug addiction and violence (Horannisian, Sabagh, 1999).

NEGATIVE REACTIONS OF ISLAMISTS

The Muslim Brotherhood, and some Salafi representatives who joined the new party *Hizb al-watan* (Nation Party), expressed their dislike of President A. F. Al-Sisi and started to organise various demonstrations, mass rallies or roadblocks. However, the violent pacification of the protests, arrests of top leaders, as well as the closure of official TV channels, newspapers and journals, forced the religious opposition to revive underground activities and propaganda techniques. Internet websites, social media or forums became the main communication channels for Islamists who have used that media to reach a mass audience and influence the emotions and reactions of the public (Messieh, 2013).

Moreover, the political reactions of the opposition concern two opposite images based on political statements and ideological manifestos, as well as video and audio materials or graphics, caricatures and photos. The first image reflects negative opinions about the policy of President A. F. Al-Sisi and the second concerns the sentimental features and martyrdom attributed to Islamists humiliated by the secular and military forces.

The Rabia sign became a crucial element in the campaign. It commemorates the Rabia al-Adawiya massacre, express solidarity with the victims and demonstrates the victory over President M. Morsi. After the Rabia dispersal, the symbol emerged widely in social media and protest marches. M. Morsi's followers created Internet websites describing Rabia's meanings and presenting various graphics and photos (Hellyer, 2014).

The opposition often applies particular epithets that discredits Egyptian officials who are called *inqilab* (coup d'état), *milishiyyat al-inqilab* (militias of the coup d'état) or *saffah* (killer, murder). The words are juxtaposed with the positive symbol of Tahrir Square in 2011, where thousands of protesters expressed their anger and resistance. Islamists used the symbol, and combined it with emotional epithets like *thawra* (revolution), *hurriyya* (freedom), *adala ijtima'iyya* (social justice) or *shab* (people) and *shabab* (youth) (*Muslim*, 2014).

Furthermore, the Islamic groups present information and reports describing violent acts of the security services against members of the opposition and demonstrators. Some headlines highlight the restrictive laws and regulations imposed during A. F. Al-Sisi's presidency, arrests of protesters and clashes with police (*The Rabi'a*, 2014). Media sources also include provocative photos and graphics showing the brutality of the security services, casualties among protesters and damage left after clashes. State violence is contrasted with the legitimacy of M. Morsi, the first free elections in Egypt, legal power and respect of human rights.

The propaganda materials often refer to social and economic problems such as power and water cuts, or price increases and the growing crime rate on the Egyptian streets. Tragic events like bus or train accidents are blamed on the new authorities as well. The opposition states that secularists are responsible for transport policy and the bad condition of vehicles and roads. It should be pointed out that road accidents have occurred in Egypt for a long time and they have become one of the major social problems in modern Egypt. However, the issue has always been used in political debate and has affected disputes in society between rival factions (Elshahed, 2014).

The opposition also puts forward conspiracy theories about the new authorities. Some statements stress that A. F. Al-Sisi's mother belongs to a Jewish family from Morocco (Hasanayn, 2013). Apart from historic anti-Zionist tendencies in the Arab society, the argument refers to the Egyptian constitution, underlining that the president must be an Egyptian born to Egyptian parents (*State*, 2014). This claim has been denied many times by officials, but it aroused suspicions and speculation among Egyptians.

Apart from demonstrations and a propaganda campaign, the Islamic opposition radicalised its activities and increased terrorist attacks against the central government in Cairo and local security services. It concerns groups referring to the concept of *takfir* (excommunication), which considers the state and the society as a sinful and atheistic group supporting immoral and corrupt governments. In addition, the idea of *takfir* is close to jihadist activities regarding the violent renaissance of the historic caliphate and implementation of strict sharia rules. Extremist groups also apply the defensive and offensive sense of jihad to the modern political context related to Western policy in the Muslim world (Brachman, 2008: 45–47).

Moreover, Egyptian jihadists take advantage of separatist tendencies among Bedouins in Sinai, who declare their cultural and political independence from the central government in Cairo and support the local rebels. The geo-strategic values of the Sinai, located near the Israeli border and the Suez Canal play an important role as well (*Egypt's*, 2007).

The region has also been infiltrated by neighboring groups like *Al-Qa'ida fi Jazirat al-Arab* (Al-Qaeda in the Arabian Peninsula – AQAP) formed in 2009 under the leadership of Naser al-Wuhayshi who served as a private secretary to Osama bin Laden in Afghanistan (Roggio, 2011). Al-Qaeda also supported local cells like *Kataib Abdellah Yusuf Azzam* (Abdellah Yusuf Azzam Brigades) or *Jama'at at-Tawhid wa al-Jihad* (The Groups of Monotheism and Jihad), which carried out various terrorist attacks. For example, the group was responsible for the Taba bombings in 2004, when bomb blasts targeted hotels, killing 31 people and wounding 159 others. In 2005, Sharm el-Sheikh was affected by a series of bombings that killed 88 and injured 200. In 2006, *Jama'at at-Tawhid wa al-Jihad* was involved in attacks on the tourist resorts in Dahab, where 23 tourists died and 80 persons were wounded by bomb blasts (Williams, 2005).

After the collapse of H. Mubarak's regime, the new group *Ansar Bayt al-Maqdis* (Supporters of Jerusalem) followed their comrades-in-arms and increased the terror campaign in order to put pressure on the new post-revolutionary governments and achieve political and economic privileges. However, their intensification of the terrorist campaign started after the overthrow of President M. Morsi. From July to February 2014, *Ansar Bayt al-Maqdis* conducted more than 300 attacks in Sinai. For example, on 24 October 2014, militants launched two attacks on Egyptian army positions in the Sinai Peninsula, killing at least 33 security personnel. This was one of the deadliest assaults on the Egyptian military in decades. In February 2014, a suicide attack on a bus killed 3 foreign tourists and injured 17 (Joscelyn, 2014).

In addition, another jihadist branch *Ajnad Masr* (Soldiers of Egypt) is conducting operations in big Egyptian cities like Cairo and Alexandria. The group highlighted its activities before the third anniversary of the Egypt Revolution 2011, when a car bomb exploded near the main police headquarters in the capital causing a great deal of damage, including the Museum of Islamic Art located near the target. The group is also responsible for other terrorist plots at metro stations, public buildings, politicians or security services (Al-Tawy, 2014).

Jihadist groups are also more radical in their rhetoric than other Islamists. They refer to traditional propaganda conducted by Ayman al-Zawahiri or Abdullah Yusuf Azzam, a Palestinian teacher and mentor of Osama bin Laden during the Afghan war, who supported the establishment of a worldwide terrorist organisation and drew on the ideology of fighting Western influences in the Arab-Muslim world, named a new crusade against Islam (Wright, 2006).

Ansar Bayt al-Maqdis bases its indoctrination campaign on previous traditions and applies liturgical and theological devices, such as invocations and particular quranic quotations aimed at political and ideological enemies. Its manifestos and statements also include various epithets and euphemisms, like *salibiyyun* (crusaders), *hamla salibiyya* (crusade campaign) or *kuffar* (sinners), *sihyuniyyun* (Zionists) and *taghut* (a devil, a Satan). These concern the harmful features of their political opponents and arouse negative emotions in the audience (*Al-Minbar al-ilami al-jihadi*, 2014).

The Egyptian jihadist scene is also affected by the latest offensives of *Ad-Dawla al-Islamiyya fi al-Iraq wa ash-Sham* (the Islamic State of Iraq and Syria – ISIS) or *Ad-Dawla al-Islamiyya* (The Islamic State) headed by Abu Bakr al-Baghdadi.

In November 2014, the main jihadist website *Al-Manbar al-jihadi al-ilami* (Jihadist Media Platform) published a long letter of allegiance to Al-Baghdadi declared by different organisations including *Ansar Bayt al-Maqdis*.

It should be pointed out that the old generations of jihadists still declare loyalty to Al-Qaeda leader Ayman al-Zawahiri, but young insurgents, including the Egyptian fighters, started to express their disobedience to Al-Qaeda and are fascinated by the successful military and ideological campaign in Iraq and Syria by ISIS. According to the latest statements of *Ansar Bayt al-Maqdis*, the group encourages its militants to implement sharia laws and to establish a similar caliphate in Sinai called *Wilayat as-Sina* (Sinai Province).

CONCLUSION

The analysis presented in the paper has demonstrated three major trends among Islamists in post-revolutionary Egypt.

The first factor concerns the tendencies towards reconciliation among Salafi leaders, who declare their loyalty to President A. F. Al-Sisi in line with the philosophy of classic, conservative scholars. The research shows that the secular and military authorities have reinforced state surveillance of religious debate. Moreover, religious institutions and ministries were forced to place restrictions on Muslim scholars, mosques and Friday sermons in order to avoid extremist messages and the radicalisation of believers.

The second factor reflects the propaganda and media campaign of the opposition, including the Muslim Brotherhood and some Salafists. Internet websites, social media or forums have become the main communication channels, especially since the arrest of the main leaders and the banning of the Islamist mainstream media. An Internet campaign enabled them to express their political reactions and dislikes of the current situation in the country.

The third aspect of the research regards the radicalisation of particular Islamist groups. They increased terrorist attacks against the central government in Cairo and local security services. For instance, *Ansar Bayt al-Maqdis* (Supporters of Jerusalem) launched a terror campaign in Sinai in order to put pressure on the new government and achieve ideological goals.

Moreover, Egyptian jihadists have been inspired and infiltrated by *Ad-Dawla al-Islamiyya* (Islamic State) headed by Abu Bakr al-Baghdadi. According to the latest statements published on jihadist websites, *Ansar Bayt al-Maqdis* has encouraged its militants to enforce sharia laws and to establish a similar caliphate in Sinai called *Wilayat as-Sina* (Sinai Province).

BIBLIOGRAPHY

Al-Khazraji N. (2011), *Ashari'at al-bayan*, Bayrut.

Al-Minbar al-ilami al-jihadi (2014), https://www.alplatformmedia.com/vb/index.php, 10.12.2014.

Al-Tawy A. (2014), *Cairo hit by four bomb blasts on Friday, killing 6*, http://english.ahram.org.eg/NewsContent/1/64/92374/Egypt/Politics-/UPDATE—Cairo-hit-by-three-bomb-blasts-on-Friday,-.aspx, 30.11.2014.

Brachman M. J. (2008), *Global Jihadism: Theory and Practice*, New York.

Cunningham E. (2014), *Egypt's Salafist Nour party in tenuous political alliance with president-elect Sissi*, "The Washington Post", 01.06.2014.

Egypt's Sinai Question (2007), International Crisis Group, "Middle East/North Africa Report", No. 61.

Elshahed M. (2014), *Road Rage*, "The Cairo Review of Global Affairs", 24.08.2012.

Hasanayn S. (2013), *Harb ash-shai'at didda wazir ad-difa' al-misri la tantahi*, "Elaph", 14.08.2013.

Hellyer H. A. (2014), *Egypt should engage global community on Rabia*, http://www.al-monitor.com/pulse/ru/originals/2014/08/egypt-violent-actions-against-pro-morsi-sit-ins.html, 22.11.2014.

Horannisian G., Sabagh G. (1999), *Religion and culture in medieval Islam*, Cambridge.

Jones L. (2012), *The Power of oratory in the medieval Muslim world*, Cambridge.

Joscelyn T. (2014), *Al-Qaeda's expansion in Egypt. Implications for U.S. Homeland security*, "Foundation for Defense of Democracies", 11.02.2014.

Lewis B. (1988), *The Political language of islam*, Chicago.

Maher A. (2014), *Egypt mosques: Weekly sermon themes set by government*, http://www.bbc.com/news/world-middle-east-25983912, 10.12.2014.

Messieh N. (2013), *Muslim Brotherhood Leader Arrests*, "Atlantic Council", 06.09.2013.

Muslim Brotherhood official Internet website (2014), http://www.ikhwanonline.com/Article.aspx?ArtID=208586&SecID=480, 22.11.2014.

Qutbuddin T. (2008), *Khutba. The Evolution of early Arabic oration*, in: *Classical Arabic humanities in their own terms: festschrift for Wolfhart Heinrichs on his 65th birthday*, eds. B. Gruendler, M. Cooperson, Leiden.

Rashdi R. (2014), *Nunshiru bi-at-tafasil nusus wa mawdu'at khutab al-juma al-muwahadda ala mustawa masajid Maar*, "Al-Fajr", 29.01.2014.

Roggio B. (2011), *AQAP leader pledges oath of allegiance to Ayman al Zawahiri*, http://www.longwarjournal.org/archives/2011/07/aqap_leader_pledges.php#ixzz39u3GeMW4, 29.06.2014.

State Information Service, Your Gateway to Egypt (2014), http://www.sis.gov.eg/En/Templates/Articles/tmpArticles.aspx?ArtID=66477#.VHFSfhFmxDA, 22.11.2014.

The Rabi'a Massacre and Mass Killings of Protesters in Egypt (2014), "Human Rights Watch", http://www.hrw.org/reports/2014/08/12/all-according-plan, 22.11.2014.

Williams D. (2005), *Egypt gets tough in Sinai in wake of resort attacks*, "The Washington Post", 02.10.2005.

Wright L. (2006), *Looming Tower: Al Qaeda and the Road to 9/11*, New York.

Artur WEJKSZNER
Adam Mickiewicz University, Poznań

THE DEMOCRATIC TRANSFORMATIONS IN EGYPT AS PERCEIVED BY THE REPRESENTATIVES OF THE GLOBAL JIHADIST MOVEMENT

INTRODUCTION

At the beginning of 2011, Egypt and other Arab states entered a new stage in their history. In the opinion of Western observers, the pro-democratic revolt initiated by the events in Tunisia, and later in Egypt, gave the Arabs the hope of achieving political freedom and civil liberties they had never previously experienced. The Western perception of the revolution in North Africa and the Arab Peninsula, however, lacks a considerable aspect, namely the point of view of the Muslim world, rooted in its exceptionally complicated history, culture and utterly different motivations for the social and political activities of Muslims. The ousting of the authoritarian regimes resulted in the disclosure of a number of political groups and movements that had formerly operated in a clandestine manner. The global Salafi jihadist movement deserves to be mentioned here. The term 'Salafism' is primarily associated with the renewal movement of the Muslim world, initiated by Muslim traditionalists at the turn of the 19th century – Jamal al-Din al-Afghani and Muhammad Abduh. The most fundamental call of Salafists is to pursue the path (follow the example) of their devout ancestors (*al-Salaf al-Salih*) ruled by the righteous caliphs. It has become very popular among Muslim activists, in particular those in North Africa. In the opinion of Farhard Khosrokhavar, jihadism is the greatest modern utopian and anti-Western social movement aiming to achieve its essential goals, including the establishment of a Muslim order, by use of violence (Khosrokhavar, 2009: 1). The events in Egypt and other states in the region have posed a serious strategic challenge for jihadists. They were not actually ready for such a challenge, as it was the jihadist *avant-garde* rather than pro-democratic movements that was supposed to initiate the process of rapid, revolutionary changes, leading to the new order to be established (Zerate, Gordon, 2011: 103–104). In the view of the most prominent representatives of the jihadist movement, the idea of democratic reforms appears to contradict the idea of reform through jihad, advocated by Ayman al-Zawahiri, among others. The response of jihadist ideologists to the events in Egypt and other MENA countries is distinctively reactive. Neither in terms of organisation nor ideology, was the jihadist movement ready to assume control over the process of revolutionary transformations in the largest Arab

state. The anti-nationalism of jihadists was the main obstacle in their developing a coherent vision, strategy and operating tactics corresponding to the situation in Egypt and other countries in this region. The analysis of the events in
terms of strategy, however, allowed jihadists to distinguish two hostile groups
that exerted an influence on the situation at the time: a close enemy (secular,
anti-Muslim regimes) being aided by a distant enemy (Western regimes led by
the US). This actually meant that the battle field stretched far beyond the area of
the Muslim states covered by revolutionary turmoil. The typical and broadly
promoted jihadist, anti-democratic and pro-Islamic vision of social relations
did not find a sympathetic ear in Egypt or in other countries in this region. Was
this due to its anachronism, which was inconsistent with the expectations of the
most active participants in the Egyptian revolution? Was that why the jihadists
remained passive, failing to take the lead in the process of political transition?
Does their radical vision stand a chance of being implemented in the foresee-
able future, given the attempts to restore the old order?

OSAMA BIN LADEN AND THE ANTICIPATION OF THE ISLAMIC REVOLUTION

Until his death in 2011, Osama bin Laden, a co-founder of al-Qaeda and one of
the most influential ideologists of the global jihadist movement, was actively
trying to promote the foundations of jihadist ideology, criticising the situation
of Muslims in states ruled by secular regimes. His proclamations and speeches
were extensively distributed in jihadist circles, providing a reference point in
discussions on the strategic and tactical goals and the methods of fight and response to the events taking place everywhere jihadist groups were active. Regardless of the local or regional contexts, or the evolutionary stage of the jihadist
movement, bin Laden was always hopeful about the radical Islamic youth
(*fatyan al-Islam*) which found inspiration in the beginnings of Islam and the
achievements of its first followers (*li'ahdi ajdadihim*) (Lahoud, al'Ubaydi, 2013:
29); bin Laden believed that young people were the main force behind the
changes which were to take place in the area of Dar al-Islam.

In his speeches from before the revolution, bin Laden frequently indicated
the directions of changes that should be considered by Muslims living in
Maghreb and the Middle East. He also anticipated the necessity to take control
over future events, writing that "[i]t would be nice to remind our brothers in
the regions to be patient and deliberate, and warn them of entering into confrontations with the parties belonging to Islam, and it is probable that most of
the areas will have governments established on the remnants of the previous
governments, and most probably these governments will belong to the Islamic
parties and groups, like the Brotherhood and the like" (Joscelyn, 2015); he also
added that "[o]ur duty at this stage is to pay attention to the call among Mus-

lims and win over supporters and spread the correct understanding [...] as the current conditions have brought on unprecedented opportunities and the coming of Islamic governments that follow the Salafi doctrine is a benefit to Islam" (Joscelyn, 2015). He also envisaged that "[t]he more time that passes and the call increases, the more the supporters will be of the people, and the more widespread will be the correct understanding among the coming generations of Islamic groups" (Joscelyn, 2015). Right before his death, bin Laden recorded one of his last speeches, where he took an unambiguous stance concerning the first successes of Islamic young people in North African states, noting that "we watch with you this great historic event and share with you joy and happiness and delight and felicity [...] so congratulation to you for your victories" (Wilner, 2011: 55). Osama bin Laden could only anticipate the future success that was, however, impossible to be achieved in his lifetime.

AYMAN AL-ZAWAHIRI: TOWARDS THE ISLAMIC REVOLUTION IN EGYPT

Ayman al-Zawahiri was among the co-founders of the global jihadist movement. Since the very beginning of al-Qaeda, he was among the closest associates of Osama bin Laden and the leadership of the group (for instance, he was a member of the al-Qaeda Consulting Board). After the demise of bin Laden, he continued his legacy, taking the post of the emir heading the central authorities of the jihadist movement.

Holding such a prominent position in the movement, he used it to present his own point of view on the current developments in Muslim states, named the Arab Spring. His reflections were included in a series of eleven speeches addressed at Egypt's Muslims. They are an important voice in the discussion on the future of the Muslim world, and call for active participation in the increasingly strong global jihadist movement. The issue of Egypt was one of the focal points of reference in A. al-Zawahiri's speeches and publications (at least 226 mentions before the outbreak of the revolution), second only to the issue of the principal enemy of jihadists – the United States (mentioned over 600 times) (Nasira, 2011a: 6).

The fundamental part A. of al-Zawahiri's reflections concerns the reception of events in Arab states and their historical perspective. In his opinion, secular regimes – whether authoritarian or democratic – are conducive to the spread of corruption and social injustice. This is the case in the fields of politics, economy, society and morality. The word 'secular' is equivalent to 'atheist' for the leader of the jihadist movement, who treated Egypt's regime as such. Egypt promoted an anti-Islamic, Western point of view on the functioning of social and political structures. Order based on Islamic law was consciously rejected in favour of a secular order rooted in the positive legislation made by Egypt's decision-

-makers. In A. al-Zawahiri's opinion, this system of governance is pervaded by injustice (*jahiliyya*). He believes that democracy equates to an opportunity to make the majority of decisions with no reference to axiology and defying all moral standards. It is the nature of democratic regimes to be secular, hence atheist. In his opinion, the societies that introduced this order, that is Western societies, usurp the right to being called civilised. This is contradicted by the fact that the interests of minorities, especially religious minorities, are frequently neglected or blatantly ignored by the majority (Wejkszner, 2011: 60).

It is irrelevant for a Muslim whether he lives in an authoritarian or democratic state, since none of these systems takes the order of the Quran into consideration. Explaining this aspect of his reflections, A. al-Zawahiri contrasted the concepts of citizenship and nationalism with those of Islamic community/commune (*umma*). The only solution that is accessible to Muslims to abandon oppressive anti-Muslim regimes is therefore the establishment of a caliphate based on Islamic law (*Sharia*). A. al-Zawahiri sees the colonial past as the source of the enslavement of the Muslim world and its contagion with the virus of democracy. In the context of the geographical area he refers to (that is North Africa and the Arab Peninsula), France and the United Kingdom are the main perpetrators. In the second half of the 20th century they were joined by the United States and Israel. The promotion of democratic values is strictly related to their particular interests that have nothing in common with the interests of Muslims whatsoever (Wejkszner, 2011: 60).

One of the fundamental reasons for the civilisational backwardness of the Muslim world (A. al-Zawahiri mentioned the technological and military aspect) was its division into a number of small states, with borders drawn up by the European colonisers applying artificial and political premises. The European powers were the ones who decided that introducing an Islamic order was against their interests. Their political supervision over the Arab world in the early 20th century was replaced by its economic subordination in the second half of the same century. Western regimes backed authoritarian governments (supplying them with financial means and weapons) that were oppressive towards Muslims. In this context, the promotion of democratic values is another step aiming to permanently subordinate the Muslim world to the West (Wejkszner, 2011: 60–61).

According to A. al-Zawahiri, the reasons for revolutions in Arab states should not be associated primarily with demands for democracy, but rather with the social reception of the situation that directly led to the revolutions. Among many other reasons, the jihadist leader mentions corruption, secularism and the policy of secular regimes towards Muslims that triggered social protest and the desire to change the *status quo*. Western politicians do not realise that one of the main postulates voiced by a considerable portion of Muslims who directly or indirectly back the transformations in the Arab states concerns the establishment of a new order rooted in Islamic law. A. al-Zawahiri harshly criticised the pro-democratic activities of the United States. Referring to the examples of academic publications by the RAND Corporation, he accused the US of promoting secular and modernist solutions and attempting to marginalise Islamic circles. He stated that the activities of American authorities reflect their hypocrisy and applying double standards, which was reflected in their defying the decisions made in the electoral processes conducted in Muslim states when these decisions were not in the interests of the US and its ally, Israel (for instance, Hamas assuming power in the Palestinian Autonomy). Before that (in the 1990s), the Islamists who won parliamentary elections in Algeria were denied rule. In this light, democracy becomes a tool the West uses in order to enslave Muslims and maintain Christian and Jewish influences in Islamic states. In the margins of his reflections, A. al-Zawahiri also referred to the condition of Western democratic regimes, which was far from perfect, especially in the United States. Their weakness lies in hedonism and the dearth of moral principles, which should lay the foundations of human acts. A fair socio-political system can be established only by founding it on Islamic law. In his opinion, it was Islamic order that would ensure the full implementation of the principles of justice (Wejkszner, 2011: 61).

The objective of the Egyptian revolution should be to establish such an order. The Egyptians and Muslims from other Arab states should bear in mind the experience of the period after the 1952 revolution, which was a period of suffering and persecution for Islamists. Applying the Western, secular point of view, it was believed then that Islamists were seeking to introduce a radical vision of socio-political relations. In the opinion of A. al-Zawahiri, the experience of recent decades indicates that the only chance of establishing Islamic order is to fight all those who are against this objective. Jihadists should not participate in the democratisation process of Arab states, thereby actively backing the interests of Western states. The sole reference point of jihadists should be Islam. Islamic order is both a religious and state order. Its revival had been anticipated by Hasan al-Banna. However, for this vision to come true, it will be necessary to undertake the enormous effort to overcome local regimes leading anti-Muslim policies and to deprive Western empires of their influence in Muslim states. A. al-Zawahiri believes that the US fears that Islamists might take power. One of the reasons for this is the unconditional support the US offers to Israel. The Muslim effort will concern jihadists taking all measures available in order to implement the ultimate goal of restoring the caliphate and reviving the *umma*. Jihadists should primarily target the enemies of the Islamist vision of the new order (Wejkszner, 2011: 61–62).

A. al-Zawahiri realises that the jihadist avant-garde (al-Tali'a al-jihadiyya) is no longer the only power that has influence on the political transformations in Arab states. At the same time, he believes that both jihadists and other revolutionaries have the same enemy (Lahoud, al'Ubaydi, 2013: 52), backed from the outside. What makes A. al-Zawahiri's standpoint different than other, more moderate approaches is his call for fighting both the external and internal enemies. The external enemies include, in his opinion, US allies (such as Jordan, Morocco and Poland). The internal enemy, especially in Egypt, encompassed all those forces that opposed order based on the Quran from being implemented there.

ATIYYATALLAH AL-LIBI: THE REVOLUTIONARY OPTIMISM AND JIHADIST ACTIVISM

Atiyyatallah al-Libi was among bin Laden's close associates. Until his death in August 2011, he endeavoured to promote the ideas of jihadist activism. He believed that the active participation of jihadists in the struggle against authoritarian regimes is a necessary condition for achieving strategic goals. Revolutionary turmoil can only be instigated by a skilful combination of propaganda and Islamist education. A. al-Libi rejoiced at the collapse of dictatorships in Egypt and Tunisia, believing that it would initiate a process of profound socio-political transformation, enabling jihadists to assume control in these countries (time showed that he was wrong). He contrasted jihadist ideology with nationalistic ideology, believing that the goal of Islamist revolution should be to reject the segregationist nature of nationalism, that leads to the petrifaction of artificial borders within Islamic community (Lahoud, al'Ubaydi, 2013: 43). A. al-Libi repeatedly emphasised that a revolution that leads to permanent transformations cannot be peaceful. The collapse of the old order has to be accompanied by acts of violence (such as confronting the security forces of secular state). Another important issue concerned the differentiation between the goals of, say, protesting students in Egypt and the goals of jihadists. The latter fight for "a radical and a genuine revolutionary change, the objective of which is to make God's Word reign supreme" (Lahoud, al'Ubaydi, 2013: 45). A. al-Libi believed that jihadists would be able to take advantage of the revolutionary turmoil and commence the implementation of their own strategic endeavours. On the other hand, though, he was taking another scenario into consideration, one in which some jihadists could join the protesting nationalists, whose main pursuit was merely overthrowing the authoritarian order. In his proclamations, he repeatedly resorted to incredibly vivid figures of speech, such as "the tree of jihad," when he stated that "the path of jihad is long and arduous, it tastes sweet to those who have savored the sweetness of the faith" (Lahoud, al'Ubaydi, 2013: 45).

ABU YAHYA AL-LIBI: CRITICISM OF A FALSE DEMOCRATIC REVOLUTION

Abu Yahya al-Libi was a member of the core of the most important ideologists of the global movement of Salafi jihad. He was renowned for his eloquence and oratorical skills. Before he died in August 2012, he published a number of addresses to Muslim young people, calling them to tread the path of jihad and sacrificing their life to Islam.

A. Y. Al-Libi primarily addressed the people of Libya, Egypt and Tunisia, who were protesting against the secular, authoritarian regimes that had been dragooning the Islamic community for a number of decades. He deemed their collapse to be unavoidable. He did not appreciate the objectives of mass protests, however, including the calls to set up secular political parties and introduce a democratic order. He believed that such goals were utterly anachronistic and imposed from the outside; they did not fulfil the expectations of the *umma*. Consequently, the democratic revolution would only be an episode of history that sooner or later would lead to the reinstatement of the old order. He believed that jihadists should be a revolutionary *avant-garde* indicating the direction of changes to others. Their own struggle was to abound in sacrifice and set an example for undecided and hesitant Muslims. This would undermine the plans of those impostors (*ahl al-dajal*) who deceived Islamic youth with a mirage of democracy, pluralism and freedom of speech. The vocation of young people is to fight for Islamic rather than democratic objectives since "God's religion is about the unity of this umma... while the religion of democracy is about shredding the Islamic umma in the name of plurality" (Lahoud, al'Ubaydi, 2013: 49).

HUSSAM ABD AL-RAOUF: JIHADIST VISION OF A NEW EGYPT

Sheikh Hussam Abd al-Raouf is among the most influential jihadist ideologists. He has had his share in establishing the fundamental strategic and tactical principles of the jihadist movement. He is also co-responsible for the propagandist activities of the structures in charge of the jihadist movement.

One of his speeches outlines an image of a new, Islamist Egypt which respects social justice and where order is rooted in Islamist law (McGregor, 2012: 9). This order should be gradually introduced and its consecutive stages should be extensively explained in the media. The new authorities should hold the representatives of the old, discredited regime to account as soon as possible. The President of Egypt should break the tradition of living an extravagant and costly life and focus on implementing the jihadist vision of socio-political relations instead. This would also encompass restricted diplomatic activities, including closing Egypt's embassies down in states hostile towards (or not interested in co-operation with) the new authorities, as well as terminating those international agreements that permanently inhibit the economic growth of Egypt. Political and economic relations with Arab and Islamist states should be advanced. The entire security and judiciary apparatus of state should undergo reforms. Political prisoners and prisoners of conscience should regain their liberty as soon as possible. H. A. Al-Raouf backed changes in some business sectors, including tourism. In his opinion, the tourist industry should be Islamised, meaning re-placing Western tourists with Muslim ones. Western tourists could use tourist facilities, provided that they previously pledge to behave in conformity with Muslim morality (McGregor, 2012: 9). H. A. Al-Raouf's remaining postulates seem even more radical. He proposes ensuring food security and the gradual fulfilment of other social needs (housing, employment and so on) while failing to actually indicate the sources to finance these needs (apart from loans from friendly Arab states). This Islamist vision confirms the anti-democratic attitude to political solutions and seems to be an attempt at solving a number of key so-cial issues of Egypt.

CONCLUSIONS

Given the standpoints presented in this paper, the answer to the question on the attitude of jihadists towards the transformations in the world of Islam, includ-ing Egypt, seems obvious. Despite the initial revolutionary optimism and at-tempts to influence the direction of the transformations, the jihadists failed to achieve their key objective, to introduce an order based on Quranic law. The jihadists seem not to have been prepared for the events in Arab states, including Egypt. Even the less radical Muslim Brotherhood was ambivalent about the transformations that were taking place and was unable to develop a coherent standpoint or take the steps to introduce key political changes in Egypt. This is confirmed by the analysis of the strategic goals of Islamist and jihadist circles. The democratic revolutions did not fit the scenario of jihadist activities, and they were actually an enormous negative surprise for the leaders and partici-pants of the jihadist movement. Many of them, for example A. al-Zawahiri, tried to interpret these events, resorting to the extremely orthodox Salafi vision of the new political order. The dispute concerning the selection of objectives and operating methods of different Islamist groups has continued for a long time (Nasira, 2011b: 5–6). It has acquired an exceptional dimension in the largest Arab state. On 18 February 2011, Sheikh Yusuf al-Qaradawi, one of the leaders of the Egyptian Muslim Brotherhood, addressed the young crowds gathered in Tahrir square in Cairo. He warned that those who did not take part in the revo-lution, or opposed it, should not expect to share its fruits. He directly criticised the representatives of the old regime who were not eager to share power. He called for political prisoners to be liberated, the Egyptian security services to be dissolved and the blockade of Gaza by Egypt to be terminated. He promoted vi-olence-free activities that were to result in permanent socio-political changes. Their objective was to establish a secular state based on Islamist foundations (*Transcript*, 2011). The contradictory standpoint of the jihadists, represented in Egypt by the followers of the Egyptian Islamic Group can be presented, promot-ing a Salafi vision of socio-political relations. Both before and during the revolution, they called for the necessity to replace the existing order with an Islamic order based on Sharia law (Nasira, 2011c: 3–4). They did not offer unanimous support to the young fighting the old regime as they feared two consequences. One concerned the protesters, postulating that the authoritarian order be replaced by a democratic one. Either model of governance seems unacceptable for jihadists and other Salafi circles. Another consequence was about the need to take active part in the transformations, which created an impression of anarchy and chaos. Egyptian jihadists opted for tactics involving observation and waiting for the right time to commence the implementation of their own targets. These tactics are actually popular among the global jihadist movement (Wejkszner, 2011: 55–57).

The jihadist vision remains contradictory to the postulates formulated by the clear majority of the young people supporting the democratic transformations and some Salafi groups (Black, 2011: 7–8). The jihadist vision, where democratic order is replaced with an Islamic one seems to correspond to the expectations of a large proportion of Muslims. The results of opinion polls conducted in the ten largest Muslim countries before the democratic transformations by the Gallup Organization demand deeper reflection. Over sixty percent of Egyptians opted for Islamic law to be the only foundation of the socio-political order. Over half of respondents in Pakistan, Jordan and Bangladesh shared the same opinion (*Islam*, 2006: 2–3). On the other hand, however, a significant proportion of Muslims are for political liberty, freedom of speech and assembly, and social justice. Conforming to some jihadist values does not mean, however, that a large part of society supports or sympathises with them. The opposite seems to be the case, in fact. The majority believe that democracy and Islam can co-exist. The events of the Arab Spring seem to confirm this conclusion. Public debate raises certain expectations and hopes that have failed to be met, as shown in Egypt.

BIBLIOGRAPHY

Black A. (2011), *Egypt's Muslim Brotherhood: Internal Divisions and External Challenges in the Post-Mubarak Era*, "Terrorism Monitor", Vol. IX, Issue 29.

Islam and Democracy. Special Report: Muslim World (2006), Princeton.

Joscelyn T. (2015), *Osama Bin Laden's Files: The Arab revolutions*, http://www.longwarjournal.org/archives/2015/03/osama-bin-ladens-files-the-arab-revolutions.php, 10.03.2015.

Khosrokhavar F. (2009), *Inside Jihadism. Understanding Jihadi Movements Worldwide*, Boulder–London.

Lahoud N., Al-'Ubaydi M. (2013), *Jihadi Discourse in the Wake of the Arab Spring*, The Combating Terrorism Center at West Point.

McGregor A. (2012), *Al-Qaeda and the Muslim Brotherhood: Alternative Visions of an Islamist Egypt*, "Terrorism Monitor", Vol. X, Issue 16.

Nasira H. (2011a), *Al-Qaeda's Egyptian Ideologues Planning Caliphate's Return to Egypt*, "Terrorism Monitor", Vol. IX, Issue 27.

Nasira H. (2011b), *After Mubarak: Egypt's Islamists Respond to a Secular Revolution*, "Terrorism Monitor", Vol. IX, Issue 8.

Nasira H. (2011c), *After Mubarak: Egypt's Islamic Struggle to Adapt to the Egyptian Revolution*, "Terrorism Monitor", Vol. IX, Issue 12.

Transcript of Qaradawi's February 2011 Friday Sermon in Tahrir Square (2011), http://wiki-islam.net/wiki/Transcript_of_Qaradawi%27s_February_2011_Friday_Sermon_in_Tahrir_Square, 15.02.2015.

Wejkszner A. (2011), *Jihadism and democracy. Democratisation of Muslim countries as received by the representatives of radical Islam circles*, in: *The Arab Spring*, ed. B. Przybylska-Maszner, Poznań.

Wilner A. S. (2011), *Opportunity Costs or Costly Opportunities? The Arab Spring, Osama bin Laden, and Al-Qaeda's African Affiliates*, "Perspectives on Terrorism", Vol. 5, Issues 3–4.

Zerate J. C., Gordon D. A. (2011), *The Battle for Reform with Al-Qaeda*, "The Washington Quarterly", Vol. 34:3.

Mohammad HOUSHISADAT

Tehran University

THE IMPACTS OF THE PROBABLE FOURTH ARAB AWAKENING IN THE MIDDLE EAST ON THE EUROPEAN NEIGHBOURHOOD POLICY

INTRODUCTION

The recent uprisings in the Middle East and North Africa (MENA) have led to an awakening of the Arab population who have lived under the rule of dictators for more than four decades, during which national fortunes were wasted, corruption was widespread, and injustice prevailed. Professor Tariq Ramadan from Oxford University, in his newly published book, entitled *The Arab Awakening: Islam and the New Middle East*, has argued that the term "awakening" includes both revival and renaissance, which is an assessment of the recovery of Arab consciousness at stake in the uprisings.

What appeared to be protests across MENA, led to civil uprisings in Bahrain and Yemen, pushing Syria and Libya in to civil war, revolutions in Egypt and Tunisia and protests in almost all other regional states. Generally, the Arab Spring represents popular and grassroots movements born from disillusionment associated with economic decline, unemployment, corruption and authoritarian rule (Kelly, Nicholas, 2013: 217–234). Crucially, these are revolutions in the Arab world that could be called "the third Arab Awakening," but they are not like the army coups of the 1950s and 1960s (Ajami, 2012). In this sense, they are the first genuine upheavals in the modern Arab world, and they are being achieved without foreign assistance or interference (Davidson, 2011). This was not the first time people in MENA had taken to the streets demanding fundamental changes. The story of the Arab national movements opens in Syria in 1847, with the founding in Beirut and Damascus of a modest literary society under American and some European patronage (Antonius, 2010). The first Arab Awakening, as a new pan-Arab consciousness, reflected an outbreak of nationalist sentiment against European masters. The desire to create one pan-Arab state, derived from the Arab national ethnicity, out of the ruins of the Ottoman Empire's Arabic-speaking provinces was dashed on the altar of British and French ambitions. The state system and boundaries that emerged after the First World War, reflected the economic and geostrategic interests of London and Paris, rather than the popular preferences on the streets of Cairo or Damascus. These states, mostly successors of the Islamic Ottoman Empire, maintained a supra-state identity, despite inter-Arab competition for leadership during the

1950s and 1960s (Hinnebusch, 2003: 61, 65). The second wave of Arab Awakening rose against Arab governments that were doing the bidding of colonial powers. The period of conflict began following the Egyptian Revolution of 1952, closely followed by Syria (with which it briefly united in the United Arab Republic 1958–1961) and lasted until 1970. The differentiating factor was between Arab nationalist republics, usually quasi-socialist and pan-Arab in orientation, and the traditional monarchies, with a quasi-feudal or rentierist economic structure.

Now, there are numerous signs that a revolutionary upsurge may soon be on the agenda in the Persian Gulf Sheikhdoms. Therefore, it seems that the West, in particular America, might not be so lucky in the next wave of revolutions in the Persian Gulf, entitled "the Fourth Arab Awakening."

Of particular importance to the Persian Gulf monarchies, then, are the answers to the following questions:

- In the wake of the Arab Awakening and Uprising, which has spread throughout MENA, to what extent have the Persian Gulf monarchies been affected by popular protests?
- Will the current circumstances in the Sheikhdoms play a major role in determining the future of the Arab Awakening?
- How could the possible demise of the Persian Gulf Sheikhs be called the Fourth Arab Awakening?
- What are the main impressions of the Fourth Arab Awakening on the European Union's policies and security in the future?

The first part of this paper examines the Subordinate System Theory, as the main theoretical framework for this essay. The second part highlights the anti-colonial struggles during the first Arab awakening, followed by the third section dealing with the rise of the post-colonial Arab state in the framework of the second Arab awakening. In the fourth part, areas receiving specific attention are the EU's plans and initiatives in MENA, followed by the so-called third Arab awakening, and Europe. In the case of the dramatic spread of Arab uprisings to the Arab Sheikhdoms, a fourth Arab awakening could occur. The last section will take this in to account and analyse it and its possible effects on the EU's policies and security in the future.

There is, of course, a variety of groups that have been involved in the Arab Awakening, with their differing demands, expectations, motivations and ideologies, ranging from liberals, seculars and socialists, to Islamists and the ordinary religious people. Obviously, one of the main roots of the post-2011 Arab uprisings, in addition to the economic situation in MENA, is that the Arab nations follow their ideas and identities on the basis of pan-Arabism, Islamism, etc. to establish the normative order in their own countries. In his excellent book about the role of Islam for the Arab awakening, Tariq Ramadan points out that the coming key challenges across MENA include debates on "the nature of the state, the role of Islam, the basic principle of equal rights for all citizens" (Ramadan, 2012: 3). He notes that the future of democracy in the region will be deeply intertwined with the ability of Islamic-oriented political actors to achieve greater social equality and economic justice.

However, some analysts shy away from acknowledging the impact of Islam (Grand, 2011; Rock, 2011). As witnessed, Islamist parties joined the recent protests at a later stage. This particular approach of Islamist politics is strongly associated with the post-Islamism thesis, advanced by scholars such as Asef Bayat (2007) and Olivier Roy (Roy, 1994; Roy, 2004). The principle behind Post-Islamist Theory is the possibility of Muslim modernity emerging through a gradual shift from Islamism toward post-Islamism, particularly after the post-2011 uprisings.

As the last part suggests, however, modernisation is at the heart of post-Islamism. The modernisation approach states that urbanisation, high literacy rates, freedom of thought and speech, more transparency and accessible information sources, as well as technological advancements lead to democratisation in societies (Welzel, 2009). The hierarchy of human needs is another theory, proposed by the renowned psychologist Abraham Maslow (Maslow, 1943: 370–96). This theory is often portrayed in the shape of a pyramid with the largest, most fundamental levels of needs at the bottom, including physiological (metabolic requirements for human survival), followed by safety, love or belonging; esteem, and finally the need for self-actualisation at the top, and all are interrelated rather than sharply separated. With their physical needs relatively satisfied, an individual's safety and security, comprising personal, financial and health security, as well as protection against accidents/illness needs take precedence. Nevertheless, on the basis of the fourth level, all humans have a need to feel respected in two aspects. While a lower version may include a need for status, recognition, fame, prestige and attention, the higher version manifests itself as the need for dignity, self-determination, self-confidence, independence and freedom. The latter version takes precedence over the former one, and unmet human needs may lead to tense and violent conflicts (Kök, 2007). According to Maslow and the conflict scholar John Burton (1979), the essentials go beyond just food, water, and shelter. They include both the physical and non-physical elements needed for human dignity and identification. On this basis, the Arab revolutions involve the unmet needs of identity and security. Therefore, countless Arabs feel that their legitimate identity, dignity and rights are being denied by their own rulers.

As mentioned, the concept of dignity (*karama*) and identity are useful in understanding the recent Arab uprisings which united Arabs from Libya to Oman. Cheryl Duckworth in her recent workshop on Human Dignity and Humiliation Studies in 2012 argued that humiliation is the opposite of dignity, and it is precisely this that seems to matter so much to the kinds of socio/political/economic conflicts in the Arab Awakening, and it cannot be negotiated away. She believes dignity is related to natural politics, social and economic ideas such as participation, and matter to the kinds of socio/political/economic conflict in the Arab Awakening. It is the awakening of national pride, dignity, freedom, justice and equality (Abdul Hadi, 2013: 1). Nevertheless, democratisation and modernisation theories have ignored the core theme of "Arab indignity" (Hashemi, 2013). Arab citizens are demanding dignity, identi?cation and recognition of their Islamic, political, economic and social rights, regardless of their own territories, because they believe in a larger Islamic *Umma*, while the Arab states and the current boundaries have been the product of Western conquerors (Hinnebusch, 2003: 54). In Anthony Giddens' Structuration Theory, agents interact with structure, which must respect their norms; otherwise it lacks legitimacy (Giddens, 1998: 77). Constructivism highlights the significance and role of norms, values, dignity and identity in the formation of political decisions. It also points out the mutual construction of agents and structures at the same time (Reus-Smit, 2009: 212). As such, the new well-educated generation across MENA has become the main agent of change during the Arab uprising. Ideas of human rights, freedom, social equity and dignity flooded across the region and weakened the political structure, comprising oppressive anachronistic dictators and monarchs.

THEORETICAL FRAMEWORK

Louis Cantori, and Steven L. Spiegel argued that the Subordinate System Theory, as a regional subsystem in international relations (Cantori, Spiegel, 1970: 5, 378) consists of a core or centre sector, a peripheral section and an intrusive player(s). They added that the states within the core sector of a region or subordinate system have shared social, political, economic, religious or organisational backgrounds. The peripheral sector includes all those states which are separated from the core sector to some degree by economic, organisational, social, religious or political factors, but play a role in the politics of the subordinate system.

The peripheral members often attempt to manipulate the security objectives of the intruding powers (Cantori, Spiegel, 1970: 171). The intrusive or penetrating part consists of the external power(s) participating in the region politically, militarily and also in an organisational cohesion process (Cantori, Spiegel, 1970: 293, 297). Therefore, this external power impacts on policies of both core and peripheral players, as well as regional affairs.

In the Persian Gulf region, the GCC is considered as the core section, due to the common features amongst the states, despite certain differences. Non-Arab Iran and the non-GCC Arab Iraq are peripheral players with disagreements with the GCC, but these states have the power to exert an influence on regional policies. The intrusive part consists of the external power(s) participating in the regional orders; mainly the US followed by a number of EU member states, such as the UK and France.

THE FIRST ARAB AWAKENING

In the aftermath of four centuries of Ottoman Empire/Caliphate reign, Arab national ethnicity developed dramatically (Ahmadi, 2014) and was then reinforced, particularly by a number of opposition associations, leading to an Arab renaissance. The Associations of the Enlightenment Movement, as the major agency, intended to revive Arab self-awareness and the identity of Arab nationalistic ethnicity after the middle of the 19th century (Abdul Hadi, 2013: 3). The phrase of the first Arab awakening, which took place from 1908–1922, was coined by George Habib Antonius in his book of the same title in 1938. The first Arab awakening started with calls for separation from Ottoman rule, then autonomy, and became a fight for independence on the basis of Arab national ethnicity. Not only did the first Arab awakening not continue as a fight for democracy, freedom and pluralism (Muasher, 2014), but also the Arabs were unable to reach their own primary targets, excluding separation from Ottoman Empire and the start of the independence process (Ahmadi, 2014).

THE SECOND ARAB AWAKENING

Human consciousness is one of the most powerful tools for structural change. The awakening of pan-Arab identity was a product of the spread of mass education and literacy, especially in the 1950s (Hinnebusch, 2003: 58), so this trend led to demands for more militancy towards Western imperialism and collective solidarity against the common Israeli threat, too (Hinnebusch, 2003: 65–6). The military coups d'état that were staged by army officers as the major agencies in Syria, Egypt, Yemen, Iraq, Libya and Sudan in 1949, 1952, 1962, 1963 and 1969 respectively, came mainly as a response to the *Nakba* and to the failure of the Arab ruling elites and humiliation of the Arab nations to prevent the partition of Palestine in 1947. These military national revolutions resisted the establishment of Western alliances, as well as the economic and political domination of the West. The Arab regimes adopted the goals and ideologies of the leftist movements in advocating social justice, freedom and democracy in order to lead to Arab unification, so-called pan-Arabism (Abdul Hadi, 2013).

As Malcolm Kerr said (1965), the Arab cold war, with a huge gap appearing in the Arab world, was an important outcome of the second Arab awakening, creating nearly two decades of rivalry between Arab nationalist republics, usually quasi-socialist and pan-Arab in orientation, and the traditional monarchies, which were the main Western allies in the Middle East.

113

THE THIRD ARAB AWAKENING AND THE EU

It has been observed that the Arab uprisings originated from a combination of an economic deficit, a political deficit and a dignity deficit (Behr, Aaltola, 2011). The constructivist Michael Barnett (Barnett, 1998: 10–11, 25–27) believes that the sovereign Arab states are embedded in a supra-state community with norms deriving from a shared Arab identity. "Three years of the Arab uprising have shown the bankruptcy of all the old political forces in the Arab world", as the Carnegie scholar and former foreign minister of Jordan, Marwan Muasher argued in his newly-published work *The Second Arab Awakening and the Battle for Pluralism in 2014*. The post-2011 third Arab awakening (Ajami, 2012; Ahmadi, 2014) witnessed a series of uprisings that had many different influences and motivations. An eye-opening survey of the recent Arab revolutions and their political consequences shows that many of these revolutionary heroes of the second Arab awakening and their inheritors had themselves become murderous tyrants, leading the people to rebel for a third time. As a primarily local and then national-level phenomenon, the post-2011 uprisings constituted a massive demand for justice, equality, identity and dignity by encouraging citizens to resist authoritarian brutality. Within months, it entered the third stage of regionalisation (El-Alaoui, 2013). By January 2014, rulers had been forced from power in Tunisia, Egypt (twice), Libya, and Yemen (entering the second phase of revolution); civil uprisings had erupted in Bahrain; Syria had descended into civil war; major protests had broken out in Algeria, Jordan, Kuwait, and Morocco; and minor protests had occurred in Mauritania, Oman, Saudi Arabia, Djibouti, Western Sahara and the Palestinian territories.

This new regional discourse has drawn upon classic concepts of pan-Arab unity through new forms of communication technologies and media broadcasts (El-Alaoui, 2013). Arab regimes spent most of this time wasting resources, spreading corruption and injustice, oppressing the Arab people and also establishing alliances with the West. However, the ruling structures were unable to respond to the new norms, values and newly-shaped identities. The Arab upheaval of 2011, being a war of norms and ideas (Muasher, 2014), is a wholly indigenous movement driven forward by the brave agency of young people in the Middle East (Dodge, 2012: 10). The Arab protesters have rebelled against their existing rulers without any significant foreign involvement (Sarıhan, 2012). In various countries, the Arab uprisings brought together Arabs who had long felt disenfranchised and wanted not only an improvement in their economic situation, but also, and more importantly, a government that recognised their social, political and civil rights to fulfil their own destiny with dignity.

The EU, as the only major international actor, which is tied to the MENA by both political and security relations, as well as trade, economic and development interests, initially reacted slowly and reluctantly, in sharp contrast with the attention they subsequently received. The Arab Spring became a serious test for the EU's Common Foreign and Security Policy (CFSP) and Neighbourhood Policy.

Since the mid-1990s the EU's policies with Maghreb and Mashreq countries have been pursued under the initiatives of the Euro-Mediterranean Partnership (EMP), the European Neighbourhood Policy (ENP) and now the Union for the Mediterranean (UfM). The ENP is an important tool for engaging countries neighbouring the EU, willing to enter partnership with the Union with separate regional strategies. The general aims of the ENP, comprising stability, security, and societal well-being, do not substantially differ from those of the EMP (European Commission, 2004). Unlike the ENP, the EMP constitutes unilateral, instead of EU-centric policy-making. While the ENP targets long-term goals in order to reform partner countries, it introduces short-term goals of enhancing economic relations and European security.

The Barcelona Conference or Declaration in 1995 established the central multilateral instrument to govern Euro-Med relations, and instituted political, economic, and cultural co-operation between the then fifteen EU member states and twelve Mediterranean partners.

The EU has a vital interest in political and social stability on its borders, and regional stability is a central concept in European policy. Furthermore, implementation of the Greater Arab Free Trade Area (GAFTA), negotiated in 1997, has varied considerably from country to country.

The search for a new incentive in Euro-Med relations resulted in the 2008 creation of the Union for the Mediterranean (UfM), upon the initiative of French President Nicolas Sarkozy (Emerson, 2008)[1]. The 2008 UfM was characterised by intergovernmentalism and with an apolitical approach, focuses on project-based, commercially sponsored cooperation. Concretised commercial missions were oriented to maintain the status quo, rather than to pursue political objectives, democracy or sustainable prosperity (Colombo, Tocci, 2012).

It should be noted that a number of Arab States are also included in other EU regional programmes: Northern African countries are part of the EU-Africa framework (European Council, 2008a). The development of good relations with two of the Barcelona Process partners, Israel and the Palestinian Authority, is incorporated in the Middle East Peace Process.

The multilateral Euro-Med framework was complemented with bilateral instruments. The Euro-Mediterranean Association Agreements and ENP Action Plans are the two most prominent examples, such as the EU–Syria negotiation in 2004 in accordance with the 1977 Cooperation Agreement.

---

[1]Along with the twenty-seven member states, members are sixteen Mediterranean, African, and Middle Eastern countries: Albania, Algeria, Bosnia and Herzegovina, Croatia, Egypt, Israel, Jordan, Lebanon, Mauritania, Monaco, Montenegro, Morocco, the Palestinian Authority, Syria, Tunisia, and Turkey.

The neighbourhood matters for the EU's profile as an international actor willing to provide security and opportunity in its own backyard and beyond. The EU, with its close historical, geographical, and cultural links with MENA, has been moulding its policies vis-à-vis the Arab world for decades, according to the Joint Declaration of the Paris Summit for the Mediterranean in 2008. The relationship, nowadays, comprises an economic (in terms of trade, finance, energy, but also migration) and a political (predominantly security, stability) dimension (*Regional Strategy Paper*, 2007–2013). According to the recent FRIDE-Chatham House report, entitled "Empowering Europe's Future: Governance, Power and Options for the EU in a Changing World," the broad region around the Union holds over 60% of proven global oil reserves and about 80% of proven gas reserves. The EU already depends on oil imports for 85% of its consumption and on gas imports for 62% in 2010, and the Union is expected to import nearly 80% of its gas and LNG demand by 2030 (BP, 2012: 79), all coming from the broad neighbourhood.

Relations with the Persian Gulf countries, furthermore, remain prominently connected to the ENP. So, the EU has even attempted to establish a link between southern Mediterranean states and Persian Gulf countries to more productively work together under a broader Middle East regional framework (Burke, et. al., 2010: 1). The role of the Persian Gulf countries is key to the political stability of fragile states in MENA. The future of Syria depends on a deal between Iran, Russia, Saudi Arabia and Turkey (Grevi, 2014).

As of December 2010, events in the MENA region have resulted in new challenges for the EU. Initial reactions to the uprisings showed European reluctance and indecisiveness, as the EU and certain member states were unsure about which side to support (see: *Joint statement*, 2011). In early February 2011, the European Council recognised the citizens' democratic aspirations. It committed to provide effective support to those pursuing political and economic reforms including through existing mechanisms, the EMP, UfM, and the ENP (European Council, 2011a).

In the course of 2011, three instruments, intended to set out the broader EU-MENA strategy, were presented or renewed. The first comprehensive initiative was the Joint Communication of the High Representative and the Commission on "A Partnership for Democracy and Shared Prosperity with the Southern Mediterranean," of March 2011 (European Commission, 2011a). Second, in May 2011 the High Representative and the Commission presented the renewed ENP, according to the Joint Communication by the High Representative of the Union for Foreign Affairs and Security Policy and the European Commission in 2011. Third, in September 2011 the Commission launched its SPRING programme (Support for Partnership, Reform and Inclusive Growth) as a strategic and financial instrument to support democratic transformation, institution-building, and economic growth (Press release, 2011). To realise these goals, in the years 2011 and 2012, a moderate EUR 350 mln was provided.

The EU has focused on the three major challenges, often interlinked and even overlapping, since the 2011 Arab Uprising; encompassing security and defence, economic concerns, and human rights, as well as the democratic aspirations of people in the Arab world.

The Union has let security and stability concerns prevail in its relations with MENA during the post-Arab Uprisings (Roth, 2012). Policies were driven by member states' fear of radicalism, migration, and terrorism. Regional conflicts, combined with rising radicalism in the Arab world, were mentioned in the 2008 "Report on the Implementation of the European Security Strategy as Factors Leading to Instability" (European Council, 2008b). Two security aspects can be discerned: an external (unrest in Arab countries) and an internal one (threats to the EU caused by spill-over effects).

Thus far, the EU has made little use of the CSDP instruments to respond to the Arab awakenings, despite repeatedly declaring that it had a "responsibility to protect" (Wouters et. al., 2012). One such failed attempt to use CSDP instruments occurred in the case of the post-2011 uprisings in Libya and the lack of a common understanding within the EU on how to handle this crisis within the NATO and also the closure of the EUFOR Libya in November 2011 (European Council, 2011b).

The EU sees itself as a normative actor in global governance, and prioritises the promotion of human rights, democracy, good governance and the rule of law, and seeks to develop relations and build partnerships with third countries and organisations that share these values. The upheavals in the Arab region underlined the need for the EU to revisit its role, in accordance with the above-mentioned rules and its contribution to reforming institutions in partner countries (Treaty on European Union, 2010).

The Arab Spring has extended the region beyond the Mediterranean basin. It is thus difficult to talk about Euro-Mediterranean relations without taking into account the effects that the Arab uprisings are having on regions bordering the ENP countries, particularly the Persian Gulf area.

THE FOURTH ARAB AWAKENING AND THE EUROPEAN NEIGHBOURHOOD POLICY

As mentioned above, there are four main immediate factors that have contributed to the emergence of the Arab Awakening, including the people's struggle for social and economic justice, their demand for social and political liberties, their desire for dignity and identity, as well as Islamism.

It is no secret that most MENA societies have for a long time been ruled by autocratic dictators who have oppressed their own people with an iron rule, particularly through military and police violence and an accompanying security apparatus. Coupled with the lack of basic social and political freedoms, these economic hardships might be said to have created a great potential for revolt.

Members of the Gulf Cooperation Council (GCC) are at the forefront of the Eastern camp. The evidence from the Persian Gulf States' responses to the Arab uprisings, as a process not an outcome (El-Alaoui, 2013), is not encouraging (Davidson, 2012a), while the monarchies, both rich and poor, are not immune to the challenges facing the rest of the region (Muasher, 2013).

Meanwhile, in 2014 the US-based think tank Fund for Peace, in its annual *Failed States Index*, placed Saudi Arabia and Bahrain in the situation of high warning of state failure compared with the other Arab Sheikhdoms. Fragile states are typically defined as those whose institutions lack accountability, capability, legitimacy, or a combination of the three (Castillejo, 2014: 48).

Nonetheless, Saudi Arabia, Qatar, Kuwait and the UAE have attempted to intervene in regional upheavals, particularly in Libya, Egypt and Syria, and have contained the unrest generated by the Arab uprisings (Ulrichsen, 2012: 2). The civil uprisings in other Arab republics galvanised popular opposition in the Persian Gulf, starting in Bahrain on 14 February, 2011, the so-called "Day of Rage". The protestors voiced demands for greater political freedom and equality for all Bahrainis, and targeted the regime's promotion of sectarian divisions, as the house of Khalifa is Sunni Muslim in a majority Shia country. However, the Al-Khalifa ruling family responded by confronting the dissenters through the use of GCC, Saudi-led forces and demonstrators received draconian jail sentences, while censorship and electronic surveillance remain the order of the day. Under the House of Saud, moreover, there are no guaranteed rights, no separation of powers, no checks and balances, and no written constitution. Representative bodies are sometimes chosen or nominated, but they are purely consultative and have no power to block or implement any policy (Davidson, 2013a). It is notable that widespread demonstrations took place in Saudi Arabia and Oman contemporaneously to the Bahraini uprising. Meanwhile, in the United Arab Emirates, officials responded to demands for political reform by arresting prominent human rights and opposition activists, closing down NGOs and international think-tanks, in addition to taking over local civil society organisations. Constant street protests against corruption and royal intrusion in the Parliament's affairs have undermined the Al-Sabah family, though the December 2012 elections were boycotted by the opposition. Only Qatar, given its fortuitous combination of large hydrocarbon wealth and a small population, escaped unrest (Tobias, 2012: 629).

Four years have passed since Yemeni strongman Ali Abdullah Saleh was ousted and Abd-Rabbu Mansour Hadi, Yemen's vice-president under A. A. Saleh, took over as the head of a transitional government. He also stepped down on January 23, 2015. The Yemeni revolutionaries under the Houthi Shiates, known as Ansarallah, have staged rallies and sit-ins to protest against the government's failure to meet their political and social demands. So, the anti-government protesters from 2011 are now entering a fourth year of uncertainty; however, it is still a revolution, with the same goals (Al-Jazeera, 2015). The GCC in general, and Saudi Arabia in particular, have in recent months repeatedly stated their own concerns over the development in Yemen, as there is a famous proverb in the Arab Peninsula stating that "Yemen is the main entrance of Saudi Arabia."

It can be argued that Arab Absolutes (Davidson, 2013a) enjoy a degree of legitimacy in public, being rooted in religion (Levins, 2013: 200), using it to justify their rule and retain some degree of popularity and immunity (Hamid, 2011) that the region's authoritarian presidents of republics do not (Hinnebusch, 2003: 68–69).

On the other hand, the main member states within the GCC have struggled to prevent the growth of the MENA uprisings and more militancy in the region. Britain's news daily "The Guardian", citing Wikileaks (2010), quoted that then US Secretary of State Hillary Clinton called Saudi Arabia the world's largest source of funds for radical Islamist militant groups, such as al-Qaida and the Taliban. "Donors in Saudi Arabia constitute the most significant source of funding to Sunni terrorist groups worldwide," she said. Furthermore, the Islamic State of Iraq and Syria (ISIS) or the Islamic State of Iraq and the Levant (ISIL), has served to bring together thousands of Islamic extremist militants from as many as eighty countries, and have for years been funded and indoctrinated by the Saudis, Qataris, and Kuwaitis, with the Wahhabi-Salafi version of orthodox Islam. What is more, the European Parliament resolution (2014/2843(RSP)) regarding the ISIS offensive, in addition to other acts, has very recently announced that IS fighters have been receiving funds from wealthy donors in the Persian Gulf, particularly in Saudi Arabia, Qatar, Kuwait and the United Arab Emirates. Clearly, these situations could threaten the Good Neighbourhood Policy of the EU.

Unlike Egypt, Tunisia, or Algeria, the Persian Gulf monarchies have had hydrocarbon-financed means, such as wealth distribution strategies, subsidies, public sector employment, housing or education to buy off protesters and keep the masses off the streets (Davidson, 2013b) and attempted to implement largely "reforms from above" (Muasher, 2013) to keep the governments ahead of the street. However, these unsustainable economic and energy patterns, mostly oil and gas rents, are an Achilles heel that will pose an existential threat to the survival of the regimes in their present form that lies at the heart of the social contract between ruler and ruled (Davidson, 2012b). The Arab Sheikhdoms have the best infrastructure in place, due to the oil revenues from previous decades, which has created a new, modern class in the population (El-Alaoui, 2013), while most of the Arab revolutions have predominantly grown from the middle class, religious groups and democratic elites (Sarıhan, 2012: 81). For this reason, some monarchies have also attempted to enter the post-rentierism period by submitting parts of their own economic power to civil society and the

aforementioned new, modern middle class (Reem, 2013). An important consequence of this youth-led movement, as the major agency of the new norms, values and identity against the ruling structure, is that it will remain part of the
national consciousness for years to come, as this new generation grows into
adulthood and middle age with memories of the principles they fought for. Regardless of the barely suitable economic situation in the Persian Gulf monarchies, this new understanding of basic rights, dignity and justice is most likely
to endure. Hence, the new generation's ambitions led them to sacrifice their
lives while calling for the replacement of the humiliation and dehumanisation
they have long experienced with human rights, democracy, equality and legitimate governance on the basis of new norms and values. Given the rise of the
population size and declining ability of the Sheikhdoms to continue subsidising
their citizens in return for their political acquiescence, due to the decrease in resources, these monarchies will most likely have some political economy concerns and feel high pressures in the future (Krane, 2012). Apart from economic
ties, several monarchies have close political and military relations with Western
countries, and there is no doubt that several key regional states, first and foremost Saudi Arabia and Qatar, are crucial players in the global energy market.
The stability of these countries is also strongly supported for economic and strategic reasons by the United States (Houshisadat, 2013: 164–167). In addition, the
rulers have been able to combine elements of autocratic rule with modern resources. Therefore, this stands in contrast with many other parts of the Arab
world (Davidson, 2012a). As a result, there is more likelihood that the overthrow of the Bahraini regime, followed by the toppling of the House of Saud
and the other Sheikhdoms would send shockwaves around the world and accelerate the transition from the uni-polar world domination exercised by the
Anglo-Americans after 1992, towards world normalisation on a multi-polar basis (Davidson, 2013a). To qualify as a real revolution, a political upheaval needs
to create a lasting institutional change. This could be "the overthrow of the
monarchy, the ousting of a foreign colonial power, a land reform capable of
breaking the power of the latifundists, the abolition of slavery and the existing
situation for foreign workers," and so on (Davidson, 2013a). In sum, the Persian
Gulf monarchies face various sorts of challenges in the short- and me-
dium-terms, consisting of demographic pressures stemming from youthful
populations, increasing demands for civil rights, saturated public sectors and
weak private sectors that are unable to generate sufficient jobs, subsidies and
unproductive rent-seeking patterns of economic behaviour, improper increases
in both public expenditure and unsustainable fiscal policies and dramatic rises
in domestic energy consumption at greatly subsidised prices (Levins, 2013:
384). Nonetheless, there is a shaky calm at present, but the core problems remain unresolved. For the time being, the responses by Arab governments to
the agents' norms and values will determine whether those societies will
make a smooth transition to democracy, or at least become more constitutional

and less monarchical (Hertog, 2011), or whether the street confrontations will persist for some time and finally raise the question of whether the Arab postcolonial states can transit to "post-postcolonial" (Owen, 2012), at least quasi-democratic states. Most of the upheavals in the Arab republics happened in accordance with the physiological and safety levels of the Human Needs Theory proposed by the renowned psychologist Abraham Maslow (Maslow, 1943), however, the fourth Arab awakening will possibly take place on the basis of the higher version of the esteem and, to some extent, the safety levels. Furthermore, the coming Arab Awakening will probably enter a fourth stage. In this phase, after being a local and then national-level phenomenon during the third Arab Awakening, this regional wave will become more internationalised, with an overseas arena of confrontation (El-Alaoui, 2013) and, likely, a little more involvement of the external powers. The "third forces" for democracy, human rights and the ethics of pluralism will emerge in this new transformation and pass through a transitional period, as credible alternatives both to the religious and secular opposition (Muasher, 2014). There can be no question that the call for basic rights and the spread of new communication technologies are critical to the success of the Arab revolutions and the continuation of the Arab Awakening in the future.

CONCLUSIONS

The human consciousness is a potent tool for structural change. The Arab nations have already experienced three awakenings since the middle of the 18th century, with demands of dignity, identi?cation and recognition of their Islamic, political and economic as well as social rights. The first Arab Awakening reflected an outbreak of nationalistic ethnic sentiments within the Ottoman Empire, in addition to the Western interventions. The Associations of the Enlightenment Movement, as the major agency, intended to revive Arab self-awareness and the identity of the Arab nationalistic ethnicity. Consequently, the fall of Ottoman rule and the start of the autonomy process were the main outcomes of the first Arab consciousness.

The awakening of pan-Arab identity was as a result of mass education and literacy throughout the 1950s and 1960s, resulting in national military coups led by army officers. These events were a definite reaction to Western domination, and also the humiliation resulting from the Israeli invasion of Palestine.

The post-2011, entirely indigenous uprisings have been a huge demand for justice, equality, identity and dignity by resisting authoritarian brutality, and within months they became a regional issue. On the other hand, the ruling structures were unable to respond to these new demands, driven forward by the youth-led movement. The upheavals in other Arab republics galvanised popular opposition in the Persian Gulf starting in Bahrain. Unlike the other protestors in the Arab world, the demonstrators in the rich monarchies have looked for more freedom and equality, rather than economic improvement. Conversely, considering the increase in the population and decrease in resources, these monarchies will presumably feel high pressure in the future. The existing social contract between ruler and ruled on the basis of the rent-seeking patterns are an Achilles heel for the survival of the Arab Sheikhdoms (Davidson, 2012b). Several monarchies have close relations with the West, some of whom are key energy players in the world. It is most likely that any "Gulf Stream" or so-called fourth Arab awakening would be more internationalised, rather than the post-2011 regionalised Arab uprisings.

The Arab uprisings provide unique opportunities to revise the EU's relations with countries during the transition period in MENA. The EU has now embraced security, economic, socio-economic, political, social and diplomatic challenges. Ultimately, the EU's quest for stability in the MENA region is still reflected in all its instruments.

The EU has a lot at stake in its neighbourhood, chiefly its profile as a norms-based international actor and the credibility of its role in the world. The EU's influence will depend, in large part, on its capacity to shape a new strategic approach to neighbouring countries and regions (Grevi, 2014: 15).

The EU made convenient use of the strategic revision of its ENP framework to stress the importance of universal values of human rights and democracy in its neighbourhood policies, on the basis of the Joint Communication by the High Representative of the Union For Foreign Affairs and Security Policy and the European Commission (European Commission, 2011b: 2).

The EU has already engaged with the UN in responding to the Arab uprisings, such as the Annan plan in Libya and also the Action Group for Syria. As such, the Union's engagement with regional multilateral organisations, including the African Union (AU), the League of Arab States (Arab League), the Organisation of Islamic Cooperation (OIC), and the Gulf Cooperation Council (GCC) should be developing at different speeds (Joint Communiqué, 2011). The United States is, to be sure, indispensable here: it has greater influence over regional actors and can give individual parties credible security guarantees. But to achieve fair solutions and secure them politically and economically, Europe has to play its part. If the EU wants a resilient neighbourhood it must be prepared to share risks with its neighbours, whether by providing security, underwriting investment or offering more sustained political engagement (Castillejo, 2014: 54). Regarding the Persian Gulf's atmosphere, the balance of interests and security, based on confidence–building, mutual defence pacts, détente even with foreign powers, and cooperation over regional security matters amongst the core, peripheral states and also intrusive players, instead of a balance of power and zero-sum game, can guarantee stable inter-regional relations in the future. For this reason, the "EU+[GCC+2] Partnership", as a win–win game, sounds perfect (Houshisadat, 2015). The EU is well advised to work with regional actors in the Persian Gulf area, especially in efforts to resolve protracted conflicts.

BIBLIOGRAPHY

Ahmadi H. (2014), *The Third Wave of the Arab Awakening; the Anatomy of the Recent Uprisings in the Arab Countries*, The Institute for Middle East Strategic Studies (IMESS), Tehran.

Ajami F. (2012), *The Arab Spring at One*, https://www.foreignaffairs.com/articles/libya/2012-01-24/arab-spring-one, 17.11.2014.

Antonius G. (2010), *The Arab Awakening: The Story of the Arab Nationalism*, London.

Barnett M. (1998), *Dialogues in Arab Politics: Negotiations in Regional Order*, New York.

Bayat A. (2007), *Making Islam Democratic: Social Movements and the Post-Islamist Turn*, Stanford.

Behr T., Aaltola M. (2011), *The Arab Uprising: Causes, Prospects and Implications*, http://www.fiia.fi/en/publication/174/the_arab_uprising.

BP (2012), *Energy Outlook 2030*, London.

Burke E., Echagüe A., Youngs R. (2010), *Why the European Union needs a broader Middle East's policy*, Madrid.

Burton J. (1979), *Deviance, Terrorism, and War: The Process of Solving Unsolved Social and Political Problems*, Oxford.

Cantori L., Spiegel S. L. (1970), *The International Politics of Regions: A Comparative Approach*, Englewood Cliffs, New Jersey.

Castillejo C. (2014), *State fragility in the extended neighbourhood*, in: *Challenges for European Foreign Policy in 2014; The EU's extended neighbourhood*, Madrid.

Colombo S., Tocci N. (2012), *The EU Response to the Arab Uprisings: Old wine in new bottles?*, in: *Rethinking Western Policies in Light of the Arab Uprisings*, eds. R. Alcaro, M. Haubrich-Seco.

Davidson C. (2011), *The Great Arab Revolution and the Gulf States*, "Current Intelligence", 31.01.2012.

Davidson C. (2012a), *Yes, the Gulf monarchs are in trouble*, "Foreign Policy", November 13.

Davidson C. (2012b), *The Importance of the Unwritten Social Contract*, "The New York Times", 29.08.2012.

Davidson C. (2013a), *The Last of the Sheiks?*, "The New York Times", October 18.

Davidson C. (2013b), *After the Sheikhs: The Coming Collapse of the Gulf Monarchies*, Hurst, London.

Dodge T. (2012), *After the Arab Spring: power shift in the Middle East?*, in: *The Middle East after the Arab Spring IDEAS reports*, ed. N. Kitchen, London.

Durham University HH Sheikh Nasser al-Mohammad Al-Sabah Publication Series 3, September.

El-Alaoui H. (2013), *Are the Arab monarchies next?*, "Le Monde diplomatique", January.

Emerson M. (2008), *Making sense of Sarkozy's Union for the Mediterranean*, "CEPS Policy Brief", No. 155.

European Commission (2004), *Strategy Paper on the European Neighbourhood Policy (ENP)*, Brussels.

European Commission (2011a), *A Partnership for Democracy and Shared Prosperity with the Southern Mediterranean*, Brussels.

European Commission (2011b), *A New Response to a Changing Neighbourhood, a review of European Neighbourhood Policy*, Brussels.

European Council (2008a), *The Africa-European Union Strategic Partnership*, http://www.consilium.europa.eu/uedocs/cms_data/librairie/PDF/EN_AFRICA, 17.11.2014.

European Council (2008b), *Report on the Implementation of the European Security Strategy*, Brussels.

European Council (2011a), *Conclusions of the European Council of 4 February 2011: Statement by the Heads of State or Government of the Euro Area and the EU Institutions*, Brussels.

European Council (2011b), *Council Decision 2011/764/CFSP of 28 November 2011 repealing Decision 2011/210/CFSP on a European Union military operation in support of humanitarian assistance operations in response to the crisis situation in Libya (EUFOR Libya)*, OJ L314/35, 29 November.

Giddens A., Pierson C. (1998), *Conversations with Anthony Giddens: making sense of modernity*, Stanford.

Grand S. R. (2011), *Starting in Egypt: The Fourth Wave of Democratization?*, Washington D. C.

Grevi G. (2014), *Re-defining the EU's neighbourhood*, in: *Challenges for European Foreign Policy in 2014; The EU's extended neighbourhood*, Madrid.

Hadi A. M. (2013), *The Second Arab Awakening*, second edition, *Palestinian Academic Society for the Study of International Affairs/ PASSUA*, Al-Quds.

Hamid S. (2011), *Why the Middle East Monarchies Might Hold On*, Brookings.

Hashemi N. (2013), *The Arab Spring Two Years On: Reflections on Dignity, Democracy and Devotion*, "The Ethics & International Affairs".

Hertog S. (2011), *The costs of counter-revolution in the Gulf*, "Foreign Policy", 31.05.2011.

Hinnebusch R. (2003), *The international politics of the Middle East*, Manchester.

Houshisadat M. (2015), *The Position of the Persian Gulf Gas and LNG in the EU's Goals for Security of Gas Supply by 2030*, "Polish Quarterly of International Affairs", June.

Houshisadat M. (2013), *The Coming LNG Boom; The Persian Gulf Gas Supply and the EU Energy Security*, LAP LAMBERT Academic Publishing, Saarbrücken, Deutschland/Germany.

Joint Communiqué (2011), *21st EU-GCC Joint Council and Ministerial Meeting Abu Dhabi*, http://www.consilium.europa.eu/uedocs/cms_data/docs/pressdata/en/er/121610, 17.11.2014.

Joint Declaration of the Paris Summit for the Mediterranean (2008), http://eu-un.europa.eu/articles/fr/article_8021_fr.htm, 17.11.2014.

Joint statement by Nicolas Sarkozy, Angela Merkel, and David Cameron (2011), https://www.gov.uk/government/news/joint-uk-france-germany-statement-on-egypt, 17.11.2014.

Kelly S., Ross Smith N. (2013), *The EU's Reaction to the Arab Spring: External Media Portrayals in China, India and Russia*, "European Foreign Affairs Review", Vol. 18, No. 2.

Kerr M. (1965), *The Arab Cold War, 1958–1964: A Study of Ideology in Politics*, Oxford University Press.

Kök H. (2007), *Reducing Violence: Applying the Human Needs Theory to the Conflict in Chechnya*, "Review of International Law and Politics", Vol. 3, No. 11.

Krane J. (2012), *Energy Policy in the Gulf Arab States: Shortage and Reform in the World's Storehouse of Energy*, Cambridge University Press.

M. Levins C. (2013), *The Rentier State and the Survival of Arab Absolute Monarchies*, "Rutgers Journal of Law and Religion", Vol. 14, May.

Mahdi A. (2013), *The Second Arab Awakening*, Al-Quds.

Maslow A. (1943), *A theory of human motivation*, "Psychological Review", No. 50(4), http://psychclassics.yorku.ca/Maslow/motivation.htm, 17.11.2014.

Maslow A. (1954), *Motivation and personality*, New York.

Muasher M. (2013), *Year Four of the Arab Awakening*, Carnegie Endowment for International Peace.

Muasher M. (2014), *The current Arab Awakening and the Battle for Pluralism*, Yale University Press, US.

Owen R. (2012), *The Rise and Fall of Arab Presidents for Life*, Harvard University Press.

Press release (2011), *EU response to the Arab Spring: new package of support for North Africa and Middle East*, Brussels.

Ramadan T. (2012), *Islam and the Arab Awakening*, Oxford University Press.

Reem A. (2013), *Building for Oil: Corporate Colonialism, Nationalism and Urban Modernity in Ahmadi, 1946–1992*, The Association for Gulf and Arabian Peninsula Studies/AGAPS PhD Dissertation Award 2013: Winner "Journal of Arabian Studies", Vol. 3, Issue 2.

Regional Strategy Paper (2007–2013), and Regional Indicative Programme (2007–2010) for the Euro-Mediterranean Partnership, http://ec.europa.eu/world//enp/pdf/country/enpi_euromed_rsp_en.pdf, 17.11.2014.

Reus-Smit C. (2009), *Constructivism*, in: *Theories of International Relations*, ed. S. Burchill, London.

Rock A. (2011), *Qaradawi's Return and Islamic Leadership in Egypt*, "Eurasia Review", 20.03.2011.

Roth K. (2012), *Time to abandon the autocrats and embrace rights*, Human Rights Watch World Report.

Roy O. (1994), *The Failure of Political Islam*, London.

Roy O. (2004), *Globalized Islam: The Search for a New Ummah*, London.

Sarıhan A. (2012), *Is the Arab Spring in the Third Wave of Democratization? The Case of Syria and Egypt*, "Turkish Journal of Politics", Vol. 3, No. 1.

Tobias M. (2012), *A Saudi spring? The Shia protest movement in the Eastern Province 2011–2012*, "Middle East Journal", No. 66(4).

Treaty on European Union (2010), Art 21(1), OJ 2010, C83/13, March 30.

Ulrichsen K. C. (2012), *Small states with a big role: Qatar and the UAE in the aftermath of the Arab Spring*.

Welzel C. (2009), *Theories of Democratization*, Oxford.

Wouters J., De Man P., Vincent M. (2012), *The Responsibility to Protect and Regional Organizations: Where Does the EU Stand?*, in: *Responsibility to Protect: From Principle to Practice*, ed. J. Hoffmann, A. Nollkaemper, Amsterdam.

Part II

INTERNATIONAL RESPONSE

Przemysław OSIEWICZ
Adam Mickiewicz University, Poznań

THE ATTITUDE OF SELECTED MIDDLE EAST STATES TO THE POLITICAL TRANSFORMATIONS IN EGYPT IN 2011 AND 2013. THE INFLUENCE ON THE CURRENT STATUS OF BILATERAL RELATIONS

INTRODUCTION

The political transformations initiated in Egypt in January 2011 are of unquestionable internal and regional significance. Firstly, they constitute an element of the broader transformation process experienced by many MENA (Middle East and North Africa) states. Secondly, the change of authorities in Egypt has, among other things, brought about changes in Egypt's international policy, including bilateral relations with different regional actors. The ousting of President Hosni Mubarak understandably sparked interest on an almost global scale, but it was the local politicians, observers and analysts who were aware of the fact that the transition on Egypt's political arena could trigger changes in the balance of power in North Africa and the Middle East. Thirdly, the issue of Egypt being a regional power was revived, especially in the context of competing for primacy in the Arab world.

This paper presents a detailed analysis of the standpoints taken by the authorities of the most important states in the Middle East as concerned the transformations on Egypt's political arena after 2010: Israel, Turkey, the Islamic Republic of Iran and member states of the Gulf Cooperation Council: Saudi Arabia, Bahrain, the United Arab Emirates, Qatar, Oman and Kuwait. The purpose of the paper is to determine the reasons why the authorities of the above-mentioned states decided to support the political transformations in Egypt in 2011 and 2013, or to withhold their support, and the outcomes of these decisions, assessed in 2015. The fundamental research question is whether there is a relation between the decisions made by individual countries towards the political transformations in Egypt and their current bilateral relations with Egypt. The sources entail selected monographs, academic papers, analyses, press articles and internet sources.

It should be observed that, apart from Israel, all the above-mentioned states either have authoritarian governments (Saudi Arabia, Iran, Bahrain, Qatar, the United Arab Emirates, Oman and Kuwait) or suffer from a serious deficit of democracy and oppression of their respective opposition forces (Turkey). The successful revolution in Egypt could have encouraged their internal political opponents, bringing about an outbreak of social unrest. Still, the authorities in some of these countries openly advocated the ousting of H. Mubarak. Is this policy evidence that they gave priority to foreign policy, seeking to strengthen their own respective positions in the region at the cost of potential internal social tensions?

ISRAEL'S STANDPOINT

It is worth commencing the analysis of the standpoints of the most important states in the region with Israel, whose attitude is the most complex in historical, political and economic terms. Israel was clearly the state that had the most to lose in the wake of the replacement of Egypt's authorities. Egypt and Israel maintained correct relations after signing the Camp David peace treaty in 1978. During the period of H. Mubarak's government, both states collaborated in terms of both politics and economy. This was best evidenced by the 2005 Egypt-Israeli contract for the construction of a submarine gas pipeline and supplies of gas from Egypt to Israel. The conditions of concluding this contract later came to be used in the indictment against H. Mubarak.

Therefore, the violent anti-government demonstrations staged in Egypt raised considerable concerns among Israel's authorities. The removal from office of President H. Mubarak made it very likely that the mutual relations of both countries might deteriorate considerably, and in the case of the Muslim Brotherhood's members, or Islamists assuming power, diplomatic relations might be broken off altogether. Additionally, an uncontrollably developing situation in Egypt could jeopardise regional peace and leave Israel almost entirely surrounded by hostile Arab regimes again. Consequently, the Israeli authorities seriously feared a repetition of the situation from the first half of the 1970s. Additionally, this scenario would also pose a threat to the regional security system primarily designed by the United States, that also safeguarded the *status quo* after the Camp David agreement. Israel-Egypt co-operation constituted one of its essential elements.

Israel's standpoint on the political transformations in Arab states was primarily influenced by its singular status in the region, and in particular its disadvantageous geopolitical location. Alongside Jordan, Egypt was the only state in the region that collaborated with Israel. According to Itamar Rabinovich, "Israel looks at the Arab turmoil through a fractured lens: that of a powerful but anxious state, an important actor in the Middle Eastern politics not fully integrated in the region, at peace with some Arab states and in conflict with other parts of the Arab and Muslim world" (Rabinovich, 2014: 1). At the same time, however, it has to be stressed that the opposition in Egypt did not seek Israel's support. Quite the opposite, as such potential support could have discredited opposition members not only in the eyes of many Egyptians, but also in the Arab world.

The fears of Israel were best encapsulated by President Shimon Peres, who several months after President H. Mubarak stepped down thanked him for sparing the country from war. At the same time, he characteristically remarked that the "[e]lections in Egypt are dangerous. Should the Muslim Brotherhood be elected they will not bring peace. Democracy without peace is not a democracy. We fear there will be a change in government without a change in the circumstances which led to this state" (*Peres praises*, 2011). The eventual victory of the opposition in February 2011 did not herald any significant changes in contacts with Israel. It was only the increasing political importance of the Muslim Brotherhood, and their assuming power in the end that posed a true threat for Egypt-Israel collaboration. "Since the fall of the Mubarak regime, the conventional wisdom in Israel has suggested that an Islamist government in Egypt would necessarily be hostile to the Jewish state. Egypt's parliamentary elections, in which the Muslim Brotherhood won close to 50 percent of the vote, only reinforced this notion, which Prime Minister Netanyahu viewed with a suspicious 'wait-and-see' attitude. On this part, the MB's Freedom and Justice Party seems equally unwilling to change their posture towards what they still call the Zionist entity" (Ben-Meir, 2014: 51). The predictions of Israeli authorities began to come true in April 2012, when Egypt terminated the contract for gas supplies for Israel, negotiated for a period of twenty years. Earlier, the pipeline running across the Sinai Peninsula had been targeted by over a dozen sabotage attacks and opponents of Israeli-Egypt collaboration had staged protests in numerous cities and towns (Adib-Moghaddam, 2014: 4). Many Egyptians believed that owing to the disadvantageous terms of the 2005 contract, Israelis were buying Egyptian gas at prices way below market prices. Responding to the decision taken by the Egyptian authorities, Israeli Minister of Foreign Affairs Avigdor Lieberman stated: "[i]t is not a good sign, but I think that to turn a business dispute into a diplomatic dispute would be a mistake" (Sherwood, 2012). Collaboration was resumed after a relatively short break, when President Abdel Fattah el-Sisi assumed power in Egypt.

The removal of the Muslim Brotherhood from power was highly beneficial for Israel in political and economic terms, but also from the point of view of the security of the state. Israelis managed to avoid being surrounded by hostile Arab regimes. It was also significant that the new authorities in Egypt were not going to collaborate with Iran, as was the case during the period of Mohamed Morsi's presidency.

TURKEY'S ATTITUDE TO THE POLITICAL TRANSFORMATIONS IN EGYPT

When the Justice and Development Party (AKP) took power in November 2002 it brought about an essential change in Turkey's foreign policy. The concept to build 'strategic depth' involved fostering a 'zero problems with neighbours policy,' including Syria (Davutoğlu, 2001). The new authorities were also going to reinstate the old Ottoman influence zone, by means of normalising relations or developing co-operation with selected states of North Africa and the Middle East, as well as by reaching further into Africa and Asia. As concerned Egypt, Turkey was hoping to expand mutual co-operation. The Turkish concept of foreign policy, drawn up by Ahmet Davutoğlu, was assessed as a constructive and ambitious project. It was emphasised that it could enable Turkey to become a stabilising agent in the region, as evidenced, among other things, by Turkey's commitment to the attempted rapprochement of Israel and Syria. Graham E. Fuller was right to observe that "never has the modern state of Turkey been so engaged in affairs of the Middle East" (Fuller, 2014: 4).

The events the Arab world witnessed at the turn of 2010 and 2011 astonished Turkey, as well as the authorities of many other states, so much that Turkey was not ready for rapid political changes, including the ousting of H. Mubarak and the change of the balance of power in the region. A. Davutoğlu neither could nor did foresee such developments in the Middle East. The fundamental assumptions of Turkey's foreign policy were jeopardised as was soon to be evidenced by Syria.

The Turkish government adopted a 'wait and see' position, taking no sides. In December 2010, nobody could have predicted that the events in Tunisia would result in a domino effect in the MENA region. Eventually, Ankara supported the new authorities, but it did so only after Zine El Abidie Ben Ali truly lost power in the country. In the case of Egypt, the Turkish government faced another dilemma of whether to back H. Mubarak's regime or take the side of the Egyptian protesters. Whereas Prime Minister Recep Tayyip Erdoğan stalled his official support for the Tunisian opposition, in the case of Egypt, Turkey was active. Before the representatives of other states did so, the Turkish PM officially demanded that H. Mubarak fulfil the postulates voiced by the protesters and step down. In the opinion of Ali Omidi, the Turkish authorities quickly drew conclusions from the developments in Egypt, and noticed the potential for the Muslim Brotherhood assuming power there. By this token, Turkey would be able to promote its political model, dubbed the Turkish model, in the region. Additionally, Turkey would keep a strong ally in the Arab world, thereby strengthening its international position when the process of political transformations in the region came to an end (Omidi, 2012: 33).

G. E. Fuller observes that "Turkey was torn between acting on the basis of 'a principle' that soon became contradictory: on the one hand, maintenance of overall good relations with all neighbours where possible, and, on the other, support for democratic change. And all preferably without western intervention" (Fuller, 2014: 194). As was the case in Syria and Libya later on, Turkish authorities eventually opted for offering their support to the protesters in Egypt. However, prior to taking an official standpoint in this respect, the authorities cautiously analysed the developments. The demonstrators won political backing from Ankara only when their victory was already certain. Turkey's decision can therefore be approached as pragmatic and rational. Turkey's priority remained to avoid any tensions in the region and its government also wanted to be ready for H. Mubarak retaining his office.

When the Muslim Brotherhood led by President M. Morsi took power in 2012, Turkey supported them politically. The price for this support soon turned out to be exceptionally high. The Turkish authorities unequivocally condemned the coup d'état, the ousting of the Muslim Brotherhood and the army taking power in Egypt in July 2013. The Turkish standpoint caused a diplomatic crisis, which culminated when Turkish ambassador was expelled from Cairo at the end of November. In the opinion of some scholars, the case of Egypt, among other things, evidenced the failure of the Turkish concept of 'strategic depth' (Kaczorowski, 2014: 215). Ironically, several months before, the Turkish governance model was presented as a model to be followed by the Muslim Brotherhood (Pupcenoks, 2012). It should also be added here, however, that the Turkish brotherhood was actually critical of the Turkish model. Lawrence Rubin emphasised that "after first receiving a hero's welcome in the region, Prime Minister Erdogan's tour exposed the limits of Turkey's appeal. During Erdogan's visit to Cairo, he advised Egyptians, particularly Islamists, not to be afraid of secularism. These and other remarks were interpreted as patronizing and (mis)interpreted as a call for secularism, angering the Muslim Brotherhood" (Rubin, 2014: 124).

Another significant paradox of Turkey's foreign policy should be noted. Whereas Turkey officially supported the opposition in Arab states, the Turkish authorities did their best to prevent a similar scenario from developing in their own country. This is well evidenced by the brutal pacification of demonstrators protesting in June 2013. Taksim Square in Istanbul and the adjacent Gezi Park came to symbolise them. The government of Recep Tayyip Erdoğan learned their lesson from the fate of numerous Arab regimes, and decided to resort to violence and a series of repressions to be applied right from the beginning.

Supporting Egypt was contrary to the goals of Turkey's foreign policy, seeking to strengthen its position as a local power. Beyond doubt, Egypt was and continues to be one of Turkey's essential competitors in the Middle East, especially considering its influence in the Arab world. Additionally, Turkey's clear political commitment and strengthening ties with the new authorities in Egypt could have resulted in infringing the interests and plans of other states, such as the Islamic Republic of Iran and other influential Arab states. Nevertheless, prior to the coup d'état, Egypt-Turkey relations could be described as at least good. The authorities of Turkey realised that by collaborating with Egypt they could strengthen their position in the region, while confrontation would jeopardise it.

Assessing the situation in 2011–2015 one can say that Turkey is among those states that lost most on account of their policy towards Egypt. At the beginning of 2015, both countries are clearly more divided than sharing common causes. The Egyptian ambassador was considered a *persona non grata* in Turkey, and the Turkish ambassador was expelled from Egypt. Politicians in both states resort to very strong language; Egypt accuses Turkey of failing to recognise the massacre of the Armenians in 1915 as genocide and of interfering with Egypt's internal affairs, and attempts to destabilise the situation by offering support to banned organisations. The spokesman of Egypt's Ministry of Foreign Affairs, Badr Abdelatty, stated in public that Turkey "is attempting to influence public opinion against Egyptian interests, supported meetings of organizations that seek to create instability in the country" (*Egypt expels*, 2013). Turkey's President, R. T. Erdoğan, refers to President A. F. el-Sisi as a tyrant, and calls for his predecessor, M. Morsi to be liberated. During one of his speeches he also declared: "I will never respect those who come to power through military coups" (*Egypt expels*, 2013). According to Ahmet Uysal, "Libya, Turkey and Qatar were the only nations that wished success for a democratic Egypt. Turkey sees democracy as a way to ensure development in Egypt" (Uysal, 2013).

Therefore it can be assumed that as long as the AKP Party stays in power in Turkey, and President A. F. el-Sisi is the head of Egypt, it is unlikely that mutual diplomatic relations will normalise. It should be stressed, however, that President R. T. Erdoğan is famous for his pragmatic attitude and frequent changes of position. It is therefore quite likely that Turkey and Egypt might establish political co-operation. This is facilitated by the increasingly aligned standpoints of both countries as concerns ISIS, although the Turkish policy towards Islamic State is far from straightforward (Yegin, Özertem, 2014).

ATTITUDE OF THE ISLAMIC REPUBLIC OF IRAN

The rapid political transformations in Arab states surprised the authorities of the Islamic Republic of Iran as well. Iran's government could interpret them in two ways: either as a threat to the stability of Iran's political system, in case they inspired opposition in Iran, or as an opportunity for Iran to increase its influence in the Arab world, for instance by means of supporting the new authorities. There also emerged in this context the issue of the Shia minorities in Egypt and Syria, as well as the Shia majority in Bahrain. Iran was also assuming that the transformations in Arab states could result in the weakened influences of the West, in particular of the US, in the region (Marashi, Parsi, 2013: 133).

The Iranian authorities could see the opportunity to strengthen their regional position, taking advantage of the political transformations in Arab states. Tehran was only against the anti-government rallies in Syria (Parsi, Marashi, 2011: 103). As concerned Egypt, Supreme Leader Ali Khamenei deemed it a better solution to support the opposition in Egypt, the more so as Iran's authorities treated President H. Mubarak as an enemy. The main accusation concerned his close collaboration with Israel and the US. The change of the regime could result in deteriorating relations between Cairo and these two states, thereby reinforcing the position of Iran in the Middle East. Additionally, Ali Khamenei assessed the events in Egypt and other states in this region to be a manifestation of the outbreak of Muslim anger in the Arab world. He applied the meaningful name of the 'Islamic Awakening' to these developments. Therefore, there emerged interpretations linking the process of political transformations in Arab states to the revolutionary process initiated in Iran in 1979 (Ayoob, 2014: 411).

It cannot be ignored, however, that soon after the success of Egyptian demonstrators; street protests were staged in Tehran which were suppressed by the Basij almost immediately. The protesters referred to the political changes in Egypt and Tunisia. Jerzy Zdanowski was right, however, observing that there were a number of differences between the protesters in Iran and those in other Arab states. Most importantly, "the opposition in Egypt was born outside the establishment circles whereas in Iran it is part of these circles" (Zdanowski, 2011: 206). Here, the events of 2009 deserve to be mentioned, and the wave of protest within the 'green movement.' Iranian protesters, headed by Mir Hossein Mousavi, demanded not so much a change of the system, but a change of the ruling elite, in particular the removing from office of President Mahmoud Ahmadinejad whose electoral victory was falsified in their opinion.

A sudden political change, and the consequent ousting of H. Mubarak, could facilitate improved Egypt-Iran relations. Representatives of Iran backed the Egyptian protesters from the very beginning, while H. Mubarak was dubbed the 'Pharaoh of Egypt' in official statements (Omidi, 2012: 37). Mutual relations improved as early as early 2011, as evidenced by Egypt's permitting the transit of Iranian warships through the Suez Canal for the first time in thirty years (Maloney, 2011: 262). When the Muslim Brotherhood assumed power later on, the conditions were created facilitating the normalisation of mutual relations despite ideological differences. One of the more important elements of the rapprochement was provided by the visits of high ranking officials, which would have been unfeasible at the time of H. Mubarak. The visit of President M. Ahmadinejad in Cairo deserves to be mentioned in this context. In the opinion of L. Rubin, "when the president of Iran visited Egypt in 2011, there was tremendous concern. However, the visit turned out to be a diplomatic fiasco. During President Ahmadinejad's historic visit to Cairo, protesters hurled shoes at him and he was publicly berated by one of Egypt's top clerics" (Rubin, 2014: 121). Even such incidents, however, did not change the assessment of the Iran-Egypt rapprochement by other states in the region, in particular by Saudi Arabia, and elsewhere.

The diplomatic rapprochement of Cairo and Tehran raised the greatest concerns in the United States and Israel. The July 2013 coup d'état dismissed the threat that the balance of power in the region might change, and antagonised Egypt and Iran again. Iran did not recognise the change of President and openly criticised the detention of President M. Morsi.

BAHRAIN

Bahrain was among the countries that were vividly interested in the development of the situation in Egypt. King Hamad bin Isa Al Khalifa feared that the success of the Egyptian demonstrators could encourage some of his subjects to take an open stand, demanding political transformation or even his abdication. Another danger would be posed by the Muslim Brotherhood possibly assuming power in Egypt. Egypt could then try to intervene in the internal matters of other Arab states and coax them to reject monarchy. The Bahrain authorities' concerns seemed justified when the first demonstrators took to the streets in the capital city of Manama. The opposition was composed primarily of Shia muslims, who could count on the support of Iran's authorities. H. I. Al Khalifa learned his lesson from the mistakes committed by H. Mubarak and opted for a violent confrontation with protesters, which was tangibly supported by Saudi Arabia and the United Arab Emirates. In the opinion of Radosław Bania, "the events started by the mass protests in Bahrain's capital, Manama, were directly inspired by the collapse of the government of Egypt's President Hosni Mubarak, but they should be perceived as one of the elements of cyclical socio-political upheavals this country has witnessed since it regained its independence" (Bania, 2014: 204).

The fact that the Muslim Brotherhood assumed power in Egypt was received in Bahrain as a factor destabilising the situation in the region. The King of Bahrain shared the same point of view as the leaders of Saudi Arabia and the UAE, and was anxious to see neighbouring Qatar supporting the new authorities in Egypt. The situation changed after the coup d'état in Egypt in July 2013. The King of Bahrain supported the new authorities headed by General A. F. el-Sisi.

SAUDI ARABIA

Saudi Arabia was most concerned about the developments in Egypt. Successive months showed that the concerns of the ruling elite that the wave of protests might spread across the region were justified. It suffices to mention the violent demonstrations in neighbouring Bahrain or, more importantly, the protests in the eastern part of Saudi Arabia, where Shias predominate (Matthiesen, 2012: 628).

Artur Pohl is right to note that "in the case of Tunisia and Egypt, Saudi Arabia took the side of the contemporary regimes it had good relations with, but it took no action against the protesters. The Saudis backed the regimes of Mubarak and Ben Ali until the end, the latter found harbour there after he had been deposed and fled his country" (Pohl, 2014: 152). The King of Saudi Arabia, Abdullah, committed himself personally to defend H. Mubarak. In late January 2011 he said, in a very firm way: "[n]o Arab or Muslim can tolerate any meddling in the security and stability of Arab and Muslim Egypt by those who infiltrated the people in the name of freedom of expression, exploiting it to inject their destructive hatred" (*Saudi king*, 2011). Ironically, this made Saudi Arabia and Israel the strongest allies of the Egyptian President in the region, although for very different reasons.

Saudi Arabia feared that members of the Muslim Brotherhood in Egypt could gain power. Although in the past it frequently offered shelter to Brotherhood members who were persecuted in Egypt and elsewhere, now Saudi Arabia treats them as the source of a threat to both internal and regional security. This explains why Saudi Arabia approved of the July 2013 coup d'état in Egypt. The toppling of President M. Morsi limited the influence of Qatar, Turkey and Iran in Egypt, which was highly advantageous for the Saudis. According to Thanassis Cambanis, "Saudi Arabia and other Gulf countries spent more than 12 billion USD to bring Sisi to power and promised further payments to keep him there" (Cambanis, 2015: 248).

THE UNITED ARAB EMIRATES, KUWAIT AND OMAN

The Emir of Kuwait, Sabah IV Ahmad Al-Jaber Al-Sabah, explicitly condemned the anti-government protests in Egypt in early 2011. Al-Sabah "condemned riots, looting, sabotage and terrifying of citizens in Egypt, and affirmed Kuwait's solid support to the Egyptian government and people" (*Al Diwan*, 2011). Nonetheless, soon after President H. Mubarak stepped down, Kuwait took a more pragmatic attitude, counting on profits from its current and potential investments. A special investment fund with a start-up capital of USD 1 bln was established for this purpose. A similar decision was made by the management board of the Kharafi Group, which invested over USD 7 bln in Egypt before 2010. In April, Kharafi allocated yet another USD 80 bln for investment in Egypt (Haniyeh, 2012: 135).

The Sheikh of Dubai and Vice President of the United Arab Emirates, Mohammed bin Rashid al-Maktoum, firmly rejected the accusations by some countries that the UAE had benefited from the political instability in the region after 2010. During a government summit in 2013, he stated that "[o]ur strategic trade partners do not include any Arab Spring countries. Indeed, none of our top ten partners is an Arab state, apart from the Kingdom of Saudi Arabia. Worldwide investments in the UAE were flowing strongly long before the Arab Spring. They have continued, and will continue, to flow" (Al-Maktoum, 2013: 69). On the other hand, the considerable involvement of the UAE in activities to counter the political changes in the region, perceived in terms of a threat to internal security, should also be noted. In this context, particular attention should be paid to the decided negative approach the UAE's authorities took towards the government of the Muslim Brotherhood, which led to tensions in relations with

Egypt in 2012–2013. "Around January 2013, several members of the Egyptian Muslim Brotherhood living in the UAE were arrested, accused of holding secret meetings and recruiting Egyptian expatriates, and raising large amounts of money and spying. Ninety four were put on trial, which caused major tensions with Egypt" (Rubin, 2014: 121). Dubai's police chief Dhahi Khalafan stated even that "the Brotherhood poses a greater security risk than Iran" (Rubin, 2014: 121).

Similarly to the authorities of Bahrain, Oman also "saw serious and sustained unrest with a wave of protests that began in February 2011 and then resisted a variety of determined government attempts to quell them" (Maloney, 2011: 181). Even before that, the Sultan of Oman, Qaboos bin Said Al Said, considered the Arab revolution to be a threat on account of the possible domino effect and the outbreak of violent anti-government protests in numerous countries of the Middle East.

The policies of Kuwait, the United Arab Emirates and Oman towards Egypt, in particular at the turn of 2012 and 2013, were the result of the fears of Arab monarchies that the ideas propagated by the Muslim Brotherhood may spread. This is the explanation for their decisive steps towards the Brotherhood's followers, as well as the support given to General A. F. el-Sisi after the July 2013 coup. In the opinion of Mohamed Abdel Kader, "the Muslim Brotherhood's ambitions put Egypt at odds with other state fearing the Muslim Brotherhood's encroachment on their national security, revitalizing regional fears about the export of revolutions, this time with an Arab Islamist hue rather than the Persian Islamist case of Iran post-1979" (Kader, 2014: 408).

QATAR

In contrast to, for instance, Saudi Arabia, Qatari authorities perceived the political changes in many Arab states as an opportunity to strengthen their influence and achieve a number of interests. This was one of the reasons why they decided to back the opposition forces in Tunisia, Syria, Yemen, Libya and Egypt. Qatar "had welcomed the change in regime in Egypt, having had testy relations with the Mubarak government for some time" (Anderson, 2013: 31). For the same reason, Qatar backed the opposition in Libya, whose leader Muammar Gaddafi was among the greatest critics of Qatar's policy in the Arab world.

In the majority of cases, Qatar aided first and foremost members of the Muslim Brotherhood and political groups of Islamists (Katulis, 2013). In Egypt's case, Qatar supported the Egyptian authorities dominated by the Brotherhood mainly in financial terms, and it offered extensive political backing to President M. Morsi. Significantly, soon after the July 2013 coup, Qatari authorities decided to withhold its entire economic aid to Egypt. They did not acknowledge the political change and condemned the arrest of M. Morsi (Badawi, Farid, 2013). Thereby, Qatar lost all influence in Egypt when President A. F. el-Sisi took power there.

The intensifying tension in bilateral relations was reflected by the Qatari ambassador being recalled from Egypt after the representative of Egypt, speaking at the forum of the League of Arab States, accused Qatar of supporting terrorist groups. This incident occurred in February 2015, several days after Egypt started shelling the locations of ISIS militants in nearby Libya (*Egypt seeks*, 2015). Additionally, for over a year before, the Egyptian authorities detained journalists working for the Qatar TV station Al-Jazeera (*Egypt Al Jazeera*, 2015).

CONCLUSIONS

The political transformations in Egypt brought about significant changes on a regional scale and were received with considerable interest by the authorities of the most important states in the Middle East. President H. Mubarak was coerced to resign, having been among the most important and influential politicians in the region for nearly thirty years. When the Egyptian revolution was beginning, H. Mubarak could count on the support of several important actors in the region, including, interestingly, both Saudi Arabia and Israel.

The leaders of some Middle East states, in particular the monarchs from the Persian Gulf area, followed the reports from Cairo with concern. Although unpopular in the region, H. Mubarak guaranteed a stable and predictable government, as opposed to the opposition. Additionally, the success of the Egyptian demonstrators could be taken as an example and encouragement for the citizens of Bahrain, Oman and Saudi Arabia who were dissatisfied with their respective authorities. The risk that similar anti-government protests would break out on a mass scale was also likely in Iran and Turkey. The leaders of the above-mentioned states learned their lesson from the fate of Z. A. Ben Ali in Tunisia and H. Mubarak in Egypt. This is evidenced by, among other things, the brutal pacification of protesters in Taksim square in Istanbul and the violent suppression of protests in Bahrain.

The authorities of nearby Israel were equally concerned with the developments, as a rapid political change in Egypt could be particularly threatening for their country. Therefore, the opposition in Egypt could not count on support from the Israeli authorities, which they did not want, anyway. On the contrary, such support could only discredit the Egyptian opposition in the eyes of part of society. Therefore, the Israelis believed that the best scenario involved President H. Mubarak maintaining power. The Israeli authorities feared that the government in Egypt would be seized by the Muslim Brotherhood or Islamists. In early 2011 it was commonly believed that this scenario would undermine the stability of mutual diplomatic relations. Additionally, uncontrolled developments in Egypt could jeopardise regional peace and leave Israel almost completely surrounded by hostile Arab regimes once more. The only exception, but no-one could say for how long, would be Jordan. Therefore, Israeli authorities seriously feared that the situation from the first half of the 1970s could be repeated. Egypt's termination of the gas contract in 2012 seemed to justify these fears. Many analysts believed that it was only the beginning of serious diplomatic tensions. The situation considerably improved, however, after the members of the Muslim Brotherhood were removed from power.

Concluding, it can be said that the Egyptian political transformations in 2011 benefitted Turkey and Iran most, while Israel lost most. The situation reversed after the July 2013 coup d'état, when Israel recovered its position, primarily in economic terms, while Turkey and Iran lost the political influence they enjoyed while the Muslim Brotherhood was in power. The situation of Qatar was similar, whereas Saudi Arabia and the remaining Persian Gulf monarchies clearly benefitted from General A. F. el-Sisi coming to power. The influence the decisions made in 2011 and 2013 had on mutual relations in early 2015 are illustrated in the table below.

State	Attitude to the political transformations in Egypt in 2011 (+/–) positive/negative	Attitude to the political transformations in Egypt in 2013 (+/–) positive/negative	Bilateral relations with Egypt as compared to 2012–2013 (March 2015) (+/–) positive/negative
Saudi Arabia	–	+	+
Bahrain	–	+	+
The Islamic Republic of Iran	+	–	–
Israel	–	+	+
Qatar	+	–	–
Kuwait	–	+	+
Oman	–	+	+
Turkey	+	–	–
The United Arab Emirates	–	+	+

Source: Author's analysis.

BIBLIOGRAPHY

Adib-Moghaddam A. (2014), *On the Arab Revolts and the Iranian Revolution: Power and Resistance Today*, New York.

Al-Maktoum M. R. (2013), *Flashes of Thought: Inspired by a Dialogue at the Government Summit 2013*, Dubai.

Anderson L. (2013), *Early Adopters and Neighbourhood Effects*, in: *The Arab Spring: Will It Lead to Democratic Transitions?*, eds. C. Henry, J. Ji-Hyang, New York.

Ayoob M. (2014), *Turkey and Iran in the Era of the Arab Uprisings*, in: *The New Middle East: Protest and Revolution in the Arab World*, ed. F. A. Gerges, Cambridge.

Badawi N., Farid D. (2013), *Following Morsi's ouster, Qatar's support to Egypt in question*, http://www.dailynewsegypt.com/2013/07/14/following-morsis-ouster-qatars-support-to-egypt-in-question/, 11.02.2015.

Bania R. (2014), *"Arabska Wiosna" – doświadczenia arabskich monarchii subregionu Zatoki Perskiej*, "Przegląd Politologiczny", Vol. 19, No. 1.

Ben-Meir A. (2014), *Spring or Cruel Winter? The Evolution of the Arab Revolutions*, Washington D.C.

Cambanis T. (2015), *Once Upon A Revolution: An Egyptian Story*, New York.

Davutoğlu A. (2001), *Stratejik derinlik: Türkiye'nin uluslararasý konumu*, Istanbul.

Egypt expels Turkish ambassador, Turkey retaliates (2013), http://www.reuters.com/article/2013/11/23/us-egypt-turkey-idUSBRE9AM03Y20131123, 30.01.2015.

Egypt seeks UN backing for air strikes against ISIS in Libya (2015), http://www.theguardian.com/world/2015/feb/17/egypt-seeks-backing-air-strikes-isis-libya, 20.02.2015.

Egypt: Al Jazeera journalists released on bail (2015), http://www.inquisitr.com/1835466/egypt-al-jazeera-journalists-released-on-bail/, 20.02.2015.

Fuller G. E. (2014), *Turkey and the Arab Spring: Leadership in the Middle East*, Bozorg Press.

Haniyeh A. (2012), *Egypt's Orderly Transition: International Aid and the Rush to Structural Adjustment*, in: *The Dawn of the Arab Uprisings: End of an Old Order?*, eds. B. Haddad, R. Bsheer, Z. Abu-Rish, London.

Kaczorowski K. (2014), *Stambulska recepcja Arabskiej Wiosny i idei "tureckiego modelu" demokracji*, Kraków.

Kader A. B. (2014), *Contradictory Paths: Islamist Experiments of Egypt and Turkey*, "Turkish Review", Vol. 4, No. 4.

Katulis B. (2013), *Qatar, Saudi Arabia Diverge in Battle to Shape Changing Middle East*, http://www.worldpoliticsreview.com/articles/12988/qatar-saudi-arabia-diverge-in-battle-to-shape-changing-middle-east, 11.02.2015.

Kuwait Amir condemns riots, looting, sabotage in Egypt, affirms support to Egyptians, 29 January 2011 (2011), http://www.da.gov.kw/eng/newsroom/searchArchive.php, 3.02.2015.

Maloney S. (2011), *Iran: The Bogeyman*, in: *The Arab Awakening: America and the Transformation of the Middle East*, ed. K. Pollack, Washington D.C.

Maloney S. (2011), *Kuwait, Qatar, Oman, and the UAE: The Nervous Bystanders*, in: *The Arab Awakening: America and the Transformation of the Middle East*, ed. K. Pollack, Washington D.C.

Marashi R., Parsi T. (2013), *The Gift and the Curse: Iran and the Arab Spring*, in: *The Arab Spring: Change and Resistance in the Middle East*, eds. M. L. Haas, D. W. Lesch, Boulder.

Matthiesen T. (2012), *A 'Saudi Spring'? The Shia Protest Movement in the Eastern Province 2011–2012*, "The Middle East Journal", Vol. 66, No. 4.

Omidi A. (2012), *A Comparative Analysis of the Turkish and Iranian Foreign Policy Towards the Arab Revolutions*, "Discourse: An Iranian Quarterly", No. 3–4.

Parsi T., Marashi R. (2011), *Arab Spring Seen From Tehran*, "Cairo Review", No. 2.

Peres praises Mubarak for his contribution to peace (2015), http://www.ynetnews.com/articles/0,7340,L-4024283,00.html, 3.02.2015.

Pohl A. (2014), *Arabia Saudyjska wobec Arabskiej Wiosny*, "Przegląd Politologiczny", Vol. 19, No. 1.

Pupcenoks J. (2012), *Democratic Islamization in Pakistan and Turkey: Lessons for the Post-Arab Spring Muslim World*, "The Middle East Journal", Vol. 66, No. 2.

Rabinovich I. (2014), *Israel and the Arab Turmoil*, Stanford.

Rubin L. (2014), *Islam in the Balance: Ideational Threats in Arab Politics*, Stanford.

Saudi king expresses support for Mubarak (2011), http://www.reuters.com/article/2011/01/29/egypt-saudi-idAFLDE70S08V20110129, 3.02.2015.

Sherwood H. (2012), *Egypt cancels Israeli gas contract*, http://www.theguardian.com/world/2012/apr/23/egypt-cancels-israeli-gas-contract, 30.01.2015.

Uysal A. (2013), *Insights for Egypt's and Tunisia's Islamists from Turkish Experience of Democratic Transition*, "Insight Turkey", Vol. 15, No. 4.

Yegin M., Özertem H. S. (2014), *Parameters of Engagement and Turkey's Limits in the Coalition Against ISIS*, The German Marshall Fund of the United States, "Analysis", 13.11.2014.

Zdanowski J. (2011), *Bliski Wschód 2011: bunt czy rewolucja?*, Kraków.

Artur POHL
Adam Mickiewicz University, Poznań

EGYPT-ISRAEL RELATIONS AFTER 2010

The Arab Spring,[1] or the process of political and social transformations in Arab states in the Middle East and North Africa, which started in December 2010 in Tunisia, has become one of the most significant events of the early 21st century. Observers and researchers dealing with this region were surprised by how dynamic and widespread this phenomenon was, the more so that one of the characteristics of states located in the Middle East and North Africa was their political systems' resistance to change (Fiedler, 2014: 39). The stability of autocratic regimes that frequently oppressed their own peoples in the name of combating Islamic fundamentalism and terrorism has turned out to be illusory, which was indisputably revealed by the Arab Spring. In an avalanche effect (also called the domino effect, contagion, spread and competition) which Samuel Huntington refers to in his *The Third Wave* (Huntington, 2009: 109–116), the transformations triggered by the self-immolation of the Tunisian shop-owner Mohamed Bouazizi (De Soto, 2011) have spread to include numerous Arab states and, to a varying degree, influenced their internal situations (for more see: Pohl, 2014: 143–154). The consequences of the Arab Spring have been significant also for other, non-Arab entities and affected bi- and multilateral relations in the Middle East.

Israel is one of the non-Arab actors who have been most strongly influenced by these events. Israel has not been recognised by a majority of Arab states in the Middle East and North Africa, and has formally remained in a state of war with several of them since 1948. Regardless of Israel's disadvantageous geographical location, in the late 2000s, the country did manage to stabilise the situation in its neighbourhood and build a certain order and security, based on the following three pillars:

– political and military alliance with the US;
– military and technological edge over other states in the region (including nuclear weapons);
– peace treaties and co-operation with Egypt and Jordan.

The latter factor has changed under the influence of the Arab Spring, though. Whereas Jordan did not witness any serious transformations that could endanger the relations and security of Israel, the replacement of Hosni Mubarak's regime and the Salafi Muslims and politicians from the Muslim Brotherhood

---

[1] Other terms used with reference to these events include "Islamic awakening," "Arab revolution," "Arab awakening," and "e-revolution;" Przemysław Osiewicz observes, however, that the term "Arab Spring is most widely spread in the literature on the transformations in the Arab world after 2010" (for more see: Osiewicz, 2014: 7–17).

143

taking power in Egypt could have an adverse impact on the bilateral relations of both states. Therefore, the purpose of this paper is to analyse Egypt-Israel bilateral relations after 2010. The study is based on the assumption that the replacement of H. Mubarak's regime has led to a crisis in Egypt-Israel relations. The research primarily involves the analysis of media coverage and the statements of politicians in respective countries.

EGYPT-ISRAEL RELATIONS BEFORE 2010

Egypt and Israel established official relations on 26 March, 1979, after both countries signed a peace treaty (*Peace Treaty*, 1979). It concluded the war and the period of numerous armed conflicts which started when Israel declared independence in 1948. Over the period of thirty years, Egypt and Israel experienced four serious conflicts and a number of border incidents that led to thousands of casualties. As a result, Israel first defended its independence and later extended its territory, annexing the Sinai Peninsula in 1967, thereby demonstrating its military superiority over the more numerous Egyptian forces, additionally supported by the armies of other Arab states. The hostility of Egypt towards Israel in the first thirty years of the latter's existence was also expressed in other ways. Egypt's authorities offered active support to Palestinian *fedaeens*, inspiring their raids into Israeli territories and terrorist attacks, and they served as the spokesman of the Palestinian cause on the international stage. The degree of hostility between both states at that time was evidenced by the wars, as well as the language used by leading politicians. One day before Egypt's invasion of Israel, an Egyptian diplomat, Azzam Pasha, the first secretary-general of the Arab League, stated that "this will be a war of extermination and a momentous massacre which will be spoken of like the Mongolian massacre and the crusades" (Dayan, 1955: 253);[2] several days earlier he also said "it does not matter how many [Jews] there are. We will sweep them into the sea" (Morris, 2008: 187). Other Egyptian leaders spoke in a similar vein. In 1955, President Gamal Abdel Nasser observed that "[t]here will be no peace on Israel's border because we demand vengeance, and vengeance is Israel's death." Before the Six-Day War, he made numerous remarks on the annihilation of the Jewish state and total war. In his speech broadcast by a Cairo radio station on 25 May, 1967, the leader of Egypt said that "the Arab people is firmly resolved to wipe Israel off the face of the earth..." and added a day later that is was necessary to be "ready to undertake a total war with Israel." Another four days later, he challenged the Israeli minister of defence to try all their weapons against Arab forces that "will spell Israel's

---

[2] According to other sources, this statement was issued much earlier – during an interview given by Azzam Pasha to a journalist from the *Akhbar al-Yom* weekly, published on 11 October, 1947 (Barnett, Karsh, 2011: 87).

death and annihilation" (Tessler, 1994: 393; Bard, 2006: 41–59; Mutawi, 1987: 89). Israel perceived the threat posed by Egypt and other Arab states in terms of another Holocaust and Nazism. The Arabs were Nazified in public discourse. At a session of the Central Committee of his party, David Ben Gurion said, for instance "[w]e do not want to return to the ghetto [...] We do not want the Arab Nazis to come and slaughter us" (after: Zertal, 2010: 293). Moshe Dayan observed that "[m]illions of Jews, who were exterminated because they had no country, are watching us from the ashes of Israeli history and exhorting us to settle and to build up a land for our people. [...] [Arabs] dwell around us and await the moment when they can spill our blood" (Dayan, 1976: 190–191).

The breakthrough in Egypt-Israel contacts followed the Yom Kippur War, another war won by Israel, and upon Anwar el-Sadat assuming power in Egypt. Thanks to the mediation of the US and both parties' intention to reach agreement, it was accomplished at the peace conference at Camp David in September 1978, providing foundations for the peace treaty that marked a radical turn in mutual relations. The agreement concluded the war and normalised bilateral relations, commencing the second stage of the thirty year duration of Egypt-Israel relations, with President H. Mubarak playing the leading role.

Although these three decades are frequently named the era of 'cold peace', they can be divided into two parts. The first fifteen years did not witness any armed conflicts between Egypt and Israel, but the relations were far from good. Their normalisation was very slow, which was influenced both by Israeli policies towards Arab states and the Palestinians, as well as by the activities of the Egyptian opposition. The following events are among the main reasons for the lack of rapprochement between the two states:
– the Israeli bombing of the Iraqi Osirak nuclear reactor in June 1981;
– the Israeli invasion of Lebanon in 1982;
– the failure of talks on Palestinian autonomy;
– the continued construction of settlements in the occupied territories and too slow withdrawal from conquered territories;
– the Israeli reaction to the Intifada;
– assassinations and attacks against Israeli diplomats in Egypt;
– the resistance of Egyptian and Arab states towards the normalisation of relations.

In 1991, Israeli Prime Minister, Yitzhak Shamir described relations with Egypt in the following manner: "[n]ormalization has sunk into oblivion; there is no normalization now. So many years after signing the peace treaty, there are no normal trade relations with Israel; there is no cultural cooperation; there is no Egyptian tourism to Israel. It is as if Israel and Egypt were not living in peace but were two absolute alien and estranged countries. This situation should come to an end" (after: Stein, 1997: 312).

Egypt-Israel relations improved in the period of the second fifteen years of H. Mubarak's rule, starting with the Oslo Agreement signed by Israel and the

Palestine Liberation Organisation. The President of Egypt contributed to this success, having become actively involved in the Madrid Conference and mediating between the parties (Kumaraswamy, 2009: 168–169). Later he continued to act as an intermediary in Israel-Palestine relations, lessening numerous disputes and attempting to prevent the escalation of conflicts.[3] It is worth noting that H. Mubarak's regime took steps against the Palestinian Islamic Resistance Movement (Hamas), rooted in the Muslim Brotherhood. Therefore, the President of Egypt supported the Al-Fatah movement, the political and military rival of Hamas. An interesting example of the improved relations between Egypt and Israel at that time is provided by Egypt's closing in 2007 of the border crossing with the Gaza Strip controlled by Hamas (Sharp, 2008: 8–9). This decision by H. Mubarak's regime meant that the country actually joined the Israeli blockade of the Palestinian territory and collaborated in combating this terrorist group. The improvement of bilateral relations and the emerging trust between Egypt and Israel is also evidenced by the contract signed to deliver natural gas via the Arish-Ashkelon Pipeline, which met around 40% of Israeli demand for this energy source, and the increasing trade between the two countries[4] (Fink, 2011). Another important factor was the offer by Israeli politicians to grant political asylum to H. Mubarak after his stepping down, which confirmed the high quality of relations between the representatives of both countries (Weiss, 2011).

Although Egypt-Israel relations after 1979 were not ideal, from the point of view of Israel's security their most important aspect concerned the guaranty of peace to be maintained. H. Mubarak's government was not interested in running military operations against its Eastern neighbour as this would antagonise the West and in particular the United States, which was providing considerable financial and military aid to Egypt. Combating radical terrorist groups in Egypt, including the delegalisation and repression of opposition Islamic parties, the President contributed to stabilisation in the region and curbed the asymmetrical threats to Israel's security.

OVERTHROW OF HOSNI MUBARAK'S REGIME IN 2011

The thirty years of H. Mubarak's administration saw the gradual normalisation of relations with Israel. The problem that remained was the hostile attitude

---

[3] This involvement can be exemplified by his attempt to intermediate in the negotiations between Israel and Hamas regarding the liberation of a kidnapped IDF soldier Gilad Shalit (*Plans*, 2006), and participation in the resumption of talks between the authorities of the Palestinian Autonomy and Israel in 2010 (*Egypt's Mubarak*, 2010).

[4] According to the Israel Central Bureau of Statistics, the volume of imports to and exports from Egypt amounted to 2.7 million dollars in 1980, 11.3 million dollars in 1990, 79.6 million dollars in 2000 and to as much as 503.1 million dollars in 2010 (*Statistical*, 2011: 720).

of Egyptian society towards the Jews.[5] Despite the activities of H. Mubarak's regime, Islamic radicalism developed. Both these facts were the reasons for Israeli concerns that H. Mubarak's possible assassination or a coup d'état could result in the Islamists taking power, in particular the Muslim Brotherhood, which might mean breaking the peace treaty and supporting anti-Israeli terrorist groups. In 2008, Professor Efraim Inbar wrote in his book *Israel's National Security Issues* that "[a] successful political assassination could bring about a succession struggle and political instability. A successful Islamic revolution in Egypt, the most populous Arab country, would reverberate throughout the region. It would change the Middle East and would probably put an end to the peace treaty between Israel and Egypt – a cornerstone of the current peace process" (Inbar, 2008: 136).

The scenario presented by this Israeli scholar came to be verified several years later. The Arab Spring, starting in Tunisia, inspired the Egyptian people to take action against the authoritarian power of H. Mubarak. The first mass protests staged on 25 January, 2011, were sparked by the death of a blogger, Khalid Said, murdered by the police on 7 January. The demonstrators communicated through social media to arrange meetings in many Egyptian cities and commencing the process of internal change. In early February, the protests were backed by the Muslim Brotherhood, which supported the demands for H. Mubarak to step down and democratise the country. The brutal response of the police forces resulted in bloody clashes and hundreds of casualties. The protesters succeeded on 5 February, when the leadership of the ruling party stepped down, followed by H. Mubarak six days later. The democratic parliamentary and presidential elections allowed the Muslim Brotherhood, accompanied by a Salafi group, to take full power in Egypt (Purat, 2014: 226–227).

NEW CHAPTER IN EGYPT-ISRAEL RELATIONS

The overthrowing of H. Mubarak's regime aroused concerns in Israel as to the potential consequences for mutual relations. Even before the President of Egypt stepped down, Israeli Prime Minister, Benjamin Netanyahu voiced his concerns as regarded the future of the peace treaty and the possible Islamisation and radicalisation of Egypt, as in the case of Iran. On 31 January, B. Netanyahu observed: "[o]ur real fear is of a situation that could develop... and which has already developed in several countries including Iran itself – repressive regimes of radical Islam" as well as "[w]e are all following with vigilance, with worry and hope that indeed the peace and stability will be preserved" (*Israel's Netanyahu*, 2011).

---

[5] Politicians did not endeavour to change this, on the contrary, they maintained it as this attitude allowed them to focus the potential rage of the Egyptians on an outside entity, rather than on internal issues.

The words of the Prime Minister are a clear indication that the Israeli authorities perceived the collapse of H. Mubarak's regime and the Islamists taking power as a threat to their state and a disadvantage for mutual relations. It can be assumed that B. Netanyahu's concerns were also related to the possibility of fundamentalist Egyptian authorities entering into an anti-Israeli agreement with Iran.

The concerns voiced by the Israeli leaders were dispersed as early as two days after the collapse of H. Mubarak's regime. The Supreme Council of the Armed Forces (SCAF), acting as the provisional government, announced on 13 February, 2011, that Egypt would honour all the obligations and agreements it had signed (*Egypt military*, 2011). Although the future of the peace treaty seemed secure, at least as long as power in Egypt was vested with the military, Egypt-Israel relations began to evolve. The changes were negative from the Israeli perspective and they were rooted on the one hand in the reorientation of Egypt's foreign policy, and on the other – in the changed governing style.

One of the first issues that had an adverse impact on bilateral relations was the attitude of the new Egyptian authorities to Hamas and its conflict with Fatah. For years, H. Mubarak's regime was unsympathetic, even hostile towards the former while allying with the latter. The SCAF decided to abandon the policy of aiding one party only, and to become a partner to Hamas as well. The provisional Egyptian authorities demonstrated their good will, becoming involved in the mediation process between the representatives of both groups intending to end the conflict that had lasted since 2006. The negotiations succeeded, leading to a conciliatory agreement signed on 4 May, 2011, that concluded the fighting between Hamas and Fatah (Bronner, 2011). Less than one month later, on 28 May, the SCAF partially opened the Rafah border crossing, easing the four-year blockade of the Gaza Strip[6] (*Egypt eases*, 2011). Both these events stirred the discontent of Israeli authorities. Prime Minister B. Netanyahu said that the agreement between Hamas and Fatah was "a tremendous blow to peace and a great victory for terrorism." The opening of the Rafah border crossing was met with equally great indignation. The opposition Kadima party issued a statement saying that "[t]he breaking of the blockade, with no coordination with Israel, and against its will, constitutes a diplomatic failure of the B. Netanyahu government – that because of its diplomatic weakness and inability to create coordination and cooperation with international parties, has left Israel isolated, in a position of weakened security, while Hamas has gotten stronger" (Abu Toameh, Katz, 2011). Both these statements regarding the activities of the Egyptian authorities evidence the growing discontent of Israel and its fears of the reorientation of Egypt's foreign policy in the wake of H. Mubarak's collapse.

---

[6] The border crossing remained closed for men aged 18–40, who were not allowed to use it, and for trade.

Egypt-Israel relations at the time of SCAF were challenged by increasing terrorist activities in the borderlands of Egypt, Israel and the Gaza Strip, which resulted in tensions between the two countries. The Arish-Ashkelon Pipeline was repeatedly bombed, interrupting the supply of gas (*Egypt's Hamas*, 2011). In August 2011, Palestinian militants hiding in Sinai carried out a series of attacks in Israeli territories, killing eight Israelis.[7] Following an exchange of fire between the IDF and militants, who were chased along the border with Egypt, Egyptian border guards were killed, having found themselves in the line of fire (Greenwood, 2011). This incident resulted in one of the most serious coolings of bilateral relations in over thirty years. The Egyptian authorities expressed their indignation and announced the possibility of withdrawing their ambassador from Israel (Michael, Deitch, 2011; Batty, 2011). However, the lack of actual activities and an adequate response from the SCAF intensified the long-lasting, anti-Israeli sentiments of society and triggered the outbreak of mass protests, despite official apologies. In the course of the protests, demonstrators attacked the Israeli embassy in Cairo on 9 September, 2011, enforcing the evacuation of Israeli diplomats and their return to homeland (Ravid, Khoury, 2011).

Balancing the stability of the state on the one hand, and on the other maintaining peace and correct relations with Israel, which allowed Egypt to obtain billions of dollars of US aid annually following the Camp David agreement, the SCAF decided to seal the border with the Gaza Strip. In early September 2011 the army commenced an operation aimed at locating and closing the underground tunnels used by the Palestinians, including terrorists, to illegally cross the state border and smuggle weapons later used in attacks conducted on Israeli territories (*Egypt military*, 2011). These steps were intended to weaken radical Islamic groups developing in the Sinai Peninsula, while helping to seal the Israeli blockade of the Gaza Strip and strengthen Israeli security, thereby improving bilateral relations. A further warming was accomplished thanks to the agreement between Israel and Hamas as regarded the liberation of Gilad Shalit, an IDF soldier held captive for five years, which was facilitated with Egypt's mediation (Bronner, 2011).

The Muslim Brotherhood's victory in the elections to the Egyptian parliament, held at the turn of 2011 and 2012, again stimulated increased Israeli concerns about the future of bilateral relations between both states. They were primarily rooted in the anti-Israeli rhetoric of the Brotherhood and its connections with Hamas. In 2010, Mohamad Morsi, one of the Brotherhood's leaders and the future President of Egypt called for "our children and our grandchildren [to be nursed] on hatred for them: for Zionists, for Jews" (Kirkpatrick, 2013). According to some Israeli analysts and experts, after taking power in Egypt, the Muslim Brotherhood "will try to kind of freeze or to minimize the [peace] agreement," because "[i]t is an Islamic, extremist movement. They have

---

[7] Seven died in the attacks, one in the exchange of fire with the terrorists.

said they hate Israel; they would like to see Israel wiped off the map" (Berger, 2012). Israeli forecasts seemed to have been confirmed by the events at the beginning of 2012.

In March, the People's Assembly, Egypt's lower chamber of parliament, which had been taken over by Islamists at that time, passed a resolution in which it declared that "Egypt will never be the friend, partner or ally of the Zionist entity [Israel] which we consider as the first enemy of Egypt and the Arab nation" and called for the government "[to] revise all its relations and agreements [with Israel]" (Kessler, 2012). The cooling of Egypt-Israel relations seemed to be confirmed by breaching the contract for the supply of natural gas via the Arish-Ashkelon Pipeline in April 2012. Both Egypt and Israel claimed that this was the outcome of an economic rather than a political dispute (Sherwood, 2012; Sanders, 2012). M. Morsi's victory in the presidential elections and his resumption of contacts with Israeli enemy – Iran, which he officially visited as the first Egyptian leader since 1978,[8] could have meant a further cooling between Egypt and Israel. Since his election, however, the new President of Egypt refrained from anti-Israeli and anti-Semitic rhetoric, and, what is more, declared that the 1979 peace treaty would be honoured and the foreign policy would be balanced (*Egyptian President*, 2012). Although in November 2012 the President condemned the Israeli attacks on the Gaza Strip and withdrew the ambassador from Tel Aviv, he also committed himself to mediation between Israel and Hamas. Egypt's mediation allowed the bloody conflict resulting from the IDF Operation Pillar of Defence and rocket attacks by Palestinian militants to come to an end (Karon, 2012; Zeiger, 2012). It was one of the paradoxes of M. Morsi's administration that it witnessed the strengthening and advancement of Egypt-Israel intelligence and military collaboration. It contributed to the activities of terrorist groups in the Sinai Peninsula, primarily in the borderlands, being curbed and to the alleviation of tensions between both states (Gold, 2013).

The growing social discontent with the Islamisation and strengthened autocracy of M. Morsi's power resulted in the outbreak of mass protests in 2013, eventually concluded in the military coup d'état on 3 July (Wedeman, Sayah, Smith, 2013). The deposition of the Muslim Brotherhood was welcomed with caution by the Israeli authorities. As time went by, however, they became increasingly positive towards the transformations taking place in Egypt. In an interview for the German *Welt am Sonntag*, Israeli PM B. Netanyahu stated: "I believe that over the long haul these radical Islamic regimes are going to fail because they don't offer the adequate enfranchisement that you need to develop a country economically, politically and culturally" (*Netanyahu*, 2013). Israeli diplomacy simultaneously started lobbying the European Union and the United States to ac-

---

[8] That is, since the Islamic Revolution in Iran, which ousted the pro-Western regime of Shah Mohammad Reza Pahlavi, and signing the Egypt-Israel peace treaty.

cept the new Egyptian authorities and continue the financial and military aid offered to Egypt since the agreement in Camp David (Kirkpatrick, 2013; *Washington*, 2013). The coup d'état gave Israel an opportunity to renew its informal alliance with Egypt against Hamas and to strengthen both countries' collaboration in the field of intelligence and combating terrorism in the Sinai Peninsula. General Abdel Fattah el-Sisi became the actual authority in Egypt, initiating an extensive campaign against the increasingly strong radical Islamic groups that posed a threat to both states. The importance attached to this matter by Israel can be evidenced, among other things, by allowing the Egyptian army's increased presence in Sinai[9] and carrying out a number of offensives nearby the Egypt-Israeli border in its fight against terrorists (Gold, 2014: 13–140; *Israel Agrees*, 2013). Under General A. F. el-Sisi, Egypt became an Israeli partner in ensuring security as it continued the destruction of the underground tunnels used by smugglers and terrorists. The new Egyptian government resumed aiding Mahmoud Abbas and Fatah in the conflict with Hamas and strengthened the blockade of the Gaza Strip by increased limitations imposed on the Rafah border crossing (Trager, 2014). In the time of A. F. el-Sisi, the policy of Egypt towards Israel and the mutual relations are more reminiscent of the policy of H. Mubarak in the second fifteen years of his presidency. While they are increasingly correct, they are still far from a good neighbourhood based on mutual trust. President A. F. el-Sisi appears to be a pragmatic politician who wants to play the leading role in the region. Therefore, he can be expected to maintain good relations with Israel. There are a number of common interests, such as the weakening of Hamas in the Gaza Strip and fundamentalist groups in the Sinai Peninsula, maintaining the peace from Camp David, which brings aid worth millions of dollars annually, and the development of tourist and trade contacts, in particular in the energy sector, allowing the Egyptian economy to grow.

CONCLUSIONS

Overthrowing H. Mubarak's regime ended the period of the Egypt-Israel strategic alliance against Hamas and closer trade and military contacts. At the same time, it started a new stage of mutual relations, with the Islamist Muslim Brotherhood, headed by President M. Morsi, initially playing the leading role. The anti-Israeli past of Egypt's new leader and the connections between his party and Hamas aroused Israeli concerns as regarded the future of the peace treaty and the further collaboration of both states. Mutual relations cooled, which was primarily related to the change of Egypt's attitude to the operations of Hamas and its conflict with Israel, as well as the hostile rhetoric of Islamist groups and some Egyptian politicians. It should be noted, however, that even under the

---

[9] Limited by virtue of the Camp David agreement and the peace treaty that followed.

government of the Muslim Brotherhood, Egypt never renounced the peace treaty and continued intelligence and military collaboration with Israel directed against terrorist groups. It also became involved in mediations between Hamas and Israel. The coup d'état of 3 July, 2013, and the removal of the Muslim Brotherhood from power actually led to the resumption of correct Egypt-Israel relations as before the Arab Spring. The policy of President A. F. el-Sisi towards Israel and Hamas is reminiscent of H. Mubarak's policy, although the former is characterised by a larger commitment to the cooperation with Israel, in particular as concerns such a vital issue as combating Islamic terrorism. The analysis of Egypt-Israel relations after 2010 allows the hypothesis formulated at the beginning of this paper, as to the crisis of these relations, to be disproved. One should rather talk about a temporary cooling of these relations, related to the SCAF and later the Muslim Brotherhood assuming power.

BIBLIOGRAPHY

Abu Toameh K., Katz Y. (2011), *300 Gazans enter Egypt In first hour of Rafah opening*, http://www.jpost.com/Video-Articles/Video/300-Gazans-enter-Egypt-in-first-hour--of-Rafah-opening, 4.11.2014.

Bard M. G. (2006), *Myths and Facts: A Guide to the Arab-Israeli Conflict*, Chevy Chase.

Barnett D., Karsh E. (2011), *Azzam's Genocidal Threat*, "The Middle East Quarterly", Fall.

Batty D. (2011), *Egypt withdraws ambassador to Israel over police deaths*, http://www.theguardian.com/world/2011/aug/20/egypt-withdraws-israeli-ambassador-police, 4.11.2014.

Berger E. (2012), *Islamist Victory in Egypt Raises Concerns in Israel*, http://www.voanews.com/content/islamist-victory-in-egypt-raises-concern-in-israel/1246667.html, 4.11.2014.

Bronner E. (2011), *Israel and Hamas Agree to Swap Prisoners for Solider*, http://www.nytimes.com/2011/10/12/world/middleeast/possible-deal-near-to-free-captive-israeli-soldier.html?pagewanted=all, 4.11.2014.

Bronner E. (2011), *Palestinian Factions Sign Accord to End Rift*, http://www.nytimes.com/2011/05/05/world/middleeast/05palestinians.html, 4.11.2014.

Dayan M. (1955), *Israel's Border and Security Problems*, "Foreign Affairs", Vol. 33, Issue 2.

Dayan M. (1976), *Avnei Derekh, Autobiografia*, Tel Aviv.

De Soto H. (2011), *The Real Mohamed Bouazizi*, http://www.foreignpolicy.com/articles/2011/12/16/the_real_mohamed_bouazizi?page=0,2, 4.11.2014.

Egypt eases blockade at Gaza's Rafah Border (2011), http://www.nytimes.com/2011/05/05/world/middleeast/05palestinians.html, 4.11.2014.

Egypt military authorities 'to respect all treaties' (2011), http://www.bbc.co.uk/news/world-middle-east-12440138, 4.11.2014.

Egypt military begins operations to close Gaza smuggling tunnels (2011), http://www.haaretz.com/news/diplomacy-defense/egypt-military-begins-operation-to-close-gaza-smuggling--tunnels-1.382453, 4.11.2014.

Egypt's Hamas Dilemma After Israel Attacks (2011), http://www.stratfor.com/sample/analysis/egypts-hamas-dilemma-after-attacks-israel, 4.11.2014.

Egypt's Mubarak to continue mediating Israeli-Palestinian direct talks (2010), http://en.ria.ru/world/20100914/160580482.html, 4.11.2014.

Egyptian President Morsi reassures Israel that peace treaty is safe (2012), http://www.haaretz.com/news/middle-east/egyptian-president-morsi-reassures-israel-that-peace-treaty-is--safe-1.461123, 4.11.2014.

Fiedler R. (2014), *Arabska Wiosna – szanse i wyzwania dla polityki USA wobec Bliskiego Wschodu*, "Przegląd Politologiczny", No. 1.

Fink D. (2011), *Turning Off the Egyptian Gas Spigot: Implications for Israel*, http://ensec.org/index.php?option=com_content&view=article&id=313:turning-off-the-egyptian-gas--spigot-implications-for-israel&catid=116:content0411&Itemid=375, 4.11.2014.

Gold Z. (2013), *Why Israel Will Miss Morsi*, http://www.foreignaffairs.com/articles/139835/zack-gold/why-israel-will-miss-morsi, 4.11.2014.

Gold Z. (2014), *Security in the Sinai: Present and Future*, http://www.icct.nl/download/file/ICCT-Gold-Security-In-The-Sinai-March-2014.pdf, 4.11.2014.

Greenwood P. (2011), *Egyptian border guards killed during Israeli raid on militants*, http://www.telegraph.co.uk/news/worldnews/middleeast/israel/8710372/Egyptian-border-guards-killed-during-Israeli-raid-on-militants.html, 4.11.2014.

Huntington S. P. (2009), Trzecia fala demokratyzacji, Warszawa.

Israel agrees to Egypt troop movements in Sinai as ultimatum to Morsi nears (2013), http://www.haaretz.com/news/middle-east/1.533378, 4.11.2014.

Israel's Netanyahu fears Egypt could go way of Iran, http://af.reuters.com/article/egyptNews/idAFLDE70U2E420110131?sp=true, 4.11.2014.

Karon T. (2012), *How the Gaza Truce Makes Egypt's Muslim Brotherhood a Peace Player*, http://world.time.com/2012/11/21/how-the-gaza-truce-makes-egypts-muslim-brotherhood-a-peace-player/, 4.11.2014.

Kessler O. (2012), *Iran lauds Egypt house vote to expel Israel envoy*, http://www.jpost.com/Middle-East/Iran-lauds-Egypt-house-vote-to-expel-Israel-envoy, 4.11.2014.

Kirkpatrick D. D. (2013), *How American Hopes for a Deal in Egypt Were Undercut*, http://www.nytimes.com/2013/08/18/world/middleeast/pressure-by-us-failed-to--sway-egypts-leaders.html?_r=0, 4.11.2014.

Kirkpatrick D. D. (2013), *Morsi's Slurs Against Jews Stir Concern*, http://www.nytimes.com/2013/01/15/world/middleeast/egypts-leader-morsi-made-anti-jewish-slurs.html?pagewanted=1, 4.11.2014.

Kumaraswamy P. R. (2009), *The A to Z of the Arab-Israeli conflict*, Plymouth.

Michael M., Deitch I. (2011), *Egypt to withdraw ambassador to Israel over ambush*, http://www.independent.co.uk/news/world/middle-east/egypt-to-withdraw-ambassador-to-israel-over-ambush-2341011.html, 4.11.2014.

Morris B. (2008), *1948. A History of the First Arab-Israeli War*, Michigan.

Mutawi S. A. (1987), *Jordan in the 1967 war*, Cambridge.

Netanyahu to German weekly: Fall of Egypt's Morsi is sign of political Islam's weakness (2013), http://www.haaretz.com/news/diplomacy-defense/1.537105, 4.11.2014.

Osiewicz P. (2014), *Zmiany społeczno-polityczne w państwach arabskich po 2010 roku: krytyczna analiza stosowanych pojęć*, "Przegląd Politologiczny", No. 1.

Peace Treaty Between the State of Israel and the Arab Republic of Egypt (1979), http://unispal.un.org/unispal.nsf/9a798adbf322aff38525617b006d88d7/40d14c9b19a5f6dc85256ced00741c70?OpenDocument, 4.11.2014.

Plans to free solider 'sabotaged' (2006), http://www.news24.com/World/Plans-to-free-soldier-sabotaged-20060712, 4.11.2014.

Purat A. (2014), *Znaczenie Bractwa Muzułmańskiego w polityce Egiptu oraz w wydarzeniach Arabskiej Wiosny 2011 roku*, "Przegląd Politologiczny", No. 1.

Ravid B., Khoury J. (2011), *Egyptian protesters break into Israeli Embassy in Cairo; Obama expresses concern to Netanyahu*, http://www.haaretz.com/news/diplomacy-defense/egyptian-protesters-break-into-israeli-embassy-in-cairo-obama-expresses-concern-to--netanyahu-1.383574, 4.11.2014.

Sanders E. (2012), *Egypt-Israel natural gas deal revoked for economic reasons*, http://articles.latimes.com/2012/apr/23/world/la-fg-egypt-israel-oil-20120424, 4.11.2014.

Sharp J. (2008), *The Egypt-Gaza Border and its Effect on Israeli-Egyptian Relations*, CRS Report for Congress, http://fas.org/sgp/crs/mideast/RL34346.pdf, 4.11.2014.

Sherwood H. (2012), *Egypt cancels Israeli gas contract*, http://www.theguardian.com/world/2012/apr/23/egypt-cancels-israeli-gas-contract, 4.11.2014.

Statistical Abstract of Israel 2011 – N. 62. (2011), Central Bureau of Statistics, http://www1.cbs.gov.il/shnaton62/shnaton62_all_e.pdf, 4.11.2014.

Stein K. W. (1997), *Continuity and Change in Egyptian-Israeli Relations 1973–1997*, in: *From Rabin to Netanyahu: Israel's Troubled Agenda*, ed. E. Karsh, London–Portland.

Tessler M. A. (1994), *A History of the Israeli-Palestinian Conflict*, Bloomington.

Trager E. (2014), *Sisi's Egypt and the Gaza Conflict*, The Washington Institute, http://www.washingtoninstitute.org/policy-analysis/view/sisis-egypt-and-the-gaza-conflict, 4.11.2014.

Washington cuts Egypt aid despite intense Israeli lobbying (2013), http://www.haaretz.com/news/diplomacy-defense/1.551666, 4.11.2014.

Wedeman B., Sayah R., Smith M. (2013), *Coup topples Egypt's Morsy; deposed president under 'house arrest'*, http://edition.cnn.com/2013/07/03/world/meast/egypt-protests, 4.11.2014.

Weiss M. (2011), *Hosni Mubarak 'was offered asylum in Israel'*, http://www.telegraph.co.uk/news/worldnews/africaandindianocean/egypt/8679159/Hosni-Mubarak-was-offered-asylum-in-Israel.html, 4.11.2014.

Zeiger A. (2012), *Egypt delays ambassador's return to Tel Aviv*, http://www.timesofisrael.com/egypt-delays-ambassadors-return-to-tel-aviv/, 4.11.2014.

Zertal I. (2010), *Naród i śmierć. Zagłada w dyskursie i polityce Izraela*, Kraków.

Radosław FIEDLER
Adam Mickiewicz University, Poznań

US POLICY TOWARDS EGYPT VERSUS OTHER ENTITIES

US APPROACH TO EGYPT BEFORE AND AFTER THE ARAB SPRING

The United States is the most active and influential external actor in the Middle East and North Africa (MENA). During the Cold War, the Middle East was one of the most important areas of US-USSR competition. After 1945, the successive administrations had to tackle an entire range of challenges and threats that resulted from the complexity of the situation in this region. The challenges of that period involved the wave of Arab nationalism with an anti-Western slant, successive wars waged by Israel against its Arab neighbours, political instability of certain US allies, the Islamic revolution in Iran and another wave of anti-Americanism that followed, this time rooted in religious radicalism and religiously motivated terrorism (Fiedler, 2010: 45–80).

After the end of the Cold War, the United States did not manage to mediate the conclusion of the conflict between Israel and the Palestinian Autonomy. However, the gravest outcomes of US policy towards the Middle East were produced by the decision to invade Iraq in 2003. The failure to stabilise Iraq, and then Syria after the Arab Spring, has made the US consider the possibility to co-operate with Iran. The possible reshuffling of priorities in US policy towards MENA results from the threat posed by Islamic State.

Since the Cold War, US policy has been concentrated on the following objectives:

– to ensure the flow of oil, which is crucial for the development of global economy;
– to combat terrorism;
– to maintain military bases and their respective infrastructure in order to ensure US military presence in the region;
– to prevent the proliferation of nuclear, chemical, biological and conventional weapons;
– to foster economic development, human rights and democracy.

The last objective constitutes one of the non-military instruments of US policy towards MENA. In comparison with other external actors, including the European Union, the United States has proposed numerous initiatives targeted at fostering the development of civil society in the Arab world.

Table 1. Selected US financial instruments implemented in MENA

Programme/initiative	Objective
United States Agency for International Development (USAID)	The programmes were targeted at central administrations as well as NGOs. After 11 September, 2011, the main objective involved fostering democratic solutions in Arab states and encouraging their societies to attempt to create civil administrative structures.
Middle East Free Trade Area (MEFTA) in 2003	The plan envisaged the emergence of a US-Middle East Free Trade Area by 2003.
Broader Middle East and North Africa Initiative (BMENAI) in 2004	Three fields: political – by means of fostering democracy, the rule of law and human rights; socio-educational – by means of aiding the programmes to develop education in order to elevate the level of education of young people in Arab states and ensuring their free access to modern information technologies; economic – by means of seeking how to create new jobs, supporting free market mechanisms and the reforms of financial systems, increasing foreign investments and the implementation of anti-corruption solutions.
Middle East Partnership Initiative (MEPI) 2002 r.	A programme aiding civil society institutions in MENA.

Source: (developed on the basis of: Heydemann 2014: 299–317).

The initiatives and programmes developed primarily by the G. W. Bush administration did not result in the assumed breakthrough related to the political liberalisation and regional integration of MENA countries. The administration of Barack Obama was not as committed to the implementation of these programmes.

The issue of political reforms was and continues to be present in US policy, but it is of secondary importance. The scenario Washington would desire most for Egypt involves gradual modernisation and top-bottom liberalisation of the authoritarian system (Heydemann, 2007). Political reforms initiated by the authorities are safer.

It was known for decades that too rapid democratisation would mean bringing Islamic fundamentalists to power. Therefore, except for a short period after 11 September, 2001, the topic of political reforms was not a priority in US policy towards this strategic ally (Piazza, 2008; Muravchik, 2001; Kaplan, 2003: 23).

Examining the efficiency of US policy towards MENA one finds that many problems were not solved, new ones emerged, some resulting from miscalculations by Washington concerning Iraq, which had an adverse impact on regional security. Apart from failures, the US has also had some success as regards MENA. One of the most significant achievements scored by US diplomacy involved the peace agreement worked out between Egypt and Israel, which has become one of the essential elements of regional security. This was a major breakthrough that proved the strength of US leadership in the Middle East. Before that, Egypt had closer relations with the Soviet Union, whose potential to solve the Middle East conflict, however, was much more limited. The remaining key US allies, alongside Egypt, are Israel Saudi Arabia and Jordan.

Every year, the US transfers military aid to Egypt to an amount of USA 1.3 bln and a mere USD 250 mln as economic aid. Over the period 1948–2014, the US allocated a total of USD 74.6 bln as aid to Egypt (Sowa, 2014).

US policy towards Egypt, and towards Jordan, is primarily related to the issue of Israel's security. Thanks to peace treaties signed with Israel, both Arab states were able to develop closer relations and strategic co-operation with the United States.

The Arab Spring, its dynamic development and outcomes, came as a considerable surprise to the US. The predominant concern was the risk that predictable autocrats would be replaced by the chaos of internal conflicts and religious radicalisation, coupled with a new wave of anti-Americanism (Ross, 2010: 109–115). Anti-American sentiments were one of the driving forces of the 1979 Islamic revolution in Iran, and the same was justifiably feared in the case of the Arab Spring (Huber, 2015: 57–75).

The issue of anti-American sentiments was supposed to be soothed by President B. Obama addressing the Arab and Muslim world in Cairo's Al-Azhar University. Although the speech was made at a symbolic site, it was general and presented no new initiatives. The President did not refer to the need for the democratisation of Arab states, either.[1] Despite some attempts at a change of rhetoric, US policy towards the Middle East has not considerably changed, at least not the policy towards regional allies.

Whereas the events of the Arab Spring in Tunisia did not raise concerns in Washington, the situation was different in the case of Egypt. Despite the potential for chaos in Egypt after 25 January, 2011, the B. Obama administration decided, albeit with some hesitation, that the best solution would be the ousting of Hosni Mubarak. Washington was not going to back the unpopular dictator at any cost. The replacement of Egypt's leader did not infringe the system of power – the Egyptian army continued to be in charge (Laz, 2014: 48). The US 'abandoning' of H. Mubarak was condemned by Saudi Arabia and Israel, though. For the Saudi monarchy it evidenced disloyalty towards a long-lasting ally who deserved to be supported in the circumstances of political crisis, despite his difficulties (Bania, 2014: 201–214). Israel was equally critical, and expressed its concerns that after H. Mubarak religious groups, headed by the Muslim Brotherhood, would assume power, which could mean that regional security would collapse after a radical Egypt renounced the Camp David treaty (Yossef, 2013: 211–225).

---

[1] For more on the content of President Obama's Cairo speech, see: *Full Text of Obama's Speech in Cairo. President Speaks At Cairo University*, http://www.msnbc.msn.com/id/31102929/ns/politics-white_house.

The process of democratisation in Egypt primarily resulted in the representatives of the Muslim Brotherhood and other religious groups, including the Salafi, assuming power. In the first democratic parliamentary elections after the Arab Spring, both groups won a total of 68% of seats (Vidino, 2013). The civilian authorities did not exercise control over the Egyptian army, whose command (The Supreme Council of the Armed Forces) maintained independence. Regardless of the alarming signals related to the critical statements by some representatives of the Muslim Brotherhood as to whether it made sense to maintain the peace treaty with Israel, Washington stressed that the candidate of the Muslim Brotherhood, Mohamad Morsi, was the first democratically elected president in the history of Egypt. The US also appreciated his role and support for US diplomacy in finishing the exchange of fire between Israel and Hamas in November 2012 (Dunne, 2014). Another positive signal was Egypt's readiness to implement budget reforms in order to ensure a tranche of financial aid from the International Monetary Fund (Bradley, 2012).

The B. Obama administration put considerable confidence in President M. Morsi and his government, hoping that the democratic process and establishment of civil society institutions would continue to clearly indicate the direction of Egypt's transformation, and that some radical views would become more moderate over time. This confidence could be undermined on account of the intensifying crisis between the Egyptian authorities and the opposition, and the increasing curbs on civil society institutions. The Muslim Brotherhood and its allies managed to push through their own draft of the constitution, taking no account of the opinion or input of secular political circles and the Coptic Church. The new constitution was founded on religious law. The authorities resumed repressions of those NGOs that obtained financing from abroad (Hanna, 2013). In June 2013, 43 NGO workers (including 19 US citizens) were convicted for running activities without the necessary permits, even though these organisations had applied for them much earlier; their applications were never processed (Katulis, Sofer, Juul, 2013). These developments did not bring about a change in US policy towards Egypt. The co-operation in the field of security was maintained in 2013 and the resources allocated within the framework of USD 1.3 bln for aiding the Egyptian army and economic reforms were not suspended. The US hoped that the democratic elections constituted an added value of the Egyptian transformation and it realised that the democratisation process would be lengthy and full of crises.

Washington responded to the coup d'état of 3 July, 2013, in a highly critical manner (Gerbaudo, 2013: 104–113). Initially, the B. Obama administration applied diplomatic measures, trying to achieve an agreement between the Egyptian army and the toppled President M. Morsi and his followers. These diplomatic attempts of Washington were utterly ignored by the Minister of Defence, Abdel Fattah el-Sisi, who was to become President of Egypt in June 2014. Military forces carried out brutal pacifications in Cairo, leaving over 1,000 casualties among the members and advocates of the Muslim Brotherhood. Many more people died in July 2013 than in the period from 25 January and 18 February 2011, leading to the ousting of H. Mubarak (Marshall, 2013: 8–10). There were 2,528 civilian casualties between 3 July and 31 December 2013 (Rękawek, 2014). Washington deemed resorting to violence and mass infringements of human rights to be a reason to suspend weapons deliveries provided as US military aid for Egypt, which was unprecedented. It needs to be stressed that the US military aid was not suspended as a direct consequence of the coup d'état, but rather of the repressions that followed.

After several months, however, the US began to gradually soften its initial, firm standpoint towards the military authorities headed by General A. F. el-Sisi. One of the challenges to be faced after 2011 involved the deteriorating situation in the Middle East, in particular in Iraq, Syria, Yemen and Libya. In summer 2014, the crisis of the state of Iraq was vividly revealed by the rapid advances of the jihadists from ISIS (Islamic State of Iraq and Sham). The progressing destabilisation of Libya resulted in increased numbers of refugees on the one hand, and unprecedented smuggling of weapons, including anti-aircraft and anti-tank missiles, that were to arrive in Sinai and Gaza on the other.

Regional issues and challenges made Egypt an even more desirable US partner, in spite of the repressions against the opposition. US military aid was resumed on 22 April, 2014. Washington agreed to supply 10 Apache air assault helicopters to facilitate the counter-terrorist campaign in Sinai.

The significant role of Egypt in the campaign against ISIS was confirmed by another visit by John Kerry in Cairo on 12 September, 2014, when the country joined the anti-ISIS coalition. President of Egypt is going to use the campaign the US initiated to combat the terrorism of ISIS and extend it to cover the less radical religious parties, including the Muslim Brotherhood, as well as other circles and groups opposing the authorities (Aziz, 2013).

Seeking to maintain the regional anti-ISIS coalition, Washington is aware that without Cairo, it will be impossible to run an effective campaign against jihadists from the East and West of Egypt. What is a problem is that the 'normalisation' of US-Egypt relations can be condemned by Egyptians on account of the US abandoning the issues of human rights and the democratisation of Egypt. Secretary of State, J. Kerry personally intervened in the case of three journalists of the English-speaking Al-Jazeera, accused of connections with the banned Muslim Brotherhood, to no avail. Egyptian, Australian and Canadian citizens were sentenced to seven years in prison, although the allegations of their connections with the Muslim Brotherhood were not substantiated during the trial (Gordon, Kirkpatrick, 2014). Another case is the mass death sentences passed by Egypt's military courts. They mainly concern the members and advocates of the banned Muslim Brotherhood who are sentenced *in absentia* – their number reached 1,212 in 2014 (Sharp, 2014). The repressions of the new authorities of Egypt exceed those of H. Mubarak's regime, resulting in aggravated social tensions and even confrontations that may lead to President A. F. el-Sisi facing mass protests. The unconditional and indiscriminate support offered by the US to Egypt can turn out to be risky, even in the short term. After 2011, Egyptian society proved to be capable of organising itself and staging long-term mass protests (Affaya, 2013: 50–70). So far, the opposition suffered from the lack of, or highly limited co-operation of secular and religious circles. The integration of these two forces could lead to a serious crisis, comparable to the Iranian revolution of 1978–1979. The same as three decades earlier, the Egyptian authorities are using the fight against terrorism and religious radicalism to break human rights and eliminate the remnants of civil society institutions. The frustration of numerous opposition circles can breed resistance that will culminate in a political crisis. The Egyptian military elite has not reflected on the recent events that brought the apparently immovable H. Mubarak down just a few years ago.

The US instruments for exerting financial influence on Egypt are relatively limited, although still more substantial than those of the EU. They encompass military aid and a financial support package totalling over USD 1.5 bln annually. Another similar instrument is provided by the International Monetary Fund, whose financial support is conditioned on the implementation of financial and economic reforms. Much greater, and unconditional, financial aid is offered by the Persian Gulf states, such as Saudi Arabia and the United Arab Emirates, who transferred a total of around USD 18 bln, preventing the bankruptcy of Egypt. The donators from the Persian Gulf recognised President A. F. el-Sisi as guaranteeing the political and economic stability in Egypt. They have made no conditions regarding the implementation of political reforms. The US, however, is the greatest supplier of the modern weapons required by the Egyptian army, provided within the framework of US military aid.

RUSSIAN FEDERATION APPROACH TO EGYPT BEFORE AND AFTER THE ARAB SPRING

In the 1950s, Egypt, Syria and Iraq invited the Soviet Union to co-operate. This was the period of Moscow's profound involvement in the arming of Egypt, among other things (Beliakov, 2013: 272–282). The USSR, however, did not manage to create sufficient bridgeheads to set off US influences. Soviet involvement in the Middle East was seriously weakened after Egypt terminated its closer co-operation with the USSR in the early 1970s.

After 1991, Syria remained the only ally of the Russian Federation. Moscow has also developed co-operation with Iran, working on its civil nuclear programme. Russia collaborates with the US within the P5+1 group (the US, Russia, France, the UK, China and Germany) negotiating with Tehran. Additionally, alongside the US, EU and UN, Russia is also a member of a quartet established in Madrid in 2001 for the purpose of reactivating the Middle East peace process between Israel and the Palestinian Autonomy.

For over two decades following the collapse of the USSR, Russia's policy towards the Middle East has continued to try to diminish the US's influence in the region. Russia interprets US failures in Middle East policy as evidence of the US gradually losing its position there. In Moscow's opinion, this is exemplified by US inefficiency in bringing Middle East conflict to an end and its inability to tackle such threats as, for instance, ISIS.

Following the 'zero problems' principle, the Russian Federation tries to maintain good relations and extend trade exchange with as many countries in the Middle East as possible, and convince them that it is an alternative to the US.

Relations with Egypt have been developed intensively for over a year. Despite the short period of A. F. el-Sisi's presidency so far, he has already visited the Russian Federation, and President Putin paid him a return visit in Cairo in February 2015. Before the Arab Spring, 1.5 mln Russians came to Egypt for holidays, and trade exchange oscillated around USD 2 bln annually. Russia took advantage of the US-Egypt crisis in October 2013 and offered to supply weapons to Egypt. On 17 September it was reported that Russia and Egypt had reached a preliminary deal for Cairo to buy arms worth USD 3.5 bln from Moscow[2] (Akulov, 2014). The preliminary arms contract with Russia evidences that Cairo has large suppliers of arms other than the US. Russia is also going to support the development of Egypt's civil nuclear programme.

Russia is making it clear to Cairo that it is not interested in collaborating in the field of human rights and continued political liberalisation, which in Moscow's view, leads to serious destabilisation in the region.

The Egypt-Russia co-operation can transform into a more strategic partnership over time. This is also indicated by the declaration to develop civil nuclear energy in Egypt.

CHINA'S APPROACH TO EGYPT

The People's Republic of China finds the Middle East and North Africa significant on account of its energy potential. One of the more serious challenges faced by China, whose population accounts for 1/5 of the global population, is its def-

---

[2] "Russian Mi-35 attack helicopters and/or Mi-17 multipurpose helicopters are reported to be part of the just concluded deal. Egypt already has nearly 100 of these rotary wing aircraft and the older Soviet-era Mi-8 helicopters, which have troop-transport, cargo, signals-intelligence, and attack variants, the latter equipped with 23 mm guns and the capacity to carry 500 kg bombs and antitank guided missiles. Some of these systems are operating in Sinai" (quotation from: Akulov, 2014).

icit of energy resources and the generally increasing demand for different goods.[3] Chinese oil resources covered internal demand until 1992. In the years that followed, domestic production was unable to keep up with the growing demand for oil.[4] Very conservative estimates by the International Energy Agency indicate that China's demand for oil in 2030 will amount to 10 mln barrels daily, 80% of which will be imported.[5] The US Department of Energy estimates that China is going to use 14.2 mln barrels of oil daily in 2025.[6]

As in Russia, the Chinese authorities also find autocratic regimes capable of developing multifaceted co-operation with them more valuable than human rights and democratisation. Since the Arab Cooperation Forum was initiated in 2004, China's trade turnover with Arab states reached USD 190 bln in 2011. The Arab Spring turned out to pose a serious challenge to Chinese interests, though. Before 2011, China signed long-term contracts for a total of USD 18.8 bln with Muammar Gaddafi's regime. In 2012, Libya supplied 3% of China's oil imports. While the security situation in Libya was deteriorating, however, China was forced to reduce its involvement, and even to evacuate part of 35,000 Chinese workers from Libya. Its total loss amounted to around USD 20 bln. In 2011, China abstained on resolution 1973 of the UN Security Council on the military intervention in Libya. The Chinese authorities are not going to repeat this error, as they see it, in the case of Syria or another crisis in the Middle East (Sun, 2012).

China's negative experience of the outcomes of the Arab Spring in Libya translated into increased interest in Egypt as a stable and predictable actor in the region. After the Arab Spring, the Chinese stress that only secular autocrats are able to ensure the implementation of its long-term strategies towards MENA (Bacik, 2011; Sevilla, 2013: 93–107).

CONCLUSIONS

1. Since the beginning of its co-operation with Egypt, the US has stressed the strategic location of Egypt and regional security, founded on the peace treaty with Israel.

---

[3] It is worth noting that in 1985 China was still the greater oil exporter in East Asia, while in 2005 it was the second importer of oil, after the US (Zweig, Janbai, 2005: 25).

[4] In the period 1993-2002 the demand of the Chinese economy for oil increased by 90%, while the production of oil in China went up by only 15% over the same period (Leverett, Bader, 2005: 189).

[5] In 2004 there were around 23 mln vehicles registered in China; it is estimated that their number will rise to 130 mln by 2030; International Energy Agency, *World Energy Outlook*, Paris: IEA, 2004.

[6] *China Country Analysis Brief*, Energy Information Administration, U.S. Department of Energy, August 2006.

2. After the Arab Spring, and in particular following the emergence of Islamic State in the territories of Iraq and Syria, and another IS group in a part of Libya, Egypt has become even more important as a strategic partner in the peace treaty with Israel on the one hand, and as an active ally combating jihadists, aiming to destabilise the region, including US interests and allies, on the other.

3. The resumption of autocratic system in Egypt after the Arab Spring and even greater repressions than at the time of H. Mubarak pose a considerable challenge for the US's policy towards Egypt. United secular and religious opposition forces may undermine the stability of the entire system of power and recreate the situation of the first stage of the Iranian revolution in 1978–1979. This scenario is also feasible in Egypt. The Egyptians demonstrated their ability to organise themselves in 2011. Mass demonstrations may happen again, this time on an even greater scale. Washington should take this direction of events into account. In order to ensure its positive impact on Egypt also after el-Sisi has gone, US diplomacy should emphasise the importance of human rights and gradual liberalisation of the political system in Egypt, as well as seeking co-operation with the opposition.

4. The Russian Federation wants to resume closer co-operation with Egypt, as it was from the 1950s to the early 1970s. Moscow took advantage of the Washington-Cairo crisis, although it was only several months long, lasting from July 2013 to April 2014, and offered its arms supplies to Egypt, as well as collaboration in the field of nuclear energy. The potential of the Russian Federation in the region, however, is not the same as that of the US. In Egypt's policy towards the US, Russia can be used as a bargaining chip and proof that in the case of another crisis with Washington, Cairo can look for other strategic arms suppliers.

5. China finds this region important on account of its growing demand for energy resources. China had a negative experience with the Arab Spring, in particular in Libya. For Chinese policy, the most predictable partners for co-operation are regional autocrats able to ensure multi-faceted collaboration with it. Beijing follows the principle of staying away from the internal affairs of states, particularly those it intends to develop collaboration with.

6. Compared to the Russian Federation, China and the European Union, the US has a range of military and non-military instruments to influence MENA. Although it has been twenty five years since the Cold War ended, the interests of the US have not been undermined in MENA by any of the actors from outside this region. The issue is not so much the competition of different powers to make MENA their zone of influence, but a lack of interest in Washington in seeking solutions capable of solving the numerous serious issues of this region, such as the Middle East conflict, ISIS or the deficit of democracy in this region.

163

BIBLIOGRAPHY

Affaya M. N. (2013), *The 'Arab Spring': Breaking the Chains of Authoritarianism and Postponed Democracy*, in: *The Arab Spring. Critical Analyses*, ed. K. E. D. Haseeb, Routledge.

Akulov A. (2014), *Russia-Egypt Arms Deal: Major Breakthrough as US Middle East Policy Faces Another Set Back*, http://www.strategic-culture.org/news/2014/09/21/russia-egypt--arms-deal-major-breakthrough-as-us-middle-east-policy-faces-another-set-back.html, 05.02.2015.

Aziz S. (2013), *Sinai's Role in Morsi's Ouster*, http://carnegieendowment.org/sada/2013/08/20/sinai-s-role-in-morsi-s-ouster/gjd, 05.02.2015.

Bacik G. (2011), *The Arab Spring versus China*, http://www.todayszaman.com/columnist-264098-the-arab-spring-versus-china.html, 05.02.2015.

Bania R. (2014), *"Arabska Wiosna" – doświadczenia arabskich monarchii subregionu Zatoki Perskiej*, "Przegląd Politologiczny", No. 1.

Beliakov V. (2013), *The Road that Took a Quarter of a Century: On the History of Soviet-Egyptian Relations*, "International Affairs: A Russian Journal Of World Politics, Diplomacy & International Relations", Vol. 59, No. 5.

Bradley M. (2012), *Egypt Hopes for Loan as IMF Revives Talks*, "The Wall Street Journal", 23.08.2012.

Dunne M. (2014), *U.S. Policy Struggles with an Egypt in Turmoil*, http://carnegieendowment.org/2014/05/22/us-policy-struggles-with-egypt-in-turmoil/hov2, 05.02.2015.

Fiedler R. (2010), *Od przywództwa do hegemonii. Polityka Stanów Zjednoczonych wobec bliskowschodniego obszaru niestabilności 1991–2009*, Poznań.

Gerbaudo P. (2013), *The roots of the coup*, "Soundings", Vol. 54.

Gordon M. R., Kirkpatrick D. (2014), *Kerry Scours Mideast for Aid in ISIS Fight*, http://www.nytimes.com/2014/09/14/world/middleeast/kerry-visits-egypt-seeking-aid-in-isis-fight.html?_r=0, 05.02.2015.

Hanna M. H. (2013), *Clouded U.S. policy on Egypt*, http://mideast.foreignpolicy.com, 05.02.2015.

Heydemann S. (2007), *Upgrading Authoritarianism In the Arab World*, The Saban Center for Middle East Policy at the Brookings Institution, "Analysis Paper", No. 13.

Heydemann S. (2014), *America's Response to the Arab Uprisings: US Foreign Assistance in an Era of Ambivalence*, "Mediterranean Politics", Vol. 19, No. 3.

Huber D. (2015), *A Pragmatic Actor – The US Response to the Arab Uprisings*, "Journal of European Integration", Vol. 37, No. 1.

Katulis B., Sofer K., Juul P. (2013), *Preparing U.S. Policy for the Next Phase of Egypt's Transition*, Center for American Progress, http://www.americanprogress.org, 05.02.2015.

Laz E. (2014), *Sustainable Democracy and the Paradox of the Arab Spring: The Egypt Experience*, "Alternatives: Turkish Journal of International Relations", Vol. 13, No. 1/2.

Leverett F., Bader J. (2005), *Managing China-U.S. Energy Competition in the Middle East*, "The Washington Quarterly", No. 29/1, Winter 2005/2006, 05.02.2015.

Magen Z. (2013), *Russia and the Middle East: Policy Challenges*, "Memorandum", No. 127.

Marshall R. (2013), *The Coup That Wasn't: When Policy Overrides the Facts*, "Washington Report On Middle East Affairs", Vol. 32, No. 7.

Muravchik J. (2001), *Freedom and the Arab World*, "The Weekly Standard", 31.12.2001.

Piazza J. A. (2008), *Do Democracy and Free Markets Protect US From Terrorism?*, "International Politics", Vol. 45.

Rękawek K. (2014), *The Muslim Brotherhood in Egypt: No Time for Obituaries*, "Policy Papers", No. 1/15(98), http://www.pism.pl/files/?id_plik=17936, 05.02.2015.

Ross A. G. (2010), *Why They Don't Hate Us: Emotion, Agency and the Politics of Anti-Americanism*, "Millennium", Vol. 39, No. 1.

Sevilla H. (2013), *The Arab Spring and South China Sea Tensions: Analyzing China's Drive to Energy Security*, "Alternatives: Turkish Journal Of International Relations", Vol. 12, No. 3.

Sharp J. M. (2014), *Egypt: Background and U.S. Relations*, Congressional Research Service, http://fas.org/sgp/crs/mideast/RL33003.pdf, 05.02.2015.

Sowa A. (2014), *Aid to Egypt by the Numbers*, http://www.cgdev.org/blog/aid-egypt-numbers, 05.02.2015.

Sun Y. (2012), *Syria: What China Has Learned From its Libya Experience*, "Asia Pacific Bulletin", No. 152, http://www.eastwestcenter.org/sites/default/files/private/apb152_1.pdf, 05.02.2015.

Vidino L. (2013), *The Muslim Brotherhood after the Arab Spring: Tactics, Challenges and Future Scenarios*, Center for European Studies, http://martenscentre.eu/sites/default/files/publication-files/muslim_brotherhood_web.pdf, 05.02.2015.

Yossef A. (2013), *Israel and the Tahrir Revolution*, in: *Egypt's Tahrir Revolution*, ed. D. Tschirgi, W. Kaziha, S. F. Mcmahon, London.

Zweig D., Janbai B. (2005), *China's Global Hunt for Energy*, "Foreign Affairs", Vol. 84, No. 5, September/October.

Marek REWIZORSKI
Pomeranian University, Słupsk

THE ARAB AWAKENING AND GLOBAL GOVERNANCE: INTERNATIONAL INSTITUTIONS IN THE FACE OF TRANSFORMATION IN THE MIDDLE EAST AND NORTH AFRICA

INTRODUCTION

The tragic self-immolation of Mohamed Bouazizi, a young fruit vendor, in December 2010 led to a series of unprecedented demonstrations in Tunisia which soon spread to other Middle East and North Africa (MENA) countries. A mounting wave of unrest engulfed Algeria, Jordan, Egypt, and Yemen. The Arab streets, full of desperate individuals who fell under the same very difficult conditions, shared M. Bouazizi's experience of unemployment, but also found an opportunity to express their frustration and dissatisfaction with a corrupt system that was seen as a "law enforcement facility" against the poorest and for the increasingly flagrant theft of land and resources by the elite (UN, 2007; UN, 2008). According to Jane Kinnimont, who commented on the eruption of mass protests following the death of Khaled Said, a young man who was dragged from an internet café by the police and beaten to death in the street, in June 2010 in Alexandria: "Their demands for both political and economic rights echo in the widely chanted protest slogan, 'Bread and dignity'. Another recurring word in protest slogans across the region has been 'justice', encompassing concerns about corruption and wealth distribution as well as human rights and the rule of law" (Kinnimont, 2011: 33).

Indeed, the outbreak of the Arab Spring has been linked with the critical socio-economic development in the authoritarian states of the Middle East, undertaking economic liberalisation without political reforms. In this context, demographic changes have become the issue of primary concern. From 1970 to 2010, the population in the Arab world nearly tripled, going from 128 mln to 359 mln inhabitants (Hegasy, 2011: 41). An estimated 41% of these people live below the poverty line (UNDP 2009: 22), and nearly 30% of the population is between the ages of 20 and 35 (Perthes, 2011: 30). M. Bouazizi's suicide, which sparked the Arab uprising, has revealed a huge and still expanding informal sector, where workers lack contracts and benefits. UNDP figures showed, that Algeria, Egypt, Morocco and Tunisia have very large informal sectors comprising between 40 and 50% of non-agricultural employment (UN, 2007; UN, 2008).

Among the most important factors which have pushed protesters to despair there were: the "ruling bargains" that underlined authoritarian systems, state trade policies, statism, development of a "semiformal" sector in Middle Eastern economies (Kamrava, 2004: 96–112), and broad access to digital media (Howard, Hussain, 2011).

The first of the features – authoritarian ruling bargains – kept Arab economies out of greater integration into the global economy, because the state provided for the needs of politically relevant social classes, in return for their acceptance of a lack of political accountability and representation. This state of play in the internal policy brought about an eruption of statism and economic nationalism which undermined the economic and political opportunities countries can gain from globalisation.

Referring to the second and third of the features – state trade policies and statism – according to the influential "The Economist", on the eve of the Arab Spring in Egypt, where over 40% of the economy is in state hands: "private firms were strangled with red tape. Subsidies for food and fuel, worth some 10% of GDP, were busting the budget. The result was that Egypt faced a fiscal crunch as well as an urgent need to overhaul its economic model" (*Economic reform*, 2011). In Egypt, the transitional government has expanded subsidies and increased employment in state firms. Economic liberalisation had a poor reputation thanks to earlier reforms, the fruits of which flowed largely to the well-connected. Subsidies and increased employment in state firms were intertwined with a high degree of both tariff and non-tariff barriers protecting Arab markets against foreign products. According to Bernard Hoekman and Patrick Messlin, amongst hurdles to intra-economic cooperation and development of strong Arab corporations, we can include, "business licensing, public sector monopolies, exclusive agency rights, requirements to employ nationals, weak systems of contract enforcement, prohibitions on foreign ownership of real estate, limitations on majority equity to foreigners, corruption and red tape..." (Hoekmann, Messerlin, 2002: 13). Moreover, significant state-ownership in MENA is spurring inefficient and protected industries that further limit the successful adoption of an export strategy.

The fourth important impediment to economic development in MENA which contributed to the outbreak of Arab Spring is the so called "semiformality and parallel economy." Mehran Kamrava conceptualised these phenomena as the "economic activity of a considerable portion of the economically active population who neither fall inside nor outside of the regulatory purview of state" (Kamrava, 2004: 107–108). Putting it simply, "semiformality" means that economic activities in the sector straddle institutional formality and informality. As a good example, one can consider the typical entrepreneurs in the Arab world (i.e. shopkeepers, merchants) who are formally conducting business in accordance with the law (having the necessary licences or permits), but at the same time violating it by not abiding by the law (i.e. not paying taxes or disregarding public obligations). Another example is that since the 1980s there has been a growing number of entrepreneurs, mostly from Egypt or Morocco, expanding their activities abroad. Migrant labourers from these countries started using informal money changers to send home their remittances, in preference to banks. The problem of semiformality is exemplified by a situation that occurred in the 1980s, when a number of Egyptian investment companies operating abroad labelled themselves as "Islamic". They became the main venues among Egyptians working abroad and sending home their remittances. Soon, unofficial Islamic financial institutions became major sources of Egypt's foreign exchange – along with tourism and Suez Canal fees. That informal activity was harmful to Egypt's potential revenues. The destructive effect of semiformality on Arab economies and societies is indirect, yet long-standing and counterproductive. To the question of who loses in this business, the answer is the state. "Informal entrepreneurs" are circumventing the bureaucracy and conducting their business faster and more effectively in terms of profit, but at the same time labourers are bereft of basic social rights, which leads to multiplying serious social problems such as malnutrition, health insecurity, violence and poverty. In a situation where the government is only a kind of plumber, trying to stop leakage of resources, it is difficult to expect development of social policy, which could possibly work as a tranquiliser to the bustling Arab streets.

Last but not least, the outbreak of the Arab Spring was attributed to the broad access to social media such as Facebook, Twitter, YouTube, Skype and text messages. Martin Beck and Simone Hüser underlined that "virtual communication gave people an instrument that made it possible for them to share their resentment with like-minded people and to organize movements against authoritarian rulers" (Beck, Hüser, 2012: 7). They noticed that the Internet was a gateway, allowing the public to track the corrupt rulers' luxurious standards of living at the cost of 'average citizens', and the related inequalities, which seemed enormous when compared to Western freedoms and prosperity. After M. Bouazizi's self-immolation, social media became a channel for expressing solidarity and dissatisfaction with the political situation in Arab countries. Messages and posts allowed for the rapid mobilisation of protesters. Pictures taken by protesters using cameras and mobile phones were circulated online, and encouraged not only others to join the ranks of activists, but also to circumvent government firewalls (Howard, Hussain, 2011: 37, 44).

The Arab Spring certainly disrupted the high degree of homogeneity among stable authoritarian regimes in the Middle East, however there remains a question of whether it was a revolution or rather an uprising, a successful awakening of the oppressed towards democracy, giving opportunities to introduce economic and political reforms, or just another violent rebellion which did not change much, but temporarily lightened the political and economic burdens imposed by authoritarian regimes. This article will serve as a voice in this debate. The second, and even more important, objective is to depict and analyse the reaction of the International Monetary Fund (IMF) as an institution of global governance on the Arab Spring, as at the dawn of the 21st century, eruptions of social discontent are forcing states to reassess their place in reality, which appears to be increasingly unclear. The state-centric model of finding solutions to various problems seems inadequate, so states are looking toward the idea of governance. This is linked more with controlling rather than governing, and so with a wide range of processes used to coordinate decision-making and implement certain policies. It is noteworthy that governance consists of the adaptation of individual and collective methods of solving common issues, so as to find solutions to continually emerging conflicts, mitigate differences in interests and, as a consequence, to broaden the field of possible cooperation between heterogeneous entities. Various informal and official institutions play a key role here. Their intentions may become a catalyst of group activity (Commission, 1995: 2). Institutions, James Rosenau argues, are important for developing global governance, which "includes systems of rule at all levels of human activity – from the family to the international organization – in which the pursuit of goals through the exercise of control has transnational repercussions... Governance... encompasses the activities of governments, but it also includes the many other channels through which 'commands' flow in the form of goals framed, directives issued and polices pursued" (Rosenau, 1995: 13–14). Noting that the "international system" is decreasingly dependent on the states' will, thus becoming a network structure created by "states, non-state participants, relations and the links between them, binding the rules of international law as well as international regimes, alliances and institutions" (Łoś-Nowak, 2011: 28–29) it is therefore justified to analyse how international institutions reacted to the Arab Spring and what they did to help resolve it and transform it into progress in the MENA region. IMF policy will serve as example.

WHY (NOT) REVOLUTION AND WHY GLOBAL GOVERNANCE

The series of social unrests which shook the Arab world were labelled "revolutions". But it remains unclear if they fall into that category, especially as those protests are also referred to as 'revolts', 'uprisings', and the like. Often the word 'revolution' is replaced by 'transformation', which indicates the values of democratic leadership, legitimisation and governance (steering) rather, than ruling. Even among Arabic scholars, this remains a highly arguable issue. Al-Sayyid Yasîn, for example, pointing at "revolutionary hardware", stresses that because of the lack of political leadership, the Arab Awakening or Spring resembles more an upheaval than a revolution. He notes that one can speak of revolution once upheaval is taken charge of by a popular revolutionary leadership and is given a democratic direction (Yasîn, 2011: 291–293). Others, such as Asef Bayat

(Bayat, 2011), and John Keane (Keane, 2011), labelled the Arab unrests as "refo-lutions" – halfway between revolutions *per se* and reform measures.

Inconsistencies in this matter shall be thought over as the final months of 2014 mark two of the most transformational events in contemporary times – the 25th anniversary of the fall of the Berlin Wall, and the fourth year since the outburst of the Arab Spring. The first 'semi-revolution' was a successful demonstration of mass support for democratic and peaceful changes, in large part due to the presence of world class leaders like Lech Wałęsa in Poland, Václav Havel in Czechoslovakia, Árpád Gonz in Hungary, and Kurt Masur in East Germany. However, the broad consensus forged between the political elites in these countries was not repeated in the MENA region. The Arab Spring, after four years, in most instances devolved into scenes of violence, corruption, failure of central governments, many fatalities, widespread destruction and the calamity of millions of refugees fleeing violence (Blinken, 2014).

In a classic insight into theory of revolution, two American scholars – Raymond Tanter and Manus Midlarsky (Tanter, Midlarsky, 1968) – draw a perspective on the nature of this phenomenon. Their point of departure was the Hegelian revolutionary idea embedded in irresistible change – a manifestation of the world spirit in an unceasing quest for its own fulfilment, through a Marxist account focused on revolution as a product of irresistible historical forces, which culminate in a struggle between bourgeois and proletariat. They spotted also Hannah Arendt's interpretation of the revolution as a "kind of restoration" (Arendt, 1965: 34–40) where the insurgent is considered as an attempt to restore liberties and privileges once lost as a result of the government's lapse into despotism. Above all, R. Tanter and M. Midlarsky focused on the classification of revolution introduced to the literature by Samuel Huntington (Huntington, 1962). He grouped insurgents as: the internal war, the revolutionary coup, the reform coup, and the palace revolution (Huntington, 1962: 23–24). "The internal war" was substituted by R. Tanter and M. Midlarsky with the term "mass revolution" as long in duration, high in mass participation and high in domestic violence "fundamental change in the structure of political authority and the social system" (Tanter, Midarsky, 1968: 265). Indeed, the mass, long-lasting unrest started in Tunisia, where protests, ignited in December 2010, led to the overthrow of the president after being in power for 23 years. The region came further into focus as another North African country – Egypt – saw similar protests begin, leading to the overthrow of President Hosni Mubarak, who had ruled for 29 years. The protests spread to Algeria, Bahrain and the Yemen Republic. Libya also became the scene of prolonged bursts of mass dissatisfaction. Libyan leader Muammar Gaddafi was overthrown after months of extremely violent internal conflict and international military intervention, and was killed on October 20, 2011. Film of his execution recorded on a mobile phone was placed online providing a pure example of the cruelty of conflict. In Yemen, President Ali Abdullah Saleh resigned, and his successor Abdal-Rabah Mansour Al-Hadi formally replaced him in February 2012. Protests continue for self-determination in the southern part of the country and for equality for the majority of the Yemeni population. The fragmentation that took place in the MENA region was particularly visible in Syria and Egypt. In Syria, demonstrations demanding the ousting of President Bashar Al-Assad began in March 2011 and rapidly developed into a nationwide uprising and an ongoing, violent civil war between B. Assad loyalist and opposition forces. Egypt has witnessed the overthrow of two presidents since the start of the Arab Spring. H. Mubarak was forced to resign in February 2011, after 29 years in power and facing accusations of killing 846 people during the uprising. After parliamentary elections in 2011–2012 which led to victory of the Islamist Muslim Brotherhood's Freedom and Justice Party and the Salafist al-Nour party, the Brotherhood's candidate Mohammed Morsi was elected president in June 2012. Not only did he revoke the bill limiting his powers, but also decided to dissolve the House of Representatives (Egyptian Parliament) and changed the military leadership. In June 2013, M. Morsi was deposed in another surge of public protest by millions of Egyptians raging against the far-reaching presidential powers and the possibility of drafting an Islamist-leaning constitution. Civil disobedience led to a military crackdown on the Muslim Brotherhood. In the most dramatic moment, security forces killed almost 1,000 people at two pro-Morsi sit-ins in Cairo. A few months later, in December 2013, the Egyptian assembly drafted a new constitution, however this did not mean a shift towards democracy and stable leadership. Egypt once again was divided between an interim government protected by the Army and the Muslim Brotherhood. Looking at this course of events it could be claimed that Egypt has returned to the kind of police state which 'the revolution' aimed to remove.

The tattered results of the Arab Awakening, in 2014, four years after it started, were critically commented on by a number of scholars and journalists, underlining that the Arab Spring evolved into an Arab or Islamic Winter (Spencer 2012, Yoni Kempinski, Ari Yashar 2014, Spencer 2014), namely, total chaos brought about by the tumultuous and bloody events invading the Arab world over the years. One year after the tumultuous 2012, Richard Spencer, columnist of "The Telegraph", gave a gloomy view of the Arab Winter, showing the pictures from Syria (where more than 40,000 people died in the first half of 2012 in the uprising against the rule of President B. al-Assad), Egypt (riven with constant turmoil, and mass protests on the streets), and the politically unstable Libya (especially after the killing on 11 September, 2011, of the US ambassador, Chris Stevens, who died in the consulate in Benghazi) plunged into a rivalry between militias and government (Spencer, 2012). An even more dire account of the 'Arab Winter' was given two years later by Mordechai Kedar from Bar Ilan University and Eval Zisser from Tel Aviv University. M. Kedar, stressing the further deterioration of states like Syria, Iraq, Libya and Yemen, noted that on the ruins of these countries there are enclaves of Islamic states. He referred to Islamic State (aka ISIS) which seized power and declared statehood in parts of Iraq and Syria, as well as the Al Qaeda-linked Boko Haram terror group that similarly declared statehood in Nigeria (Kempinski, Yashar, 2014). E. Zisser went even further, expressing the view that the Arab Spring first turned out to be an Islamic Winter, which later transformed into pure chaos and anarchy. Both scholars accused the West of hypocrisy towards the developing bloodshed in the Middle East – silence over the 200,000 Syrians that have been killed, but reacting strongly when "three or four western journalists and aid workers are beheaded and all of a sudden the world starts to act" (Kempinski, Yashar, 2014).

Turning to the above-mentioned 'revolution', one could say that the Arab Spring was not in fact one, resembling rather an unsuccessful transformation towards democratic standards of governance, more sustainable development and adjusting to the demands of globalisation. Uprisings in those MENA countries were long-lasting and high in mass participation but did not bring about "fundamental changes in the structure of political authority and the social system." From Saudi Arabia to Jordan, the ruling elites have managed, through adjustments to their ruling strategies, to stay in power and face down the protestors. Fearing a loss of power, in some of the Arab oil empires governments decided to buy time and 'disarm' public anxiety. For example, the King of Saudi Arabia in February 2011, decided to allocate EUR 25.6 bln for society. The approach of King Abdullah was also marked by offering employees the equivalent of two-month's remuneration, an allowance equivalent to EUR 375.00 for all unemployed persons, increasing the domestic minimum wage to EUR 560.00, allocating funds for constructing 500,000 flats, granting the health sector about EUR 3 bln and in addition setting up a committee to fight corruption and giving a guarantee of funds for the recruitment of 60,000 police officers (Hanieh, 2011: 29). Similar action was taken in Jordan, where King Abdullah II announced increased wages for employees in the public sector, military staff, and the creation of 21,000 places of employment in the public sector, including 6,000 police. What is more, the government announced to introduce subsidies on fuel, food products and an increasing amount of funds designed to reduce differences between the regions of the country (Hanieh, 2011). These examples indicate that countries such as Saudi Arabia or Jordan are regimes which succeeded in keeping their authoritarian rule stable without implementing substantial liberalising measures. Despite echoes of the Arab Awakening, taking the form of street demonstrations, the revenues from the oil sector allowed these monarchies to maintain a policy of 'sticks and carrots', offering concessions which helped to depoliticise strategic sectors of society, and at the same time, income which was used to finance an all-encompassing security and intelligence directorate (Lacroix, 2011: 53).

In other countries such as Syria, Libya, and Yemen, the outcomes of the Arab Spring suggested a violent contest between those mobilising for change and the remnants of the regime. After initial success in maintaining the authoritarian

173

system in the past, President B. al-Assad was faced with the mobilisation of opposition. A bloody civil war led to a standoff between the supporters of stable authoritarian rule and progressive political transformation in Syria (Beck, Hüser, 2011).

Finally, there are countries that began transition after overthrowing a regime, like Egypt and Tunisia. In Egypt, severe internal divisions make it more wishful thinking than a real opportunity. Since the fall of 2011, the country has been shaken by massive riots. The whole country is politically and economically unstable. The massive problem blocking democratic transformation is strength of the Islamic groups, the rising popularity of the Salafists and the strength of the Muslim Brotherhood. Tunisia, where mass protests forced the ousting of Tunisian President Zine el-Abidine Ben Ali, continues to struggle with overlapping economic, security, and political challenges. Despite a new constitution being passed by Tunisian Assembly in January 2014, dropping references to Islamic law, guaranteeing freedom of worship (although Islam is the state religion) (BBC, 2014), Tunisia is facing serious problems. Its budget is hanging on the IMF credit line, agreed in June 2013 (EUR 1.74 bln). However, the loan is contingent on Tunisia making economic reforms (such as cuts in food subsidies and raising certain taxes), which according to the Fund have not yet been done satisfactorily. As a result, Tunisia is experiencing a delay in disbursements of the loan (Joyce, Smadhi, 2014). Tunisia, without proper international aid, is unable to cope with the high unemployment which gravely affects young people, reaching 35% (compared to 16% of the whole population). What is more, the interior regions of Tunisia are deprived of public and foreign investment. Lack of opportunities, and following neoliberal policies without the necessary reforms creates the vicious circle of events which in 2010 led to the outburst of mass protests. Also, the political situation is being destabilised due to the activities of terrorist groups such as Ansar al-Sharia (AST), a group with allegedly ideological ties to Al-Qaeda, which has been blamed by the State Department for the September 2012 riot at the US embassy where vandals burned embassy property and that of a nearby school (Aljazeera, 2014). After the assassination in July 2013 of Mohamed Brahmi, a Tunisian politician, founder and former leader of the People's Movement, the government came under pressure to further act against the group, declaring it illegal.

As one can observe, not only did the Arab Spring not lead to fundamental changes in the structure of political authority and the social system, but it also was devoid of strong political leadership. The problem of "leaderless movements" has been vividly depicted in the book *The Arab Uprising: The Unfinished Revolutions of the New Middle East*, written by analyst Marc Lynch. He argued that the "leaderless movements" of the Arab uprisings – fuelled by news outlets (Aljazeera) and social media (Facebook, Twitter, Skype) – substantially contributed to the ousting of dictators in the Arab world. What is more, they prevented the manipulation of the uprisings and allowed for a "people's revolution"

(Lynch, 2013). However, recent trends in Egypt are demonstrating that leaderless movements can only go so far. In the face of an absence of leadership during and after an uprising, citizens are only able to organise themselves under a common objective – the overthrow of their respective regimes – but permanent seizing of power allowing for democratic reforms is unlikely.

For these reasons, the social unrest in the Arab world should be deemed 'protests', 'uprisings', even 'riots' and 'rebellions' but not 'revolutions'. More and more accounts suggest that the Arab Spring has evolved into an Arab Winter. The surge of mass dissatisfaction was in fact an 'awakening' which burned itself out without significant positive results. The Arab Spring resulted in increased political pluralism and nascent democratic institutions, but at the same time led to instability, mass protests, clashes among former 'revolutionary' allies as well as the rise of political Islam. The early outcomes of the Arab Awakening and its political costs were presented in a study prepared by the Geopolicity think tank. The report says that only in 2011, the Arab Spring's cost to regional GDP was USD 20.56 bln. Data from the IMF shows severe losses to GDP in Egypt, Libya, Tunisia, Syria, Yemen and Bahrain, and even deeper costs for public finance in these countries (USD 35.28 bln)[1] (Table 1).

Table 1. Costs of the Arab Awakening in MENA countries

Country	Costs to GDP (in USD, bln)	Costs to Public Finances (in USD, bln)
Libya	7.67	6.49
Syria	6.07	21.22
Egypt	4.27	5.52
Tunisia	2.03	0.49
Bahrain	0.39	0.69
Yemen	0.12	0.86
Total	20.56	35.28

Source: Geopolicity (2011), *Re-thinking the Arab Spring & Road Map for G20/UN Support, Supporting Political, Security and Socio-economic Transition Across the Arab Realm*, October.

What is more, the Arab Spring negatively affected social security. In such countries as Libya, Egypt, or Syria, public revenues have fallen by as much as

---

[1] It shall be noted that decreases in GDP did not occur in the whole MENA region. The biggest oil exporters, such as the UAE, Saudi Arabia, Qatar and Kuwait, saw the increases in GDP over 2011. They forestalled internal protests and managed to direct their economies to path of growth.

95%, damaging even basic services. At the same time, the large public handouts seen in wealthy oil producers such as the UAE or Saudi Arabia widened economic rifts in the region (Geopolicity, 2011). The long-term challenges for the region remained, and in the wake of the sharp economic slowdown, have become more pressing than ever. Amongst the most important challenges were rising unemployment, inefficient subsidy regimens and low trade diversification. After the fall of revolutionary zeal on the streets, the economics again have become the very core of deliberation, shaping the political situation in MENA countries. In 2012, GDP in the region reached low levels alongside FDI flows and incomes generated by tourism (Figure 1).

Figure 1. Economic impact of the Arab Spring on MENA countries (2010–2012)

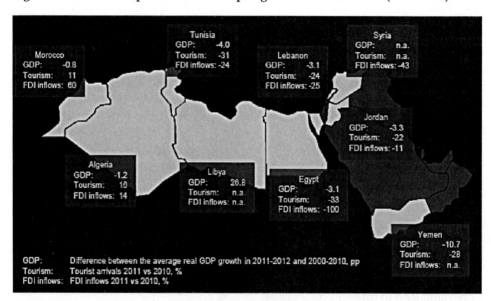

Source: UNCTAD, IMF, National Authorities.

According to the World Bank, the economic situation in the MENA region is still far below pre-uprising levels and it is difficult to presume that this will change in a short term. The political transitions which continue to unfold, with a number of elections being held in 2014, are delaying measures to address persistent structural challenges. The situation is becoming tense, especially in Egypt, where the political transformation roadmap is proceeding at the expense of a more inclusive democratic process. Uncertainties remain also in Lebanon, where after a year of political vacuum a new government was appointed. With the 2014 elections in Iraq and Algeria and scheduled voting in Yemen (2015), the whole region seems to be on fire. This political tumbling negatively affects the economy throughout the region (Tab. 2).

176

Table 2. Middle East and North Africa economic indicators (2010–2015)

	2010	2011	2012	2013	2014	2015
GDP at market prices, developing countries[1]	4.7	–0.8	0.6	–0.1	1.9[f]	3.6[f]
GDP per capita (units in US$)	3.0	0.2	–3.3	–1.4	0.6	1.2
PPP GDP[2]	4.5	1.7	–1.3	0.4	2.2	2.7
Private consumption	3.5	2.1	1.2	0.8	2.2	3.3
Public consumption	1.4	3.1	3.3	2.9	3.7	3.8
Fixed investment	4.4	–1.8	–0.9	1.5	0.7	2.1
Net exports, contribution to growth	0.8	–1.6	–3.0	–1.2	–0.1	–0.4
Current account bal/GDP (%)	1.6	2.7	–0.7	–3.4	–3.3	–3.6
Fiscal balance/GDP (%)	–1.9	–1.7	–7.4	–7.3	–6.6	–6.1

(1) GDP at market prices and expenditure components are measured in constant 2010 U.S. dollars. Geographical region (MENA) includes also high-income countries: Bahrain, Kuwait, Oman, Qatar, Saudi Arabia, and United Arab Emirates;
(2) GDP measured at PPP exchange rates;
(f) forecast.
Source: World Bank (2014), *Middle East and North Africa, Global Economic Prospects*, Chapter 2, June 2014.

According to the estimates of the World Bank report, the forecasted GDP in high-income MENA countries (Bahrain, Kuwait, Oman, Qatar, Saudi Arabia, United Arab Emirates) in 2014 (4.1%) is significantly higher than the average for poorer countries such as Tunisia, Egypt or Yemen, which is 2.7%. It is worth noting that in 2010, just before the Arab Spring started, this ratio was different. High-income MENA countries in 2010 accounted for 4.4% (the same as Egypt), while poorer ones achieved 4.5% (World Bank, 2014: 65). The main problems which undermine transformation in MENA are those of economic nature. Finding a solution might lead to further political stabilisation and disarming of the revolutionary mood in Arab societies. MENA countries will have to face large fiscal costs, rising public debt, uncertainty on stock markets, unemployment, weak fiscal balances, growing and inefficient subsidies, declining private capital flows and declining foreign currency earnings from remittances (Masetti, Körner et al., 2013).

The lack of efficiency of MENA states in coping with the results of the Arab Awakening indicates a need for employing multilateralism in the successful transition towards more democratic regimes. Multilateralism refers to collective, cooperative action by states (Keohane, 1990: 731) in concert with non-state actors to deal with those common problems and challenges which are best managed collaboratively at the international level. International institutions and significant states may help to achieve and maintain stability in such areas as peace and security, economic development and trade, human rights, functional and technical cooperation amongst Arab states. They operate in an environment influenced by processes of global governance, characterised by the evolution of non-state actors and international institutions able to facilitate global responses to the most pressing problems. Some 30 years ago, its role was underlined by Robert Keohane in his work *After Hegemony* (1984). His assumption was that individually rational action by states could impede mutually beneficial cooperation. Institutions could provide help for states to find a cooperative solution, reduce transaction costs and provide a greater degree of transparency, rendering cooperative rules effective (Simmons, Martin, 2001: 195–196). Noting this, one should ask the question how international institutions such as the IMF reacted to the Arab Awakening, what have they done to resolve it and transform it into progress in the MENA region.

INTERNATIONAL MONETARY FUND AND THE ARAB AWAKENING

Since the Arab uprisings, IMF has focused mostly on the social dimensions of its macroeconomic policy advice. Its activities concerned three issues: inclusive growth, health and education spending and income inequality and redistribution (Tab. 3). It is worth noting that the first IMF goal – inclusive growth – was not included in the Fund's MENA policy before the Arab uprisings. However, after it began, the Fund put emphasis on "equity, equality of opportunity, and protection in market and employment transitions" (Anand, Mishra, Peiris, 2013). Before the Arab uprisings, the Fund, instead of inclusiveness, preferred to separate economic growth and socio-economic inclusion, viewing them as two variables. However, after 2011, the IMF observed that the political transitions have created not only new opportunities for economic transformation but also the necessity to accelerate economic reform. The IMF therefore decided to focus on "strong economic management, and policies to bolster the business environment, which are needed to avoid a vicious circle and create in its place a virtuous one, where the right policies revive economic confidence and generate inclusive economic growth" (Finger, Gressani et al., 2014: 3). In other words, the IMF noticed that better economic conditions can help reduce discontent and thereby smooth political transitions. That was the reason why economic growth and inclusiveness were put together.[2]

Table 3. The IMF policy on the social dimensions of economic policy

Morocco	2006	2007	2008	2009	2010	2011	2012	2013
Inclusive growth	–	–	–	–	NA	X	X	X
Strengthen health care and education	–	–	–	–	NA	X	X	X
Improve redistribution and inequality	–	–	–	–	NA	X	X	X

---

[2] On measuring inclusive growth see: A. Ifzal, H. Hwa Son (2007), *Measuring Inclusive Growth*, "Asian Development Review", Vol. 24, No. 1, pp. 11–31.

Tunisia	2006	2007	2008	2009	2010	2011	2012	2013
Inclusive growth	–	–	–	–	–	NA	X	X
Strengthen health care and education	–	–	–	–	–	NA	–	X
Improve redistribution and inequality	–	–	–	–	X	NA	X	X
Egypt	2006	2007	2008	2009	2010	2011	2012	2013
Inclusive growth	–	–	–	NA	–	NA	NA	X
Strengthen health care and education	–	–	–	NA	–	NA	NA	X
Improve redistribution and inequality	–	–	–	NA	X	NA	NA	X

Note:
X explicit recommendation given by the IMF to improve stated policy objective;
– lack of explicit recommendation given by the IMF to improve stated policy objective;
NA no comparable data available.
Source: (IMF 2013a; IMF 2013b).

As can be seen from Table 3, since 2011, the IMF has promoted inclusiveness as a key requirement of growth in Egypt, Morocco and Tunisia. After the outbreak of the Arab uprisings, the IMF has been suggesting that failure to achieve inclusive growth would have detrimental effects on macroeconomic growth. Recognition of inclusive growth and social cohesion led the Fund to recommend important economic reforms to reduce high structural unemployment, deliver a more equitable distribution of income, enhance business and investment conditions, increase trade openness, improve stability and access to the financial system and improve social safety nets. For example, to tackle fiscal challenges, the IMF advised to undertake the following reforms (Finger, Gressani et al., 2014: 27–28):
– simplifying tax systems;
– enhancing tax compliance (facilitating business operations, reducing unequal tax treatment across companies, building a large, efficient tax payers' department fighting tax evasion);
– strengthening the capacity of revenue administration (by the retention of high-quality staff, who are necessary to successfully implement reforms in this area);
– advancing customs administration reforms, which would substantially raise yields on import VAT, excise, and international trade taxes.

The IMF considered undertaking economic reforms as a means of ensuring success of its loan programs. To put it in simple words, following the Arab uprising, the IMF is advising MENA governments to lay the ground for a comprehensive set of reforms to achieve higher and more inclusive growth, and reduce unemployment in a sustainable way. The Fund encourages them to find a right balance between measures needed to maintain macroeconomic stability and protect the poor during the transition, on the one hand, and those laying the groundwork for faster growth and job creation, on the other (Finger, Gressani et al., 2014: 94). This involves adjusting fiscal deficits and putting fiscal balances under control. To achieve this aim, the IMF has already committed about USD 10 bln in financial arrangements with Jordan, Morocco, Tunisia, and Yemen and engaged in possible financial arrangements with Libya and Egypt aimed at policy dialogue and capacity-building.

The Arab Awakening led to changes in the IMF's attitude towards health and education spending. As Table 3 shows, prior to the Arab uprisings, the Fund made no recommendations to address that issue. After the Arab uprisings, the IMF recommended improving and reorienting the educational system in order to facilitate meeting the needs of the private sector, with primary focus on writing skills, critical thinking, and problem solving. In the 2013 Article IV consultation report concerning Morocco, the IMF focused on promoting high and more inclusive growth recommended "a major reform of education [...] to help rationalize the system and upgrade human resources and skills" (IMF, 2012a: 4). Also, in Tunisia and Egypt the Fund began to promote education and health spending as a factor of inclusive growth, fearing that the negative outcomes of Arab uprisings may undermine progress in the area of education, health and other public utilities and basic services. The case of Tunisia shows that despite intra-regional disparities a success story is possible. By 2010, Tunisia's illiteracy rate had dropped to less than 22%. Around half of the population aged 10 years or more had a secondary or higher education. This, compared to the early 1960s, when the illiteracy rate was more than 65% and more than 90% of the population had little or no education, can be described as a significant achievement (Boughzala, Hamdi, 2014: 4). Also, in access to water, electricity, transport, communication infrastructure and basic health care in all urban areas and in a large extent of rural areas, there has been visible development since the 1960s. Below, Table 4 shows the level of education of the Tunisian labour force between 1966 and 2010.

Table 4. Level of Education of the Tunisian Labour Force 1966–2011 (% of total labour force)

Education Level	1966	1975	1984	1994	2001	2004	2010
Higher	1.2	1.4	3.3	7.0	10.0	7.9	17.0
Secondary	7.1	12.8	20.0	29.0	30.0	32.0	38.0
Primary	26.2	32.6	34.4	40.1	40.2	37.0	34.9
None	68.0	56.1	46.4	37.2	24.3	23.1	10.1
Total	100.0	100.0	100.0	100.0	100.0	100.0	100.0

Source: National Institute of Statistics – Tunisia (INS) and Boughzala, Hamdi (2014), *Promoting inclusive growth in Arab countries. Rural and Regional development and Inequality in Tunisia*, Global Economy & Development Working Paper 71, February 2014, p. 5.

The IMF, emphasising the value of spending on social infrastructure centred on education and health, advised Tunisia to reform its subsidy system toward reallocating fiscal resources to meet social demands. According to Nemat Shafik, Deputy Managing Director in the IMF, an 'Economic Spring' in the MENA region is dependent upon freeing up resources through better targeting subsidies. As she pointed out, energy subsidies consume almost USD 200 bln in the region, while only 20% of that benefits the poor. Redirecting resources by investing in education and infrastructure is essential to create the 50–75 mln jobs needed in the next decade for the fast growing generation of Arab Spring protesters (IMF, 2012b). Indeed, by outlining the necessity of shifting budgetary resources to education, health and infrastructure, the IMF highlighted the problem of subsidies, which remain large and inefficient in the region. According to the estimates of the World Bank, food and fuel subsidies in Tunisia amount to 5% of GDP, more than 9% in Egypt and Yemen, and even 11% in Libya (World Bank, 2014: 63). Historically, subsidies have been motivated as a tool of social protection, but there is growing evidence that they are disproportionally benefiting the well-off segments of the population, while adding to both fiscal and current account pressures (World Bank, 2014: 63). Still, however, reforms in this area are undermined by poor growth and fear of rising prices, which eliminates whole sectors from reform, therefore making it ineffective. As an example, we can consider the gas sector in Egypt. Despite a doubling in prices of gas in 2014 for consumers connected to the gas distribution network, electrical generation facilities and bakeries were granted exemption from the hike, which seriously diminished fiscal savings. Without breaking the vicious circle of subsidy-led policy, redirecting resources to education and health sectors is problematic.

The issue of subsidies leads to the third goal of the IMF – improving redistribution and inequality. As before, this approach was employed by the Fund after the outbreak of the Arab uprisings. Prior to the unrest in the MENA region, the IMF had focused on fiscal consolidation, characterised by cuts in public spending and welfare policies, which resulted in rising unemployment, due to savings made in government involvement in securing socio-economic stability. In the wake of the Arab Awakening, the IMF changed its strategy and advised MENA countries shift from a subsidy-led policy to well-targeted transfers for the poor, made possible by developing so called "social safety nets" (Finger, Gressani et al., 2014: 27–28).[3] By doing so, the MENA followed approximately 80% of developing countries which are either developing or plan to develop or strengthen their social safety nets (World Bank, 2012). Masood Ahmed, Director of the IMF's Middle East and Central Asia Department indicated a link between

---

[3] Social safety nets (SSNs) are defined as noncontributory transfers targeted to the poor or vulnerable. They include income support, temporary employment programs (workfare), and services that build human capital and expand access to finance among the poor and vulnerable. Such programs are usually introduced during transition periods (e.g. in Eastern Europe after the collapse of the former Soviet Union, decentralisation in Indonesia, and regime change in Brazil and Portugal), but they may as well remain in place afterward.

inclusive growth and giving better-targeted help to poorer households, stressing "...it is crucial that governments help poor households, and even more so during difficult periods. To address the fiscal constraint without necessarily reducing other important expenditures (such as on infrastructure), it is important to improve and modernize the existing safety nets to make them both well targeted and enduring. In contrast to generalised subsidies that benefit everyone, well-targeted social safety nets provide assistance only to those most in need of government help. Thus, needy people could receive benefits on a more enduring basis, yet at reduced fiscal costs" (IMF, 2011). In general, social safety nets are programs designed to ease chronic poverty and high vulnerability. The most vulnerable group are children. More than a quarter of children in the bottom income quintile in the Arab Republic of Egypt, Morocco, and the Syrian Arab Republic are chronically malnourished. By the age of 16–18, children in the poorest quintile in Egypt and Morocco are more likely to have dropped out of school than to have continued studying (Silva, Levin, Morg, 2012: X). Well constructed social safety nets along with increased social services can also "help to tackle the problem of spatial pockets of poverty in slums and rural areas by promoting the demand for safety-net services and building community assets" (Silva, Levin, Morg, 2012: X). This seems to be crucial, as about 17% of Egyptians, Iraqis, Syrians, and Yemenis have *per capita* consumption levels that are no more than USD 0.50 per day above the USD 2.00 per day poverty line (in purchasing power parity [PPP] terms) (Silva, Levin, Morg, 2012: X). Social safety nets such as Morocco's Tayssir programme,[4] the Republic of Yemen's Social Welfare Fund or Djibouti's workfare plus nutrition programme may play a very important role in developing human capital, targeting the poor and vulnerable and helping to shelter the poorest from systemic shocks.

CONCLUSION

The Arab Awakening has shaken the authoritarian regimes of MENA countries but the cost of the uprisings has been high. Four years since its beginning, the Arab Spring has devolved into an Arab Winter where the blossoming tree of democratic transition has been replaced by snow-storms of violence, corruption, failure of central governments, widespread destruction and the calamity of millions of refugees. Once again, harsh political reality demonstrated that Arab states are internally entangled in complicated dependencies which renders impossible the introduction of fundamental changes in the structure of po-

---

[4] A cash transfer program conditional on school attendance and targeting areas with high incidences of school dropouts and poverty, http://web.worldbank.org/WBSITE/EXTERNAL/COUNTRIES/MENAEXT/0,,contentMDK:22705763~pagePK:146736~piPK:226340~theSitePK:256299,00.html.

litical authority and the social system from within. The main problems which undermine transformation in MENA are primarily those of economic nature. Among them, the large fiscal costs, rising public debt, uncertainty on stock markets, unemployment, weak fiscal balances, growing and inefficient subsidies, declining private capital flows and declining foreign currency earnings from remittances are the most important ones to solve. However, the lack of efficiency of MENA states in this area calls for using mechanisms of international cooperation, shaped to a large extent by global governance institutions, in particular IOs serving as centres of global regimes such as the UN, WTO, IMF, World Bank or ILO. Such institutions could provide help for states to find a cooperative solution and render the rules of cooperation effective.

The case of the IMF shows that this organisation, focusing on fiscal rebalancing, may play a very important role in the MENA region. Loans and credit lines can boost development and aid the transition toward more innovative and competitive economies. What is more, the Fund, traditionally accused of being a rigid and immensely neoliberal institution, in the wake of the Arab Awakening, transformed its policy towards socio-economic goals. Since 2011, the IMF rightly observed that the political transitions have created not only new opportunities for economic transformation, but also the necessity to accelerate economic reform. Therefore, the Fund shifted from fiscal rebalancing towards inclusive growth built upon two variables: economic growth and socio-economic inclusion. In MENA, the Fund's activities focus on policy advice, capacity building and financing. On policy advice the Fund tends to develop regional inclusive growth through the lens of critical areas: job creation, better-targeted social safety nets, strong governance and business environments, access to finance, and greater trade access and integration. On capacity building, the IMF provides assistance to the region in designing and implementing new policies in areas such as tax collection, improved statistics, public financial management, and banking supervision. Finally, on financing, the IMF has at its disposal lending facilities and tools adapted to the financial needs in the MENA region (such as the Rapid Credit Facility for Yemen).

Despite the efforts and adjustments made by the IMF in the post-uprising environment, the effects of its activities are far from those expected. In part, the Arab countries are to blame. The example of gas subsidy reform in Egypt indicates that even well-tailored reforms may fail if they are treated selectively. However, this is only a part of the picture. Promoting inclusive growth, reducing inequality and increasing spending on education and health care can be optimised if the IMF makes some improvements. First of all, the IMF needs to narrow the scope of its analysis in MENA, identifying specific targets within larger problem areas. Secondly, IMF staff must periodically assess the performance of states in the region (e.g. with focus on country-specific Gini coefficient improvements or customised health care/education benchmarks). Thirdly, the IMF, when targeting socio-economic goals, must recruit more social scientists (mostly political scientists, development economists, public policy experts) who can improve capacity of the Fund in this area, and could be more effective than 'traditional' experts trained in macroeconomics, finance or econometrics. Most of the new analysts should represent the MENA region and previously have been employed in various environments (both public and private sector).

BIBLIOGRAPHY

Anand R., Mishra S., Peiris S. (2013), *Inclusive Growth: Measurement and Determinants*, http://www.imf.org/external/pubs/ft/wp/2013/wp13135.pdf, 16.10.2014.

Arendt H. (1963), *On revolution*, New York.

Bayat A. (2011b), *Paradoxes of Arab Refo-lutions. Jadaliyya*, http://www.jadaliyya.com/pages/index/786/paradoxes-of-arab-refo-lutions, 14.10.2014.

BBC (2014), *Tunisia assembly passes new constitution*, http://www.bbc.com/news/world-africa-25908340, 16.10.2014.

Beck M., Hüser S. (2012), *Political Change in the Middle East: An Attempt to Analyze the "Arab Spring"*, German Institute of Global and Area Studies, "Working Paper", No. 203.

Blinken D. (2014), *Arab Spring or Arab Winter? A Lack of Leadership*, http://www.huffingtonpost.com/donald-blinken/arab-spring-or-arab-winte_b_5654815.html, 14.10.2014.

Boughzala M., Hamdi T. (2014), *Promoting inclusive growth in Arab countries. Rural and Regional development and Inequality in Tunisia*, Global Economy & Development, "Working Paper", No. 71.

Commission on Global Governance (1995), *Our Global Neighbourhood*, New York.

Field M. (1985), *The Merchant, The Big Business Families of Saudi Arabia and the Gulf States*, Overlook Press.

Geopolicity (2011), *Re-thinking the Arab Spring &Road Map for G20/UN Support, Supporting Political, Security and Socio-economic Transition Across the Arab Realm*.

Hanieh A. (2011), *Rewolucja w Egipcie to nie tylko kwestia zmiany*, "Le Monde Diplomatique", No. 4 (62).

Hegasy S. (2011), *"Arabs Got Talent": Populärkultur als Ausdruck gesellschaftlicher Veränderungen*, "Aus Politik und Zeitgeschichte", Vol. 61, No. 39.

Hoekman B., Messerlin P. (2002), *Initial Conditions and Incentives for Arab Economic Integration*, "Policy Research Working Paper", No. 2921.

Howard P. N., Hussain M. M. (2011), *The Role of Digital Media*, "Journal of Democracy", Vol. 22, No. 3.

Huntington S. (1962), *Patterns of Violence in World Politics*, in: *Changing Patterns of Military Politics*, ed. S. Huntington, New York.

Ifzal A., Hwa Son H. (2007), *Measuring Inclusive Growth*, "Asian Development Review", Vol. 24, No. 1.

IMF (2011), *Mideast Needs More Focus on Inclusive Growth*, http://www.imf.org/external/pubs/ft/survey/so/2011/new021611a.htm, 16.10.2014.

IMF (2012a), *Morocco: 2012 Article IV Consultation and First Review Under the Two-Year Precautionary and Liquidity Line — Staff Report; Public Information Notice and Press Release on the*

Executive Board Discussion; and Statement by the Executive Director for Morocco, http://www.imf.org/external/pubs/ft/scr/2013/cr1396.pdf, 18.10.2014.

IMF (2012b), *A Region in Change – Hopes and Challenges By Nemat Shafik*, https://www.imf.org/external/np/speeches/2012/051012.htm, 16.10.2014.

IMF (2013a), *Morocco: Selected Issues*, http://www.imf.org/external/pubs/ft/scr/2013/cr13110.pdf, 14.10.2014.

IMF (2013b), *Arab Countries in Transition: Economic Outlook and Key Challenges*, http://www.imf.org/external/np/pp/eng/2013/041613.pdf, 16.10.2014.

Joyce R., Smadhi A. (2014), *Tunisia's Arab Spring: Three years on*, http://www.aljazeera.com/indepth/features/2014/01/tunisia-arab-spring-three-years-20141146353728616.html, 16.10.2014.

Kamrava M. (2004), *Structural impediments to Economic Globalization in the Middle East*, "Middle East Policy", Vol. XI, No. 4.

Keane J. (2011), *Refolution in the Arab world*, http://www.opendemocracy.net/john-keane/refolution-in-arab-world, 15.10.2014.

Kempinski Y., Yashar A. (2014), *From Arab Spring to Islamic Winter – to Total Chaos*, http://www.israelnationalnews.com/News/News.aspx/185578#.VEFEmRbva8o, 14.10.2014.

Keohane R. O. (1990), *Multilateralism: An Agenda for Research*, "International Journal", Vol. 45.

Kinnimont J. (2011), *Bread and Dignity*, "The World Today", August–September.

Lacroix S. (2011), *Is Saudi Arabia Immune?*, "Journal of Democracy", Vol. 22, No. 4.

Łoś-Nowak T. (2011), *Polityka zagraniczna w przestrzeni teoretycznej*, in: *Polityka zagraniczna. Aktorzy – potencjały – strategie*, ed. T. Łoś-Nowak, Warszawa.

Lynch M. (2013), *The Arab Uprising: The Unfinished Revolutions of the New Middle East*, New York.

Masetti O., Körner K., Forster M., Friedman J. (2013), *Two years after Arab Spring. Where are we know? What's next?*, Frankfurt am Main.

Perthes V. (2011), *Der Aufstand. Die Arabische Revolution und ihre Folgen*, München.

Rosenau J. (1995), *Governance in the Twenty-First Century*, "Global Governance", Vol. 1, No. 1.

Silva J., Levin V., Morg M. (2012), *Inclusion and Resilience. The Way Forward for Social Safety Nets in the Middle East and North Africa*, The World Bank, Washington.

Simmons B. A., Martin L. L. (2001), *International Organizations and Institutions*, in: *Handbook of International Relations*, eds. W. Carlsnes, T. Kisse, B. Simmons, Sage.

Spencer R. (2012), *Middle East Review of 2012: the Arab Winter*, http://www.telegraph.co.uk/news/worldnews/middleeast/9753123/Middle-East-review-of-2012-the-Arab-Winter.html, 14.10.2014.

Spencer R. (2014), *Arab Winter Comes to America: The Truth About the War We're In*, Regnery Publishing.

Tanter R., Midlarsky M. (1967), *A Theory of Revolution*, "Conflict Resolution", Vol. IX, No. 3.

Economic reform in the Middle East could prove harder than in Eastern Europe. The West needs to help it along (2011), "The Economist", 23.06.2011.

UN (2007), *Human Development Report 2006. Beyond scarcity: power, poverty and the global water crisis*, New York.

UN (2008), *Human Development Report 2007/2008. Fighting Climate Change: Human Solidarity in a Divided World*, New York.

UNDP (United Nations Development Programme) (2009), *Development Challenges Outlined in New Arab States Report*, http://204.200.211.31/contents/file/DevChallenges_Report_Vol01_Eng.pdf, 12.10.2014.

World Bank (2012), *Atlas of Social Protection: Indicators of Resilience and Equity (ASPIRE)*, http://www.worldbank.org/spatlas, 16.10.2014.

World Bank (2014), *Middle East and North Africa, Global Economic Prospects*, The World Bank, Washington.

Yasîn, Al-Sayyid (2011). *Thawra 25 yanâyir – bayn al-tahawwul al-dîmûqrâtî wa al-thawra alshâmila* (The January 25 Revolution – Between democratic transition and total revolution), Cairo.

Michał SKORZYCKI

University of Social Sciences, Łódź

THE ARAB SPRING AND THE FUTURE OF THE EUROPEAN UNION'S POLICY OF EXTENDING INFLUENCE IN THE SOUTHERN NEIGHBOURHOOD STATES

Despite the Lisbon reform, the EU remains an organisation concentrated on its economic component; thus, not infrequently it is overlooked as an agent capable of playing an independent role in international relations. In spite of all the shortcomings of the foreign policy of the EU, hampered by the necessity of seeking a compromise between the varied interests of their member states, I find such a judgment too hasty and burdened with the possibility of the incomprehension of the external influence of the EU, the strength of which should not be measured exclusively with the use of categories of the post-Westphalian world order. Jan Zielonka (Zielonka, 2007: 14, 16, 20–21) aptly defined specific methods of exerting influence by the EU on third-party states by applying his original concept of a neo-medieval empire, where centres of power are polycentric in character and where crisscrossing various submissions manifests itself through an overlap of competences of various authorities (defined functionally rather than geographically). Yet, the boundaries are fluid, enabling the external areas to enter into integration dependencies, however close or distant, with the EU. The lower level of centralisation of the said empire and its internal integration diversity (as evidenced by the EU in, for example, selective participation of member states in the Eurozone or the Schengen area) give a whole range of integration possibilities, from full membership to remaining an external entity. The area has been successively expanded since the 1970s for southern neighbourhood countries – the process gained pace after 1995, when the Barcelona Process was launched, obtaining institutional form in the Euro-Mediterranean Partnership (EUROMED).

   J. Zielonka (Zielonka, 2007: 190, 196–197) rightly remarked that the main aim of such a world power is not so much the conquest of external areas, but their stabilisation, guided mainly by political, institutional, economic and aid instruments. Nonetheless, the effect of the said action is an expansion of its influence, and consequently, the realisation of the same aim adopted by the traditional post-Westphalian powers. The EU's southern neighbourhood could unmistakably be termed an object of its influence – an influence to be expanded and intensified according to the interests of the EU itself. The convergence of those interests is not an easy process considering the various degrees of interest of member states in the countries along the southern coast of the Mediterranean. The time of gaining historical momentum, which the Arab Spring undoubtedly was, made it possible to settle the problem by imposing joint concentration on the southern neighbourhood, despite the fact that the critical 2011 presidency was held by Hungary and Poland, who were more interested in the EU's policy for the Eastern areas on account of the location of these two countries. Furthermore, the Arab Spring took place right after the introduction of the Treaty of Lisbon, which institutionally transformed the apparatus enforcing the common foreign policy – potentially increasing its efficiency.[1]

The chances of expanding the EU's influence in its southern neighbourhood are also a result of certain trends which the transformations in the region seemed initially to manifest. What I have in mind, is primarily the democratic direction of the proposed change. Both the unorganised revolutionaries and the majority of organisations opposed to the former regimes protested against them, advocating the democratisation of political and social life, which correlated with the European Neighbourhood Policy (ENP), creating the conditions for its full realisation. The image was marred by the growing popularity of Islamist groups in the revolting societies; however, the fears were appeased by the moderate course of the Tunisian Ennahda Movement – whose leader Rashid al-Ghannushi, well before the first elections, declared a commitment to the basic rights and institutional solutions associated with the European democratic system, embracing the division of powers, free elections, a multi-party system, free press and gender equality (Dudkiewicz, Sasnal, 2011: 2535) – as well as the presence of a reformist branch of the Egyptian Muslim Brotherhood seeking support among the middle class (Wickham, 2011: 93–94).

It also seemed that the new elites, forced to tackle serious economic problems, would seek financial support and trade privileges in Europe, which (thanks to adherence to the EU conditionality principle) would be an extra incentive for reforms reasserting European influences. A swift allocation of greater funds by the EU was, admittedly, not possible, but the organisation cannot be accused of inaction. The southern partners were, as soon as 2011, offered entry into a partnership for democracy and prosperity with the Southern Mediterranean – corresponding with a new concept of measures in the region of the southern neighbourhood termed 3Ms (money, market access, mobility) (*Joint Communication*, 2011; *Remarks* 2011). Soon enough, the first concrete support program emerged: SPRING (Support for Partnership, Reforms and Inclusive

---

[1] Above all, the Treaty of Lisbon has founded the External Action Service, that is, the EU's diplomatic corps, and thus, limited the awkward diarchy in the area of foreign policy of the EU, replacing the position of the High Representative of the Union for Common Foreign and Security Policy with the High Representative of the Union for Foreign Affairs and Security Policy. According to the Treaty, the High Representative has superseded the European Commissioner for External Relations assuming the chairmanship of the meetings of the Foreign Affairs Council detached from the General Affairs Council (Polak, 2009: 33).

Growth) targeted at Tunisia, Egypt, Jordan and Morocco to finance projects (with a budget of EUR 350 mln) which aimed at, among others, changes ranging from the adherence to human rights and fundamental freedoms, democratic forms of governing, expansion of the free press and other media, as well as securing citizens' freedom of expression and assembly (*EU response to the Arab Spring: the SPRING*, 2011). Altogether, Brussels allocated the sum of EUR 4 bln for southern neighbourhood states to be distributed in 2011–2013 (Przybylska-Maszner, 2011: 130).

Moreover, the Arab Spring provided an opportunity to use armed forces to secure EU interests in its southern neighbourhood. The situation created by the upheaval was the factor encouraging the elites and societies of the Arab states to support the armed intervention in one of those states. The Operation, the aim of which was to take this opportunity, admittedly, was not organised by the EU itself, but was put forward by a number of its member states, thus, the course of the operation (jointly conducted by the USA and other NATO partners) showed in practice the model of operation of a neo-medieval empire, which – as it transpired – is able to implement effective armed measures without a centralised military subsystem.

The aim of the text is to analyse if the current developments in the region continue to be favourable for the EU three years after the Arab Spring, and to assess the prospects for their exploitation, as well as to look into selected measures taken by Brussels aimed at taking advantage of the above-mentioned opportunities. I hope that the paper will contribute to answering the question of the Arab Spring's impact on the future of the EU policy of expanding its influence in its southern neighbourhood. The text is an elaboration of an article published in 2014 in "Przegląd Politologiczny" (Political Science Review) (Skorzycki, 2014) presenting an update and a verification of the prognoses included therein.

ATTEMPTS AT DEMOCRATISATION OF POLITICAL RELATIONS IN EGYPT, TUNISIA AND LIBYA

Earlier forms of institutionalised cooperation between the EU and the countries to the South showed that their originators were careful with the issue of democratic transformation and the evolution of civil society, but one should not go so far as to say that the pressure for changes in these spheres was absent in Brussels' actions. It took years of practice to develop the instruments for promoting the European socio-political model, which were successfully tested in the post-Soviet states that joined the EU. The most efficient of the functioning tools is the aforementioned European Neighbourhood Policy – within the framework of which there are projects realised in the areas defined in individually signed Action Plans. The formative communication of the European Commission entitled "European Neighbourhood Policy" reminds the signatories of the Barcelona Declaration about the duty declared therein to "[...] develop the rule of law and democracy [...], respect human rights and guarantee the effective legitimate exercise of such rights and freedoms" (*Communication*, 2004). These ideas are not only iterated in the said plans, but also supported through declarations of action for the partial adaptation of Middle East and North Africa states to European structural standards. In a document signed by Tunisia one could find, among other things, evidence of an exchange of experiences between Tunisian and European MPs, the foundation of a subcommittee (in accordance with one of the provisions of Article 5 of the Association Agreement) with a view to fostering dialogue on democracy and the rule of law, granting support to political parties so as to further strengthen their involvement in the democratic process, as well as supporting the efforts of the Tunisian authorities in the area of administration reform with a view particularly to greater transparency in public life (*EU/Tunisia*, 2005). The Egyptian Action Plan, on the other hand, encompasses promotion of public awareness and participation in elections, exchange of experiences in holding elections and cooperation in areas of shared interest by, among others, providing assistance in registering voters, supporting the efforts of the Egyptian government towards decentralisation and reform of local administrations, as well as the establishment of a formal and regular dialogue on human rights and democracy within the framework of the relevant subcommittee (*EU/Egypt*, 2007: 6). I have enumerated only some, albeit the most precise and specific, of the declared undertakings; however, their implementation did not yield any significant results prior to 2011. For it is difficult to grasp the sense of exchange of experiences with sham parliaments, or the democratisation effect of administrative reform implemented within the framework of a strictly autocratic system, the positive aspects of discussions about human rights within a subcommittee with politicians supporting such systems or the success of political party activation in a single-party system, not to mention the validity of encouraging voters to cast their votes when there is no pluralism. The intent of democratising political relations declared by most opposition groups raised hopes concerning the effectiveness of the EU's export of democracy. Further developments did not, however, bring the fulfilment of those expectations.

Ascribing a democratising character to the revolutions of 2010 and 2011 is a controversial step in itself. In Syria and Libya, social conflicts fuelled by opening the channels for voicing social discontent led to armed conflicts and an implosion of government structures (as presented further in the text). Again, in Egypt, the removal from the political scene of the symbolic figure of President Hosni Mubarak created the conditions for a silent alliance of three political forces: the army, represented by the Supreme Council of Armed Forces, the Muslim Brotherhood, represented by the Freedom and Justice Party, and a Salafi political party, Al-Nour, founded after the ousting of H. Mubarak (Behr, Colombo et al., 2012: 17). What attracted the organisations was their political interest and shared conservatism as well as political pragmatism, the expression of which was the adopted sequence of initial reformatory actions calculated to divide power between the army and the Brotherhood. The aforementioned actions included the foundation of the Supreme Council, which took control over the state and set up the Constitutional Review Committee (with the involvement of the Brotherhood representative and a religious thinker as a leader) which proposed a number of temporary amendments to the suspended constitution of 1971. Despite protests by secular parties and the Coptic community, the adjustments introduced then, mainly concerning election procedures, underwent public consultation through referendum and were approved by 77.2% of voters (with a low voter turnout at merely 41%) (Behr, Colombo et al., 2012: 18–19). In the initial agreement there was a postulate for holding presidential elections within three months, with no mention at the same time of parliamentary ones (Ostant, 2011: 228). The emerging structure of power gained the immediate advantage of not being under institutionalised public control in the initial phase of the changes. In the end, the parliamentary elections took place before the presidential ones, yet the Egyptians had to wait until 2012 for any of them.

The dampened enthusiasm of the protesters a year after H. Mubarak's ousting removed a common enemy, thus, destroying the given system and commencing a stage of ruthless political struggle where manipulations of the constitutional law and most likely also of the judicial system took place. The spoils included not only power, but also the political system of the state. The Freedom and Justice Party managed to conduct the elections before the proclamation of the constitution which was supposed to guarantee the Brotherhood's influence on its shape. The Supreme Council of the Armed Forces responded with pressure on the Egyptian Constitutional Tribunal leading in June 2012 to the dissolution of the parliament (where the Freedom and Justice Party had the majority of seats) which had been elected barely five months earlier.[2] In August 2012, President Mohamed Morsi (a member of the Freedom and Justice party) seemed to regain the advantage after decreeing the acquisition of executive power and – under the absence of the dissolved parliament – legislative power (exercised by the Supreme Council, simultaneously recalling the head of that body and at the same time the Minister of Defence, General Mohamed Hussein Tantawi and Chief of Staff, General Sami Hafez Anan) (Ostant, 2011: 230). A decided reaction of the army took place on 3 July, 2013, when, after a number of

---

[2] The army's intention to transfer some of the presidential powers to Prime Minister Kamal Ganzouri proved successful, as well as introducing an amendment to the constitution limiting the power of the head of state (among other things, filling positions in the army), and thwarting (also thanks to the Constitutional Tribunal) an attempt at introducing a ban on people holding high positions in Mubarak's regime for at least ten years from running for election, which would have closed the road to the presidency for Ahmed Shafik, backed by the army (Behr, Colombo et. al., 2012: 21; Rashed, 2012; Ostant, 2011: 230).

protests against M. Morsi's policy, the army, led by General Abdel Fattah el-Sisi carried out a coup d'état and *de facto* took over power in the country, suspending the constitution and announcing early elections (Wójcik, 2013). It seems that the army's political victory is total, which has not simplified the EU's position. It did not manage to influence the process of creating the framework for the system launched during M. Morsi's presidency, who did not even fulfil the promise of widening the composition of the National Constituent Assembly to include representatives of secular political parties (Hanna, 2013). The commitment to the continuation of state democratisation announced on 20 August, 2013, by the interim president, Adly Mansour, involving the reinstatement of a secular government, announcement of new presidential as well as parliamentary elections at the beginning of 2014 and the introduction of amendments to the constitution (Alsharif, 2013), was to the time the last attempt at persuading the USA and the EU that the Egyptian army appreciated the idea of importing Western system solutions. Brussels had to change its concept of assistance from the expert support of transformations in Egypt to attempts at intensive mediation in a conflict between the local political forces, taken up by Catherine Ashton during her numerous trips to the country (*Catherine Ashton*, 2013; *Remarks*, 2013; *High Representative*, 2013) in the second half of 2013. In the course of one of them she visited M. Morsi in his place of isolation (*Remarks*, 2013) pointing out at the same time in her speeches the necessity of including Al-Nour as well as the Freedom and Justice Party in the political process (*Remarks*, 2013).

The High Representative's efforts failed – as demonstrated by the introduction on 24 November, 2013, by the interim president A. Mansour of a restrictive law on public assembly. The law grants the Interior Ministry the right to dissolve any public gathering of more than ten people, and the police to apply coercive means, even in the case of an isolated act of petty vandalism during a demonstration. This act also introduced vague definitions of punishable acts, for example "influencing the course of justice" that give the courts a broad scope of interpretation, which is dangerous, especially in case of combining such imprecise categories with the possibility of meting out harsh punishments (*Egypt: Deeplye*, 2013). Aside from those developments, in December 2013, the Egyptian government chose to institutionalise the struggle with the largest opposition group, the Muslim Brotherhood, outlawing it and declaring it a terrorist organisation, thereby putting its members at risk of being judged on the basis of the restrictive antiterrorist act of 1992 (*Egipt: Bractwo Muzułmańskie*, 2014). The following year, the engagement of the judiciary in the political struggle reached a practical phase – as evidenced by the court in the town of Minya, which (sitting in just a few swift sessions) sentenced 683 people to death (including a spiritual leader of the Muslim Brotherhood, Mohammed Badie) for alleged participation in the murder of a policeman during riots in August 2013 (*Political*, 2014; Kirkpatrick, 2014). It should be noted that this took place barely a month after another mass sentence in the same town, and in similar circumstances (Hauslohner, 2014).

The EU moves make it clear that Europe lacks a strategy for Egypt after the recent political developments. The concept of concentrating on mediation, introduced in summer 2013, had a rational basis and involved sustaining a relationship with all parties of the conflict, but the mediations ended in a fiasco, made apparent by the confrontational policy of the new authorities against the opposition (not only religious). What is more, successive Egyptian authorities after the Arab Spring concentrated on political struggle; not certain of their future, they have not as yet shown greater interest in European instruments of reform stimulation, which has resulted in delays in the implementation of the current Action Plan adopted by the EU and Egypt within the framework of the ENP, as shown in the ENP Country Progress Report for 2013 (*ENP Country*, 2014) published by the European Commission in 2014. The document states that the key recommendations of the previous year remain pertinent, as they had not been addressed by Egypt, with the minor exception of signing the regional Convention on pan-Euro-Mediterranean preferential rules of origin (*ENP Country*, 2014). The victory of an army candidate – former Defence Minister A. F. al-Sisi – in the presidential elections held between 26 and 28 May, 2014, may contribute to the increase of political stability of the state, creating the conditions for long-term measures such as the fulfilment of the provisions of the aforementioned Action Plan. However, the measures taken by the new authorities targeted at the opposition, as described above, call into question the intentions of the Egyptian leadership, and thus, the sense of implementing the institutional reforms recommended by the EU. The procedures surrounding the presidential elections aroused similar doubts, as the government extended them by one day during the actual elections, announcing a national holiday on the second election day. Such actions were to raise the turnout to provide greater legitimacy for the expected winner, A. F. al-Sisi (Kenner, 2014). The European Union Election Observation Mission also drew attention to irregularities concerning the election "environment falling short of constitutional principles," involving, among other things, a high level of disproportion of means at the candidates' disposal, restricting by the authorities of freedom of association, assembly and expression, and restricting or harassing civil society organisations (*European Union Election*, 2014: 1–2). The EU had a dilemma regarding Egypt, one well-known before the Arab Spring, forcing Europe to choose between cooperation with an authoritarian state justifying the fact with the prospects of its democratisation, conducted with the support of trade instruments and the ENP, and imposing sanctions. In the case of Syria, Brussels chose the latter solution, but with regard to Egypt a return to the first one is more probable, as can be indicated by the EU's proposal of resuming negotiations, aimed at reaching an agreement on founding a Deep and Comprehensive Free Trade Area (DCFTA) between the parties (the issue will be discussed in greater detail later in the text).

A significantly easier task awaits Brussels in Tunisia, where the creation of the ruling system assumed a conciliatory form. An attempt at holding swift presidential elections by the government of national unity of Mohamed Ghannouchi, appointed on 17 January, 2011, and consisting of people tied with Ben Ali, did not satisfy the demonstrators. Under their pressure the cabinet stepped down on 27 February and was replaced by a new council of ministers headed by Benji Caid Essebsi and devoid of people connected with the former system (Kozłowski, 2012: 121). Elections to the National Constituent Assembly were given priority, thus, leading in October 2011 to the formation of a cabinet composed of three factions: the moderate, religious Ennahda Party, the centre-left Ettakatol Party and the Congress for the Republic. It is worth noting (after Ibrahim Sharqieh) that such a broad coalition was formed, despite the clear election success (41% of seats in the Assembly) of the Ennahda Party, whose leaders, moreover, did not decide to put forward their own candidate for the president and supported the human rights activist Moncef Marzouki, in spite of the fact that he was in favour of a secular state and that his Congress for the Republic had won a mere 13.4% of seats in the Assembly (Sharqieh, 2014). Furthermore, Tunisian parliamentary groups (mindful of the mistakes of Egyptian politicians) managed to reach a constitutional consensus, consulting the text of the constitution with NGOs, especially the largest ones comprising the so called 'Quartet' involving the UGTT Trade Union, the UTICA Employers' Association, the LTDH League of Human Rights and the Bar Association of Lawyers (Bahi, Völkel, 2014).

So far, the most serious test for the young Tunisian parliament has been the resignation from parliamentary proceedings of over fifty opposition MPs (in reaction to the murder of one of them, Mohamed Brahmi, by religious militants in July 2013) accompanied by a demand to dissolve the Assembly (Sharqieh, 2014; Ghribi, 2014). The ruling coalition managed to save not only the Assembly, but also relative political unity, thanks to the fact that it resisted the temptation of bypassing the opposition and decided to start negotiations and made some concessions, i.e. adjourning the session of the Assembly and constituting a government of national unity (Sharqieh, 2014).

By 2014, Tunisia managed to adopt a constitution, not, however, without delays, and the system itself emerging from the act diverges slightly from European standards. It was decided upon the adoption of a semi-presidential model, ensuring the head of state special powers in national security, including the possibility of resorting to "any measures" in case of "imminent danger". What is more, despite adopting the principle of the legitimisation of power by the people, the status of Islam as a national religion was upheld (Al-Ali, Ben Romdhane, 2014). Nonetheless, the constitution ensures the basis of a system coherent with the framework of the European democratic paradigm, which was confirmed by the Foreign Affairs Council congratulating Tunisians on adopting the constitution, terming it democratic and announcing that it guarantees "fundamental freedoms, the rule of law, separation of powers and the independence of the judiciary" (*Council conclusions on Tunisia*, 2014). One may venture to say that Tunisia has made the most of the chance for the Europeanisation of political relations thanks to the limited engagement of the army in public life. During the revolution, the army remained neutral, and after its end the commanders did not follow their Egyptian counterparts' example and did not display any interest in the power struggle (Dzisiów-Szuszczykiewicz, 2011: 48). Tunisia managed to avoid the awkward, for Cairo, situation where the armed forces are the only lay political power balancing the Islamists' influences.

Despite the problems typical of a newly-founded democracy and the risks concerning Islamist terrorist groups, Tunisia remains a country with the highest absorption level of the European institutional solutions that entails openness to the EU's influence. Brussels aims to make use of the successful institutional export, distinguishing Tunis through financial support and the swift upgrade of mutual relations within the framework of the ENP. At the 9th session of the EU-Tunisia Association Council in November 2012, a new Action Plan for Tunisia was agreed upon, declaring an establishment of Privileged Partnership with the country (*EU and Tunisia*, 2012). The direction of evolution of mutual relations was also reaffirmed at the 10th session of the council in April 2014. Summing up its results, the European Commissioner for Enlargement and European Neighbourhood Policy Štefan Füle tied the growth of the Privileged Partnership to a somewhat earlier (3 March) mobility partnership and initialling a Protocol on Framework Agreement on the participation of Tunisia in EU programmes, not failing to recall at the same time that Tunisia was the first beneficiary of the SPRING programme, and the amount of the EU assistance for the country assigned in 2011 and 2012 was EUR 485 mln, exceeding the initial targets more than twice (*EU-Tunisia*, 2014).

Free elections were held even in Libya, despite the complicated social structure of the country that hinders the basic centralisation necessary in any state, even if it functions within the framework of a federal system. Muammar Gaddafi's regime managed to control the country thanks to striking a balance based on an alliance of two tribes: Gaddafa and Magariha, as well as the largest Libyan group – Warfalla (Sasnal, 2011: 3–4; Wehrey, 2011: 254). The ousting of the dictator revealed the integration problems of Libyan society. A good illustration of this was the post-revolutionary situation in the birthplace of the revolution – Benghazi, which was dominated by two competing lay and Islamist militias, enjoying a high degree of independence of Tripoli and conducting single-handed actions against people linked to the former political class (Fitzgerald, Khan, 2012). In the years that followed, the process of political and military decentralisation deepened even further, not along ideological but clan and geographical lines, as illustrated by the Misrata militia operations in the capital Tripoli. One of the most notorious episodes connected with the activity of the militia took place in November 2013, when its members opened fire on protesting citizens, killing 43 people and pillaging a government army base, thereby entangling themselves in clashes with the competing militias who also carried out an assault in an attempt to seize the opportunity to weaken a strong opponent (*New clashes,* 2014).

Despite the above-mentioned problems, in 2012, Libya managed to hold general elections to an interim parliament called the General National Congress, which in September of that year chose as PM a returnee from the USA, Professor Mustafa Abushagur (*Despite,* 2012). A provisional constitution was also adopted; however, the democratisation process was hampered due to the fragmentation of the political forces manipulating the democratic procedures. This led to a political crisis after the elections to the House of Representatives, as the results were called into question by the Supreme Court located in Tripoli (*Libya faces,* 2014). The verdict helped to legitimise the so-called "national salvation government" with its seat in the capital, led by Omar al-Hasi and supported by the reinstated General National Congress operating under the auspices of "Libyan Dawn" – a coalition linked to militias from Misrata and Tripoli, as well as several other towns from the western part of the country (Fitzgerald, 2014). Chosen in the 2014 elections and enjoying international support, the House of Representatives moved to Tobruk, and supports the official government under the leadership of Abdullah al-Thinni residing in the eastern part of the country (Fitzgerald, 2014). Libya has, therefore, two competing political centres, which, in addition, do not exercise full control over their dependent areas, the borders of which are not at all precise. The lack of territorial unity and a coherent political system precludes the continuation of the process of democratic transition, restricting the prospects for the expansion of EU influence in Libya. It seems, therefore, rational that Brussels backs the UN and US actions aimed at reaching an agreement between the two parties to the conflict and appointing a "national unity government for Libya" (*Joint Statement,* 2014). The EU is ready to acknowledge the House of Representatives as the sole representative of the Libyan nation, owing to the legitimacy obtained through elections, at the same time urging its members "to reach out to all parties and engage constructively in an inclusive political dialogue, also to find a solution to the institutional crisis, as the country cannot afford to be divided" (*Council conclusions on Libya,* 2014: 1). A search for multilateral ways to solve the conflict, together with cautious participation in the multilateral mediation group, brings to mind the EU's actions in the Israeli-Palestinian conflict. The EU turned away from the unequivocal engagement of the "Unified Protector" armed operation, which could show that Brussels politicians do not believe in such a marked stabilisation of political and social situation in Libya that would allow it to incorporate the country into the Barcelona Process.

In spite of these problems, at the onset of the Arab Spring, Egypt, Tunisia and Libya undoubtedly accepted the European political and social model, the proof of which were the attempts at democratisation of the local political systems. Free elections to legislatures were conducted, new constitutions were adopted, multi-

-party political life was invigorated and attempts to institutionalise conflicts were taken (even if they failed in Egypt and Libya). Despite the fact that the role of the EU in the process is hard to assess, its southern policy before the Arab Spring was conducted in reliance on contact with the authoritarian administrations, and the belief that it was necessary to follow European political and institutional patterns became common currency in North Africa. The obstacles hindering the transformation of that belief into reality is not a result of post-revolutionary disappointment with democracy (as in the Russia of the 1990s), but of the discord between European standards and the role of the army in the society (in Egypt's case) as well as a failure in the implementation of another European political model, the nation state (in Libya and Syria's cases). If Brussels wishes to include Maghreb and Mashriq into its zone of influence – this is the very model it has to promote through its diplomatic, economic and advisory actions.

ECONOMIC DIFFICULTIES OF THE SOUTHERN NEIGHBOURHOOD OF THE EU

The Arab Maghreb and Mashriq countries are grappling with serious economic problems, the reasons for which go far beyond the present difficulties of world capitalism. Errors in nationalised enterprise management, widespread corruption, bloated armament budgets, buying social peace for food and petrol subsidies, the relatively low levels of foreign investment, lack of modern transport infrastructures and an insufficiently educated workforce are just the most important causes of the economic problems which manifest themselves in widespread areas of poverty (the majority of Egyptians live on no more than USD 4.00 a day) and unemployment, especially affecting young people (Dzisiów-Szuszczykiewicz, 2011: 42–43). The Arab Spring has not improved the situation yet. On the contrary, political disquiet has stifled economic growth, causing an outflow of capital and tourists.[3] What is more, Cairo strived to alleviate the effects of the post-revolution slump through redistribution. As a result, expenses on subsidies for the financial year 2011/2012 (mainly food and petrol) were boosted by 42% and salaries in the public sector rose by 27% (Sasnal, 2012: 2693) deepening the already substantial deficit and triggering a meltdown of foreign reserves from USD 35 bln to USD 15 bln (Sasnal, 2012: 2693). The political upheaval complicated the Tunisian economic situation as well. In 2011, income from tourist resorts plummeted by 40% (in comparison to the previous year), and the foreign investment level decreased from USD 1.8 bln in 2010 to USD 1.08 bln in 2011 (Dudkiewicz, Sasnal, 2011: 2534).[4]

---

[3] The pace of economic growth in Egypt dropped then from 5% (annually) to 0.3%, and the country's rating by Standard & Poor's was lowered from B to BB (Sasnal, 2012: 2693).

[4] It is worth remembering that the tourist industry constitutes the second most important branch of the national economy (after agriculture), producing 5.5% of GNP (in 2010), and the

The economic difficulties increased the need for outside support, creating at the same time an opportunity to widen the EU's sphere of influence. As I have mentioned before, Brussels attempted to seize the chance, although it has to be noted that the scale of the increased value of the EU's support for the southern Mediterranean states is not at all impressive, if one takes into account promises made immediately after the Arab Spring by the USA and the states of the Persian Gulf.[5] It seemed, however, that the value of the support might suddenly soar in the estimation of the biggest (in terms of population) of the states in the southern neighbourhood, namely, Egypt, after the direct attack led by the army against the Muslim Brotherhood impeded the cooperation of the government with the aforementioned donors. Immediately after the assault, the USA started to reduce military assistance for Egypt, commencing the process by delaying the shipment of four multirole combat F-16 aircraft, justifying the step by the current situation in Cairo (Kenner, 2013), and ending in the total suspension of the support. Brussels gained thereby a possibility of exerting influence on system transformation in Egypt, which it attempted to exploit. The proof thereof was a statement of the Foreign Affairs Council, which devoted the session on 21 August, 2013, to the issue of Egypt. The document informs of their empowering the High Representative of the Union for Foreign Affairs and Security Policy to carry out a review (together with the European Commission) of previous aid measures for Egypt within the framework of ENP implementation and the Association Agreement signed with the country – assuring at the same time that the support for the social and economic sectors as well as civil society in Egypt would be continued (*Council conclusions on Egypt*, 2013).

A lot, however, points to the fact that Washington will not resign from repaying Egypt in military assistance for the adherence to the agreement of 1979 with Israel. The evidence is, for instance, that the Obama administration's efforts are heading towards resuming financial support, despite some protests from Congress.[6] One has to agree with Jeremy Sharp's opinion that the USA will resume

---

country faces mass unemployment affecting 46% of university graduates (Dudkiewicz, Sasnal, 2011: 2534).

[5] The amount of annual financial support coming to Egypt from the USA is USD 1.55 bln (US, 2012), out of which USD 1.3 bln goes into military help. In June 2012, Saudi Arabia transferred to Cairo USD 1.5 bln (US, 2012) endorsing financing for projects worth USD 450 mln, as well as promising loans of USD 750 mln for the purchase of petroleum products (US, 2012). Furthermore, soon after the Arab Spring, Qatar declared aid for Egypt to the sum of USD 2 bln, and the USA promised support for Egypt's application for a USD 4.8 bln loan from the International Monetary Fund (US, 2012).

[6] An excellent illustration of the situation was – repeatedly quoted by the mass media – the declarations of Vermont Democratic Senator Jeremy Leahy, a chairman of the Senate foreign operations appropriations subcommittee, who stated "I'm not prepared to sign off on the delivery of additional aid for the Egyptian military" and "I'm not prepared to do that until we see convincing evidence the government is committed to the rule of law" (Zengerle, 2014), voiced after the second of the mass death sentences imposed by the court in Minya.

payments of the promised sums because of the interests of US defence companies, which are the main foreign supplier of Egyptian army equipment, thereby
making them the end recipient of the sums paid out (Sharp, 2014: 12). The
amendment by California Representative Adam Schiff, restricting annual military aid for Egypt by USD 300 mln (the majority of the amount would be transferred to the civil economic aid tranche) was not accepted by the House of
Representatives Appropriations Committee (Pecquet, 2014). Again, the final say
on the aid planned for 2014 is with the President's administration, since the Secretary of State has the power to confirm the accordance of Egypt's action with the
treaty of 1979, as well as the power to acknowledge the fact of holding presidential and parliamentary elections, as well as constitutional referendum in Egypt,
which are the conditions for channelling the funds (Sharp, 2014: 11–12). Aside
from that, help for Egypt has been excluded from the ban restricting support for
countries where a coup d'état took place, resulting in the ousting of the legally
elected authorities (Sharp, 2014: 12), which additionally impedes the efforts of US
adherents of influencing Cairo through curbing financial transfers.

Even if other partners of Egypt will be able to restrict the relative value of the
EU's support, proposing larger sums, it has to be remembered that the EU is renowned for stable payments, realising their declarations (the evidence of which
is the fact that the EU maintains the Palestinian National Authority administration). This raises the value of the help rendered (increasing the severity of its
suspension, if the beneficiary does not comply with the stipulated conditions).
What is more, Brussels still holds the prospect of untapped sources of influence,
in the shape of region's trade dependence on the EU market.

For all EUROMED states apart from Jordan (as well as non-member observer
states: Libya and Mauritania) the EU is the main trade partner (*Statistics*, 2011)
and there have been no alternatives so far. The level of mutual trade exchange
between these countries is vestigial, because of the lack of complementarity of
their economies, the weakness of the logistical infrastructure, the low competitiveness of their companies and the red tape. The situation is well-illustrated by
the fact that the value of trade exchange between the member states of the Arab
Maghreb Union constituted only 3% of their overall trade exchange in 2011
(Albareda, Barba, 2011: 15). A similar situation can be noticed between the signatories of the Agadir Agreement (*Statistics*, 2011). By the same token, the states
should not count on replacing Europe with the oil monarchies of the Persian
Gulf, and the distance makes a sudden increase in the economic involvement of
the US or China in the region seem improbable.[7]

A forerunner of using trade instruments by Brussels to increase its influence
was the proposal of supplementing the association agreements with selected

---

[7] The hopes of capital flowing from the latter of the countries are dampened by the ambiguous experiences of Tehran, grappling with investment delays resulting from the caution of
Chinese corporations (Krawczyk, 2009: 2024).

states of the southern neighbourhood with Deep and Comprehensive Free Trade Areas (DCFTAs). A decision about commencement of negotiations concerning the issue with the members of the WTO and signatories of the Agadir Agreement, i.e. Egypt, Jordan, Morocco and Tunisia, was taken on 14 December, 2011, by the European Council upon the motion of the European Commission (*EU agrees*, 2011). The establishment of the Areas was to broaden the range of trade privileges (including customs privileges) enjoyed by the vast majority of the states associated in EUROMED by adding other privileges – also in reference to agricultural and fisheries products – a proposal particularly appreciated by the countries of the South (*EU agrees*, 2011). Apart from the trade issues, future agreements are to apply to public procurement, technical standards, sanitary and phytosanitary regulations, as well as competition policy and investment protection (*EU agrees*, 2011). As usual in such cases, four associated countries will be granted wider access to the common market at the cost of increasing the possibilities of expansion of European companies on their territory (in terms of investment as well as purely trade) (*UE i Afryka Płn.*, 2011). Up to 2014, however, negotiations could be commenced solely with Morocco (by August 2013 two rounds of negotiations had been completed, enabling an agreement to be composed based on existing agreements regulating trade exchange, such as the Association Agreement of 2000 and the agreement on agricultural, processed agricultural and fisheries products of 2012) (*The EU's bilateral trade*, 2013). In 2014, preparations for opening negotiations with Jordan and Tunisia took place (*Fact sheet*, 2014). The biggest difficulties arose in the case of the DCFTA negotiations with Egypt, whose interim authorities rejected the offer of dialogue on mobility, migration and security, aiming towards a mobility partnership (*European Scrutiny*, 2013: 61). Preliminary discussions concerning the agreement were suspended after the removal from power of president M. Morsi (Nasralla, Lyon, 2014). However, as early as the beginning of 2014, the EU ambassador in Cairo James Moran announced a proposal of resuming negotiations after parliamentary and presidential elections (Lomas, 2014).

The decision about the commencement of the negotiation on DCFTAs taken in 2011 indicated not only French, Italian and Spanish influences in the European Council, but also that the EU tried to actually affect the development of relations with the South, which could consider itself a privileged region, as Ukraine at the time was denied the negotiations. It cannot be ruled out that the current announcement of the resumption of negotiations with Egypt is an attempt at a continuation of the policy of using economic tools to exert pressure on democratising political relations in the country. Yet, the local opposition may interpret it as a return to a dual policy, separating economic and political issues, thus, allowing European companies to expand their exports to Egypt, despite the serious incongruity of Egyptian political practice and EU standards. Such an allegation may be justified, in that the present Egyptian leadership has not succumbed to US financial pressure, which, in turn, decreases the possibility of changing course because of the temptation of signing an agreement with the EU both long-term and ambiguous in consequences.

In spite of the problems with Egypt, trade will continue to be the major potential instrument of the EU's influence on the countries of the southern neighbourhood. It cannot be known if the EU has the sufficient unity and determination, essential in the conscious political application of such measures. Entering negotiations on DCFTAs could be a signal that the conditions had been met, but it is worth remembering that in two out of four countries chosen to be the first parties of the negotiations, the Arab Spring did not exactly take place, and before its commencement, the EU had supported trade exchange as well – not insisting on too demanding political stipulations. This was clearly exemplified by the doubling in the value of the EU's trade with Egypt between 2004 and 2010, achieved despite the fact that, for most of that time, power was held by the administration of the now-condemned H. Mubarak (Nasralla, Lyon, 2014). On the other hand, the fact that the European Commission obtained a mandate to commence negotiations with a democratising Tunisia, relatively liberal Jordan as well as tentatively reformist Morocco could be a signal of encouragement for other countries to deepen their integration with the common market, and therefore, to enter the European sphere of influence. A good indicator of the EU's determination in strengthening economic links with the southern neighbourhood will undoubtedly be the period of negotiations concerning these agreements. If Brussels wants to persuade the southern neighbourhood countries to believe its commitment to the idea of their incorporation into the EU influence zone, the Commission has to speed up the DAFTA negotiations compared to those concerning Association Agreements.

PROSPECTS FOR THE EU MILITARY PRESENCE IN ITS SOUTHERN NEIGHBOURHOOD

The EU does not have independent armed forces at its disposal, and the Common Security and Defence Policy is the least developed branch of the EU's external operations, which since the beginning has shown ambivalence in the approach towards its defensive identity.[8] The situation is not conducive to the exploitation of the chances for expansion of the EU's influences which occurred thanks to the Arab Spring. MENA (Middle East and North Africa) countries, as

---

[8] The Maastricht Treaty entrusted the Western European Union with the role of the "armed component" of the integration formation, expecting at the same time its support of the "European pillar" of NATO (*Declaration*, 1992). The ambitious plans for the establishment of a European Union Rapid Reaction Force composed of 100,000 soldiers, 400 aircraft and 100 vessels ended in the implementation of the concept of European Union Battle groups, comprising an armoured infantry battalion placed by member states at Brussels' disposal (Stańczyk, 2009: 35, 38–39).

well as the organisations associating them, not only accepted intervention from the North, but even to some extent postulated it. Governments of the countries of the League of Arab States, in order to pacify public opinion, criticised, in March 2011, the methods applied by Libyan troops in conducting an offensive against the rebels in the eastern part of the country, and subsequently (12 March) the Council of the organisation demanded a ban for Gaddafi's air force and the establishment of safety zones for civilians (Lorenc, 2011: 243–244), which could have been recognised as an invitation to, among others, Europe. The idea gained the support of the Organisation of the Islamic Conference (presently the Organisation of Islamic Cooperation) as well as the Persian Gulf Cooperation Council, which described the Libyan regime as unlawful (Hunter, 2011: 261). The potential interveners did not have to face the problem of the disapproval of the Arab governments and public opinion, difficulties which George H. W. Bush had to grapple with in 1991, and George W. Bush in 2005. Europe seized the opportunity.

As soon as 18 February, 2011, and so only two days after the adoption by the United Nations Security Council of resolution 1970, the Council of the European Union took the decision to implement the provisions of that document, announcing an embargo on shipments of military equipment to Libya and introducing visa restrictions for selected people linked to the regime, simultaneously freezing their funds deposited in European banks (Lorenc, 2011: 243). Subsequently (on France's initiative) the European Council, sitting on 11 March, deemed that M. Gaddafi should relinquish power immediately (Rettman, 2011), and French diplomacy at the same time secretly recognised the National Transitional Council as a body representing Libya internationally (Kumoch, 2011: 80–81). What is more, Catherine Ashton and Herman van Rompuy found themselves among the members of the Paris summit held on 19 March, to discuss the details of the military operation based on the UN mandate granted by resolution 1973, adopted by the Security Council a day earlier and empowering member states to take actions aimed at protection of civilians (Lorenc, 2011: 246). Significantly, the NATO Secretary General was absent from the meeting, which suited the French concept of the instrumental application of NATO forces, coinciding with the idea of the EU's independence in the area of security (Lorenc, 2011: 246).

One could talk about the situation in terms of European political success, especially French and British, whose initiative resulted in a military operation, the outcome of which brought profound changes to the political situation of the country of the Southern Mediterranean (albeit not one of those engaged in the aforementioned integration projects of the EU). The Europeans proved thereby (despite the lack of inner consensus, which was shown by Germany's abstention from action) that they are able to actively expand their influences outside the continent applying methods other than economic pressure and soft power. This was displayed in the second phase of intervention within the framework of operation "Unified Protector" (led by NATO) during which, in line with Paris and London, M. Gaddafi's regime was toppled and support given to the opposition beyond merely protecting the civilian population (Trojanowski, 2014: 97), although a change of Libyan leadership was never mentioned among the official aims of the operation (Pacuła, 2011: 70).

It has to be admitted that the first phase of the intervention showed the technical and organisational inability of EU member states to lead joint offensive operations, as seen in the size of the resources used. Out of 662 bombs dropped by 28 March, 2011, 445 were of American origin (Trojanowski, 2014: 99). Moreover, until NATO took over leadership of operations, US Navy vessels fired 199 out of 206 cruise missiles, and US fighters carried out around 1,000 of the 1,600 military flights conducted by coalition air forces (Trojanowski, 2014: 95). What is equally important, the mission would have failed without the support of US military intelligence, as well as ammunition and fuel supplies. The last of these forms of support proved particularly valuable in April 2011, when the European allies ran out of reserves of precision munitions, and as a result some of them were forced to take rapid action, for instance, an intervention purchase from Israel made by Denmark (Trojanowski, 2014: 97). Nevertheless, it has to be emphasised that after the end of the aforementioned first phase of the enterprise (lasting from 19 to 31 March, 2011) during which US (Operation Odyssey Dawn), French (Operation Harmattan), British (Operation Ellamy) and Canadian (Operation Mobile) forces with some support from other states (including the EU's Italy, Denmark, Spain, Holland, Greece and Belgium) targeted Libyan air defences, command and control and other military facilities (Taylor, 2011: 6–11, 14–15), the burden of the mission was shouldered by European forces. US forces continued to support the allies with intelligence, also placing US special forces and tanker aircraft at their disposal (Pacuła, 2011: 74). However, the vast majority of strike sorties were conducted by the armies of European NATO countries who are members of the EU: the UK and France (two thirds of strike sorties) as well as Italy, Denmark and Sweden (Gaub, 2013: 7). The US withdrawal lowered the intensity of the warfare, but the European forces managed to lead to the opposition's victory, using military instruments (one needs to reiterate here that when it comes to broad joint offensive operations, US support is still necessary, so it is difficult to talk about self-reliance in Europe's security). Furthermore, as noted by Przemysław Pacuła (Pacuła, 2011: 75), the ostentatious handover of control to London and Paris of the operation was not necessarily an expression of courtesy, but a real sign of the US intention to decrease their military presence in the vicinity of Europe, thus, creating a palpable chance for the expansion of Europe's influence.

The British and French tandem is also said to be taking some part in the Syrian civil war, through providing the Free Syrian Army (FSA) with armaments (Piskorski, 2014: 205) as well as training, conducted by French and British special forces instructors operating in Turkey (Piskorski, 2014: 202). Yet, the engagement of the whole of the EU in the conflict (even on a similar scale to Libya) is very unlikely. Legal, political and military considerations all advocate such a solution. Owing to guaranteed Russian resistance, whose vessels use the harbour of Tartus, it is impossible to obtain a UN Security Council mandate for such an operation. Moreover, the density of population of the country is far greater than in Libya (100 people per square km to four people in Libya) resulting in a high number of civilian casualties in such a hypothetical intervention (Czulda, 2014: 255). Apart from that, the involved forces would be dealing with an army loyal to the president, far bigger than the Libyan one (in 2011 Libyan army totalled 76,000; at the same time, Syrian army numbered 295,000) and equipped with a greater number of anti-aircraft systems (Czulda, 2014: 255, 246–248). Apart from that, Syria lacks an opposition centre corresponding to the Libyan town of Benghazi, which could form a strategic support area for an opposition backed by the intervening powers.

More importantly, however, the European economy has no vital interests in Syria, owing to the modest size of the country's deposits of hydrocarbons and low trade volumes. Due to European restrictions, bilateral trade volumes dropped in 2013 to the level of EUR 885 mln (*Countries and Regions*, 2014), and even before then, it was lower than in the case of other southern neighbourhood states (*Statistics*, 2011) – caused, among other things, by the lack of an association agreement joining both parties.

Furthermore, the various opposition groups fighting with the government army make it unclear as to which faction would guarantee the EU's influence in case of victory. It is also not certain if any of the groups favours Europe so greatly as to justify the costs of an intervention. The initial, unequivocal support for the opposition against Bashar al-Assad's rule belonged to the EU tactic described earlier, aimed at the improvement of Europe's image among the new elites and societies affected by the Arab uprisings of 2011. Yet, the militarisation of the conflict, coupled with the emergence among the opposition of extreme Islamist groups such as Jabhat al-Nusra, Ahrar ash-Sham or Ghuraba al-Sham as well as simple organised crime groups (Piskorski 2014: 199–201), had to lead to Brussels assuming a more cautious position and to a differentiation of opposition forces. The return of the EU to supporting B. Al-Assad is, of course, impossible, due to the threat of losing credibility, and thus, a significant amount of political capital. Analytical accuracy requires me to emphasise that the application of a rational theory of international relations would lead to a conclusion concerning the validity of the move. One of the reasons for such a move would be a government army potential that continues to surpass the possibilities of the opposition forces, as well as the fact some of the demands of the opposition were met by B. al-Assad in 2012. Within the framework of the course of action towards conciliation adopted then, the state of emergency was abolished, some elements of pluralism were introduced into the system by amending the constitution, and early elections to the People's Council were announced, resigning at the same time from the monopoly of the National Progressive Front functioning under the leadership of Baas (Piskorski, 2014: 222).

The rejection by the EU of the option of supporting the Syrian government and fundamentalist opposition leaves only one working variant. A European military operation initiative would have to be built upon cooperation with the FSA, whose Supreme Military Council backs (with a part of Local Co-ordination Committees) the EU supported (*Joint Communication*, 2014) National Coalition for Syrian Revolutionary and Opposition Forces (SOC) which took place of the Syrian National Council in emigration, ineffective and showing a deficit in the level of support across the country. The SOC is, however, torn by internal divisions fuelled by rivalry between its supporters from Saudi Arabia and Qatar (Oweis, 2014), thus, the level of its control over the FSA and Local Co-ordination Committees raises too many doubts for it to be chosen as a stable political partner for an external intervention, or to give a guarantee of stability after a victory.

The described circumstances seriously limit the possibilities of the EU's military expansion of influence in the southern neighbourhood created by the precedent of Arab acceptance for a military operation in the region legitimised by Europe. This does not indicate, of course, that the implementation of such measures is out of question in the future. In the case of Syria, however, one condition would have to be met – that of a consolidation of opposition forces and of them gaining a military advantage. In the broader perspective – a strengthening of the EU's military potential through the development of a Common Security and Defence Policy or the institutionalisation of cooperation with NATO, and an increase in investment in the armed forces of member states would be required for that purpose. It is difficult nowadays to highlight any initiatives that could meet those expectations.

CONCLUSIONS

The EU's model of expansion of its influence, tested in some of the European, post-socialist states through exporting its political system and incorporating new areas into the zone of European power has not yielded results in the southern neighbourhood. The process of democratisation of political relations has been launched solely in Tunisia, which is distinguished by the EU through higher aid funds, as well as swifter institutionalisation of mutual relations. The Brussels decision-makers, including the President of the European Council, Donald Tusk, and the new High Representative, Federica Mogherini, are faced with the task of adapting the EU's policy towards the southern neighbourhood to present conditions. If they decide to choose the active variant – and not that of merely awaiting further developments in the area – they will be presented with a dilemma of whether to apply more decisively positive and negative sanctions, or rather to retreat to the line of action exercised before the Arab Spring, i.e. fostering the stabilisation and economic growth of the countries on the southern side of the Mediterranean Sea under the guise of tentative and inefficient attempts at the democratisation of authoritarian regimes. The announcement of the resumption of DCFTA negotiations is a signal that the latter of these variants is being seriously considered, which in turn would mean that Brussels does not believe in the victory of the Arab Spring anymore and has commenced work on finding a realistic mode of operation.

The ineffectiveness of the EU's economic incentives comes as a surprise, especially in the case of Egypt, whose authorities show little interest in the EU's aid and trade concessions. Their reaction must be related to the low level of the support offered, however, the distinct value systems of the two parties might also influence the decisions. The Union continues to be an organisation of economic character, based on the belief that common prosperity has primacy over other values, whereas the new Cairo leadership displays a more traditional approach to state power – measured by its independence, the cohesion of the administration as well as military power. On the basis of such a conception, the resignation from the possibility of defeating the opposition would seem to be far too high a price to pay for the EU's support.

The European Union is considered a neo-medieval empire with a certain military potential (albeit not direct) at its disposal to expand its influence. This was demonstrated during the Libyan operations. Yet the development of the political and military situation in Libya and Syria seriously limits the probability of using such measures in the future. However, it has to be pointed out that the reserves of support in the Arab world for European military intervention have still not been exhausted.

BIBLIOGRAPHY

Al-Ali Z., Ben Romdhane D. (2014), *Tunisia's new constitution: progress and challenges to come*, https://www.opendemocracy.net/arab-awakening/zaid-al-ali-donia-ben-romdhane/tunisia's--new-constitution-progress-and-challenges-to-, 05.12.2014.

Albareda A., Barba O. (2011), *Sub-Regionalism in North Africa and the Middle East: Lessons Learned and New Opportunities*, Barcelona.

Alsharif A. (2013), *Egypt's president says road map on track as Islamists protest*, http://www.reuters.com/article/2013/09/03/us-egypt-protests-idUSBRE98210520130903, 15.09.2013.

Ayad R., Gadi S. (2011), *The Future of Euro-Mediterranean Regional Cooperation: The Role of the Union for the Mediterranean*, Barcelona.

Bahi R., Völkel J. (2014), *The surprising success of the Tunisian parliament*, https://www.opendemocracy.net/arab-awakening/riham-bahi-jan-v%C3%B6lkel/surprising-success--of-tunisian-parliament, 05.12.2014.

Behr T., Colombo S., Ebeid H., Guliński S., Sasnal P., Sławek J. (2012), *Still Awake: The Beginnings of Arab Democratic Change*, Warszawa.

Catherine Ashton visits Egypt (2014), http://eeas.europa.eu/top_stories/2013/190713_ca_egypt_en.htm, 17.11.2014.

Communication From The Commission - European Neighbourhood Policy – Strategy Paper (2004), COM/2004/0373 final, http://eur-lex.europa.eu/legal-content/EN/TXT/?uri= CELEX:52004DC0373, 17.11.2014.

Conclusions of the Council and of the Representatives of the Governments of the Member States on the Northern Co-Presidency of the Union for the Mediterranean (UfM) (2012), 6702/2/12 MED 8 PESC 202, http://register.consilium.europa.eu/pdf/en/12/st06/st06981.en12.pdf, 17.11.2014.

Council conclusions on Egypt (2013), http://www.consilium.europa.eu/uedocs/cms_data/docs/pressdata/EN/foraff/138599.pdf, 17.11.2014.

Council conclusions on Libya. Foreign Affairs Council meeting (2014), http://www.consilium.europa.eu/uedocs/cms_data/docs/pressdata/EN/foraff/145200.pdf, 06.12.2014.

Council conclusions on Tunisia. Foreign Affairs Council meeting (2014), http://consilium.europa.eu/uedocs/cms_data/docs/pressdata/EN/foraff/140967.pdf, 05.12.2014.

Countries and regions. Syria (2014), http://ec.europa.eu/trade/policy/countries-and-regions/countries/syria/, 02.12.2014.

Czulda R. (2014), *Zdolności obronne Syrii w kontekście potencjalnej interwencji NATO*, in: *Fale Tsunami. Kontestacja arabska w latach 2010–2013*, eds. R. Potocki, M. Piskorski, W. Hładkiewicz, Warszawa.

Declaration on Western European Union, Treaty on European Union (1992), Official Journal C 191, http://eur-lex.europa.eu/en/treaties/dat/11992M/htm/11992M.html#0105000050, 17.11.2014.

Despite everything, it's still a success (2012), "The Economist", http://www.economist.com/node/21562944, 17.11.2014.

Dudkiewicz M., Sasnal P. (2011), *Scena polityczna w Tunezji przed wyborami do Narodowego Zgromadzenia Konstytucyjnego*, "Biuletyn PISM", No. 95.

Dzisiów-Szuszczykiewicz A. (2011), *"Arabska wiosna" – przyczyny, przebieg i prognozy*, "Bezpieczeństwo Narodowe", No. 18.

Egipt: Bractwo Muzułmańskie uznane za organizację terrorystyczną (2013), http://swiat.newsweek.pl/bractwo-muzulmanskie-uznane-za-organizacje-terrorystyczna-egipt,artykuly,277612,1.html, 18.11.2014.

Egypt: Deeply Restrictive New Assembly Law (2014), http://www.hrw.org/news/2013/11/26/egypt-deeply-restrictive-new-assembly-law, 17.11.2014.

ENP Country Progress Report 2013 – Egypt (2014), http://europa.eu/rapid/press-release_MEMO-14-223_en.htm, 21.11.2014.

EU agrees to start trade negotiations with Egypt, Jordan, Morocco and Tunisia (2011), http://trade.ec.europa.eu/doclib/press/index.cfm?id=766, 05.01.2012.

EU and Tunisia seal Privileged Partnership with agreement on new Action Plan (2012), http://www.enpi-info.eu/medportal/news/latest/31112/EU-and-Tunisia-seal-Privileged-Partnership-with-agreement-on-new-Action-Plan, 05.12.2014.

EU response to the Arab Spring: the SPRING Programme (2011), http://europa.eu/rapid/press-release_MEMO-11-636_en.htm?locale=en, 11.07.2012.

EU/Egypt Action Plan (2007), http://eeas.europa.eu/enp/pdf/pdf/action_plans/egypt_enp_ap_final_en.pdf, 27.12.2014.

EU/Tunisia Action Plan (2005), http://eeas.europa.eu/enp/pdf/pdf/action_plans/tunisia_enp_ap_final_en.pdf, 27.12.2014.

European Scrutiny Committee, Eight Report of Session 2012–13 (2014), London.

European Union Election Observation Mission. Arab Republic of Egypt, Presidential Election, 26/27 May 2014. Preliminary Statement (2014), http://eeas.europa.eu/delegations/egypt/press_corner/all_news/news/2014/20140529_en.pdf, 27.12.2014.

EU-Tunisia: More steps to deepen cooperation and support (2014), http://europa.eu/rapid/press-release_STATEMENT-14-125_en.htm, 05.12.2014.

Fact sheet on the Arab Spring (2014), http://eeas.europa.eu/factsheets/docs/factsheets_europe_day_2014/factsheet_arab_spring_en.pdf, 21.11.2014.

Fitzgerald M. (2014), *Who's Running This Joint, Anyway?*, http://foreignpolicy.com/2014/10/13/whos-running-this-joint-anyway/, 06.12.2014.

Fitzgerald M., Khan U. (2012), *The Mess We Left Behind in Libya*, http://foreignpolicy.com/2012/12/19/the-mess-we-left-behind-in-libya/, 27.12.2014.

Gaub F. (2011), *The North Atlantic Treaty Organization and Libya: Reviewing Operation Unified Protector*, Carlisle.

Ghribi Y. (2014), *Tunisia, It's Shoot First, Ask Questions Later*, http://foreignpolicy.com/2014/02/17/in-tunisia-its-shoot-first-ask-questions-later/, 05.12.2014.

Hanna M. W. (2013), *Blame Morsy*, http://www.foreignpolicy.com/articles/2013/07/08/blame_morsy_egypt?page=0,1, 17.11.2014.

Hauslohner A. (2014), *Egyptian court sentences 529 people to death*, http://www.washingtonpost.com/world/egypt-sentences-529-to-death/2014/03/24/a4f95692-6992-461e-aaf1--9bc84908a429_story.html, 17.11.2014.

High Representative Catherine Ashton visits Egypt (2014), http://eeas.europa.eu/statements/docs/2013/131002_01_en.pdf, 17.11.2014.

Hunter R. E. (2011), *What Intervention Looks Like. How the West Can Aid the Libyan Rebels*, in: *The New Arab Revolt*, New York.

Joint Communication To The European Council, The European Parliament, The Council, The European Economic And Social Committee And The Committee Of The Regions A Partnership For Democracy And Shared Prosperity With The Southern Mediterranean (2011), Brussels, 8.3.2011, COM (2011) 200 final.

Joint Communication To The European Parliament, The Council, The European Economic And Social Committee And The Committee Of The Regions Towards A Comprehensive EU Approach To The Syrian Crisis (2014), Brussels, 24.6.2013, JOIN (2013) 22 final.

Joint Statement on Libya (2014), http://eeas.europa.eu/statements-eeas/2014/141203_02_en, 03.12.2014, Brussels.

Kenner D. (2013), *America Tries Fighter Jet Diplomacy in Egypt*, http://blog.foreignpolicy.com/posts/2013/07/24/america_tries_fighter_jet_diplomacy_in_egypt, 17.11.2014.

Kenner D. (2014), *Sisi's Big Day Is a Bust*, http://foreignpolicy.com/2014/05/27/sisis-big-day-is-a-bust/, 05.12.2014.

Kirkpatrick D. (2014), *Uproar in Egypt After Judge Sentences More Than 680 to Death*, http://www.nytimes.com/2014/04/29/world/middleeast/egypt-sentences-hundreds-to-death.html?_r=1, 17.11.2014.

Kozłowski K. (2012), *Kolory rewolucji*, Warszawa.

Kumoch J. (2011), *Francja wobec arabskiej wiosny*, "Sprawy Międzynarodowe", No. 3.

Libya faces chaos as top court rejects elected assembly (2014), http://www.reuters.com/article/2014/11/06/us-libya-security-parliament-idUSKBN0IQ0YF20141106, 06.12.2014.

Lomas U. (2014), *EU Seeks To Resume Talks On DCFTA With Egypt*, http://www.tax-news.com/news/EU_Seeks_To_Resume_Talks_On_DCFTA_With_Egypt____63682.html, 22.11.2014.

Lorenc M. (2011), *The Arab Spring in Libya*, in: *The Arab Spring*, ed. B. Przybylska-Maszner, Poznań.

Nasralla S., Lyon A. (2014), *EU seeks wider free trade agreement with Egypt*, http://www.reuters.com/article/2014/02/10/us-egypt-eu-idUSBREA191QI20140210, 22.11.2014.

Ostant W. (2011), *Egypt 2011 – A new beginning*, in: *The Arab Spring*, ed. B. Przybylska-Maszner, Poznań.

Oweis K. Y. (2014), *Saudi-Qatar rivalry divides Syrian opposition*, http://www.reuters.com/article/2014/01/15/us-syria-crisis-qatar-idUSBREA0E1G720140115, 15.12.2014.

Pacuła P. (2011), *"Unified Protector" w Libii: wyzwanie dla zarządzania kryzysowego NATO*, "Bezpieczeństwo Narodowe", Vol. 18, No. 2.

Pecquet J. (2014), *AIPAC weighs in on US military aid to Egypt*, http://www.al-monitor.com/pulse/originals/2014/06/aipac-us-aid-egypt-stop-cut.html#ixzz3JQX9U94f, 18.11.2014.

Piskorski M. (2014), *Zasoby stron konfliktu syryjskiego i ich dynamika w latach 2011–2013*, in: *Fale Tsunami. Kontestacja arabska w latach 2010–2013*, eds. R. Potocki, M. Piskorski, W. Hładkiewicz, Warszawa.

Polak M. (2009), *Traktat z Lizbony – impuls do zjednoczenia czy owoc kompromisu?*, in: *Unia Europejska we współczesnym świecie – wybrane zagadnienia*, ed. J. Bryła, Poznań.

Political Executions in Egypt (2014), http://www.nytimes.com/2014/04/29/opinion/political-executions-in-egypt.html?action=click&contentCollection=Middle%20East&module=RelatedCoverage&region=Marginalia&pgtype=article, 17.11.2014.

Przybylska-Maszner B. (2011), *The Arab Spring as a Test of post-Lisbon Capabilities and Strategies of the European Union in North Africa*, in: *The Arab Spring*, ed. B. Przybylska-Maszner, Poznań.

Rashed D. (2013), *What Morsi could learn from Anwar Sadat*, http://mideast.foreignpolicy.com/posts/2012/08/14/will_morsi_be_the_next_sadat, 17.11.2014.

Remarks by EU High Representative Catherine Ashton at the end of her visit to Cairo, Egypt (2013), http://eeas.europa.eu/statements/docs/2013/131003_04_en.pdf, 17.11.2014.

Remarks by EU High Representative Catherine Ashton during her visit in Egypt (2013), http://www.consilium.europa.eu/uedocs/cms_data/docs/pressdata/EN/foraff/138449.pdf, 17.11.2014.

Remarks by EU High Representative Catherine Ashton on arrival to the Extraordinary European Council (2011), http://www.consilium.europa.eu/uedocs/cms_Data/docs/pressdata/EN/foraff/119777.pdf, 17.11.2014.

Rettman A. (2011), *EU keen to build post-Gaddafi Libya*, http://euobserver.com/foreign/31968, 17.11.2014.

Sasnal P. (2011), *Libya: Too Hot to Handle. PISM Strategic File #14*, Warszawa.

Sasnal P. (2012), *Populizm versus postęp po wyborach prezydenckich w Egipcie*, "Biuletyn PISM", No. 58 (923).

Sharp J. M. (2014), *Egypt: Background and U.S. Relations*, Washington D.C.

Sharqieh I. (2013), *Tunisia's Lessons for the Middle East. Why the First Arab Spring Transition Worked Best*, http://www.foreignaffairs.com/articles/139938/ibrahim-sharqieh/tunisias-lessons-for-the-middle-east, 17.11.2014.

Skorzycki M. (2014), *Arabska wiosna jako szansa na reset w relacjach Unii Europejskiej w jej południowym sąsiedztwem*, "Przegląd Politologiczny", No. 1.

Stańczyk J. (2009), *Grupy Bojowe jako element polityki reagowania kryzysowego UE*, "Studia Europejskie", No. 4.

Statistics (2011), http://ec.europa.eu/trade/creating-opportunities/bilateral-relations/statistics/, 17.11.2014.

Taylor C. (2011), *Military Operations in Libya*, London.

The EU's bilateral trade and investment agreements – where are we? (2014), http://europa.eu/rapid/press-release_MEMO-13-734_en.htm, 21.11.2014.

Trojanowski M. (2014), *Operacja reagowania kryzysowego NATO w Libii*, in: *Fale Tunisami. Kontestacja arabska w latach 2010–2013*, eds. R. Potocki, M. Piskorski, W. Hładkiewicz, Warszawa.

UE i Afryka Płn. otwarte na wzajemną wymianę handlową (2011), http://www.mg.gov.pl/node/15097, 17.11.2014.

US plan for Egypt aid hits roadblock (2012), http://www.aljazeera.com/news/americas/2012/09/201292901924654975, 17.11.2014.

Wehrey F. (2011), *Libya's Terra Incognita. Who and What Will Follow Qaddafi?*, in: *The New Arab Revolt*, New York.

Wickham C. R. (2011), *The Muslim Brotherhood After Mubarak. What the Brotherhood Is and How It Will Shape the Future*, in: *The New Arab Revolt*, New York.

Wójcik Ł. (2013), *Generalna głupota*, http://www.polityka.pl/swiat/komentarze/1548031,1,wojskowy-zamach-stanu-w-egipcie.read, 17.11.2014.

Zengerle P. (2014), *Senior U.S. lawmaker blocks aid for Egyptian military*, http://www.reuters.com/article/2014/04/29/us-usa-egypt-military-idUSBREA3S0NY20140429, 17.11.1014.

Zielonka J. (2007), *Europa jako imperium. Nowe spojrzenie na Unię Europejską*, Warszawa.

Anna POTYRAŁA
Adam Mickiewicz University, Poznań

TRANSFORMATION PROCESS IN NORTH AFRICAN STATES IN THE LIGHT OF THE PRIORITIES OF POLAND'S FOREIGN POLICY

The events dubbed the 'Arab Spring' in the West, and the 'Awakening' in Arab states, raised hopes that the role of societies in establishing the principles and directions of how states operate and in consolidating democracies would increase. They also exerted impact on international environment, posing a challenge for other states (and international organisations) and making it indispensable to re-define the place of the Middle East in the foreign policies of different states and external actions of international organisations. The changes that had taken place also called for establishing the principles of co-operation anew.

These were the tasks the European Union and its member states faced. The European Union, preceded by the European Community, had long been active in North African states, undertaking political, economic as well as social and cultural co-operation. While this region was within the realm of interest of the 'old' member states (which primarily followed from historic bonds), new member states did not treat North Africa as their priority.

This study – presenting the place of North African states in Poland's foreign policy – attempts to prove that the transformations these states underwent in late 2010 did not result in changed priorities of Poland's foreign policy and in re-defining the areas of Poland's international interests. When Poland assumed the presidency of the EU Council, declarations were made concerning support for democratic reforms in North African states, but they were not accompanied by the actual desire for tighter co-operation in the political or economic fields.

AIMS OF POLAND'S FOREIGN POLICY AND THE PRIORITIES OF THE POLISH PRESIDENCY

It is stipulated in the Constitution of the Republic of Poland, adopted on 2 April, 1997, that the Council of Ministers "shall exercise general control in the field of relations with other States and international organizations" (*The Constitution*, 1997: Art. 146.4.9). As concerns foreign policy, the President of Poland collaborates with the government and Minister of Foreign Affairs (*The Constitution*, 1997: Art. 133.3). This does not change the fact that the directions of foreign policy are primarily defined by the Minister of Foreign Affairs. Speaking in front of the *Sejm*, the lower chamber of Polish parliament, on behalf of the government, the Minister annually indicates the directions, objectives and tasks of Poland's foreign policy for the upcoming year, seeking the approval of MPs. The Minister of Foreign Affairs is also responsible for long-term strategies in foreign policy (*Ustawa*, 1997: Art. 32.2.1), as well as the strategies of Poland's policy inside the European Union. The Minister also participates in international relations that are significant for the interests of Poland (*Ustawa*, 1997: Art. 32.2.3).

Before the Arab Spring, the region of North Africa was not mentioned in the speeches of successive Ministers of Foreign Affairs, or in the cabinet debates; similarly to the Middle East region, it was marginal in Poland's foreign policy. Since the 1990s, Poland had prioritised its membership of the *North Atlantic Alliance*, then of the European Union, and on developing friendly relations with the United States and neighbouring countries, placing particular importance on its Eastern neighbours. After 2001, essential significance was attributed to international co-operation aimed at combating terrorism and ensuring security in the region and globally. North Africa was in a margin of Polish foreign policy and the necessity to increase commitment in countries of this region was the result of the accession to the European Union and realisation of EU foreign and development policy. In the official strategy towards non-European developing countries of November 2004, the need of economic and trade cooperation was indicated. Egypt, Algeria and Morocco were regarded as the most important political and economic partners of Poland (*Strategia*, 2004: 41–43), followed by Tunisia and Libya. Despite declarations concerning the will to strengthen cooperation, in the document of 2004 chances and threats to implementation have been pointed out, with no references to means of realisation of aims and assumptions. What is more, in the period from 2007 to 2011, the assumptions of Poland's foreign policy envisaged activities fostering the sovereignty and security of the state, ensuring advantageous conditions for economic development and reinforcing the position of Poland in the international arena. All this was to be achieved by means of maintaining friendly relations with neighbouring countries and advancing co-operation with key partners, namely the US and the largest states of the European Union – France, Germany, Spain, Italy and the UK (*Informacja*, 2008).

It was the intention of the Polish authorities that Poland's presidency of the European Union (1 July–31 December, 2011) should facilitate the achievement of Poland's foreign policy objectives. Although the programme of the presidency needs to take the interests of the entire European Union and all member states into account, in practice it makes it possible to fill the programme developed for the entire EU with a given state's own intentions and covertly include its own objectives (cf. Czachór, 2011: 27). Consequently, embarking on its preparations for the presidency programme, the government indicated the preliminary criteria essential when identifying the priorities. They included, among other things, the challenges and needs facing the EU internally and externally; the international and domestic situation; the common interests and objectives of the countries in the group presidency (trio/Troika) and the interests of Poland (*Program*, 2009: 15).

Although the programme was ready long before the actual assumption of the presidency, the revolutionary changes in North African states affected its agenda. The Arab Spring enforced the necessity to redefine the strategic objective of Poland's foreign policy, formulated as acting as the "patron and promoter of Eastern policy" in the European Union. Since dynamic and dramatic political and social transformations (perceived as the beginning of a democratisation process) had taken place in the immediate neighbourhood of the European Union, Poland could not fail to take them into account and limit itself to ensuring the implementation of the eastern dimension of the *Common Security and Defence Policy*. On the one hand, the events in North Africa could distract the attention of member states from the issues deemed important by the Polish presidency and focus it on their southern neighbours. At the same time, however, the Polish authorities were given an unparalleled opportunity to commence the debate over the reform of the *European Neighbourhood Policy* and promote the idea of establishing the *European Endowment for Democracy* (Sasnal, 2011: 10). Poland's reaction to the events in North Africa was neither rapid nor radical, though. Instead of taking *ad hoc* steps, the desire to "promote comprehensive solutions for the European Union and its environment, among others by maintaining a balance between the southern and eastern dimension" of the CSDP (Jankowski, 2011: 61) was declared.

Three priority areas stand out in the programme of the presidency: (1) European Integration as a Source of Growth; (2) Secure Europe – food, energy, defence; and (3) Europe Benefitting from Openness. The fundamental assumptions and objectives of the Polish presidency as concerned relations with external environment were defined within priorities two and three. The security of the EU and member states depended on the "development of practical aspects of Integrated Border Management and sharing best practices in border protection" (*Programme*, 2010: 6). This objective was deemed essential in the light of events taking place in North Africa and the Middle East. At the same time, the necessity to strengthen the links between the *Common Security and Defence Policy* and the *Area of Freedom, Security and Justice* was emphasised. In the third priority "the developments in the surrounding environment were strongly reflected and mutual relations between the EU and third countries were visibly stressed" (Jańczak, 2011: 140). The Polish presidency's programme stressed that it was necessary to tighten the co-operation with the Eastern Partnership members. The objective there was to sign the Association Agreements, set up "deep and comprehensive trade areas" and accelerate "the process of visa liberalisation" (*Programme*, 2010: 7). As concerned the events in Egypt, Libya, Tunisia and other states of the Southern Neighbourhood, the "cooperation based on partnership, focused on supporting democratic transformations, building modern state structures underpinned by constitutional reforms, enhancing the judicial system and security and fighting corruption" was proposed, as well as EU support in the area of "the protection of fundamental freedoms" (*Programme*, 2010: 8). The success of democratisation in these states was related to economic growth, suggesting deeper trade relations. Therefore, the Polish presidency opted for democratisation through stabilisation.

The implementation of assumptions regarding the states of North Africa was focused on four activities. "Poland tried to act as a 'democracy expert,' being able and willing to assist [...] to implement democratic reforms" (Jańczak, 2011: 144). Poland's successful experience of transformation was shared during official parliamentary visits (such as the March 2011 visit to Tunisia), ministerial visits (such as the 2011 visit of the Minister of Foreign Affairs to Egypt, Libya and Tunisia) and study visits of delegates from North African countries (such as the new representatives of Tunisia and Egypt participating in the conference to celebrate the 30th anniversary of the first convention of the *Solidarity* movement). There were also attempts to put political pressure on the states covered by the Arab Spring, by means of calling them to respect democratic values and principles and international obligations to protect human rights (for instance, the appeal to Syrian authorities in August 2011).

Polish endeavours to stabilise North African countries resulted in the Council agreeing the mandate for the European Commission to negotiate DCFTA agreements with Egypt, Jordan, Morocco, and Tunisia.

The activities of the Polish presidency were also reflected by Poland's determination to block proposals put forward by some member states which wanted to abandon the principles of the Schengen agreement. Large numbers of immigrants flowing from North African states were perceived as threat to security, and a factor that destabilised the internal situation in the EU. Therefore, the authorities of Italy, France and Germany opted for border controls to be reinstated on internal borders. The Polish presidency was backed by Belgium, seeing these ideas as undermining the idea of European integration and diminishing the significance of the freedoms lying at the foundations of the EU, in particular of the free flow of people. In the opinion of Poland, "[t]he stability of Schengen has been challenged by uncoordinated and unilateral efforts to tackle collective problems [...]. A departure from Schengen rules would have negative effects on the European economy [...]. It would also lower the level of security now enjoyed by European citizens" (*Informal*, 2011: 1). Therefore, "[t]he Presidency's role [...] was to maintain the Schengen rules as untouched as possible" (Kaczyński, 2011: 51). The security and social order of the European Union were to be ensured by extensive operational co-operation on the external borders of the European Union. By this token, the Polish presidency officially demanded that the mandate of *Frontex* be expanded, the co-operation with third countries be strengthened to protect borders, combat trans-border crime and illegal migrant flows. These demands were considered in July 2011 in Sopot, Poland, at the meeting held by Ministers of Justice and Internal Affairs of member states. As a result, the *Action Plan of the Prague Process – Building Migration Partnerships* 2012–2016 was agreed at the November 2011 conference in Poznań. In October 2011, a new directive on the *Frontex* Agency was successfully adopted, followed in December 2011 by the qualification directive concerning the *Common European Asylum System* (*Polish*, 2012: 158). The former provided for the increased operational capabilities of the Agency, *inter alia* on account of personal reinforcement, an increased number of rapid response border groups, and the possibility of offering the support of international teams to those member states that were unable to perform border controls on account of large scale migration pressure (*Regulation*, 2011: items 9, 13–14, Arts. 3(1b), 3b, 8a). The latter sets the standards for the qualification of third-country nationals or stateless persons as beneficiaries of international protection, for a uniform status for refugees, or for persons eligible for subsidiary protection.

It was a tangible contribution of Poland in the promotion of democracy in the states undergoing the democratisation processes initiated by the Arab Spring that the *European Endowment for Democracy* was established. This new financial instrument to support the transformations in EU neighbourhood by means of financing the projects of non-governmental organisations and social initiatives was approved by EU member states. As of March 2015, the EED is financing 131 projects in Algeria, Egypt, Lebanon, Morocco, Tunisia and Syria (*We support*, 2015).

PRESENT AND PERSPECTIVES

In March 2012, Poland announced the priorities of its foreign policy until 2016. They were to present the "vision, priorities and general tasks" as well as provide the foundations for future international co-operation. North African states were treated as marginal. The priorities of Poland's foreign policy were as follows: (1) a strong Poland in a strong political union and fulfilling its tasks as an ally in a stable Euro-Atlantic arrangement; (2) openness to regional co-operation; (3) increased commitment to the co-operation for development, promotion of democracy and human rights; (4) promotion of Poland abroad in order to improve Poland's image; (5) fostering contacts with Polish emigrants; and (6) improved efficiency of foreign services (*Priorytety*, 2012: 6–7).

The most important direction of Poland's foreign policy involves co-operation within the European Union, seeking deeper political and economic integration described by the slogan "competitiveness, solidarity, openness" (*Priorytety*, 2012: 8). In the context of the Arab Spring, the dearth of references to North Africa is striking. The openness which is declared in the document mainly concerns states seeking membership of the European Union, and those that will take advantage of the openness ensured within the framework of the *European Neighbourhood Policy*, where Poland is interested in Eastern Europe and the

South Caucasus. Not a word is said about North African states, in spite of the fact that the political and economic situation in this region is closely connected with the situation of the European Union and its member states. This influences internal security, as clearly indicated by the immigration crises that have intensified in the wake of the Arab Spring.

Security is another fundamental direction of Poland's foreign policy, which is not perceived by Polish authorities as one that demands increased commitment to the stabilisation in North Africa. Having taken into account historical experience, as well as the most recent events taking place in the immediate neighbourhood of Poland, it is clear that Poland deems membership of the *North Atlantic Alliance* (and close co-operation with the United States) and the European Union to be a guarantee of security. This membership should ensure protection against a potential threat posed by a third country (while this threat was assessed as minor in 2012, its potential increased after 2014) or by terrorist organisations (where the source of threat was identified in Iraq and Afghanistan). Given the growing destabilisation of North Africa, however, it is astonishing that no references are made to threats to the security of the European Union and its member states (including Poland), posed by factors visible in North Africa.

Indicating the directions of Poland's foreign policy in 2012, the need for closer regional co-operation was stressed. Key partners mentioned in this context included Germany and France (co-operation within the *Weimar Triangle*), and Ukraine and Russia in the east. The difference was that in the case of Ukraine, it mentions strategic partnership aiming at democratisation and supporting reforms there, while in the case of Russia, co-operation was described as pragmatic, and the requirement to apply the principle of reciprocity was stressed. Given the events in 2014 and 2015 this co-operation has become questionable. The development of contacts with northern partners (in particular with Sweden, Estonia, Lithuania and Latvia) is to be achieved within the *Council of the Baltic Sea States*, while in the South (the Czech Republic, Slovakia and Hungary) – within the *Visegrad Group*. In both cases the objective is to work out similar positions in political matters and "fostering the sense of common interests" (*Priorytety*, 2012: 19).

The foreign policy of Poland will also aim to increase the global activities of this state. "Focusing on the region, the European Union and its neighbourhood [practically only its eastern neighbours – A.P.] is not to mean that Poland does not have at least selective, global aspirations" (*Priorytety*, 2012: 20). It seeks to play a significant role in international organisations and to increase its influence on the decision-making processes of these organisations. On the other hand, Poland is involved in the development of economic relations with Latin America (Argentina, Chile, Mexico and Peru) and Asia (People's Republic of China, India, Japan and South Korea). In this context Poland's declaration on its activities in response to the events in the Middle East and North Africa and its "support for modernisation and democratisation transformations" in Egypt, Libya and

Tunisia (*Priorytety*, 2012: 20) are enigmatic. Since one of the priorities of Poland's foreign policy concerned the promotion of democracy and human rights, as well as commitment to co-operation for development, it provided an opportunity for Poland's stressing its role in relation to North African countries. In the 2012 document it was stated, however, that this priority would be applied to neighbouring countries. The support for development, propagation of democratic values and commitment to the protection of human rights should foster the stabilisation of situation in neighbouring countries and prevent conflicts, thereby ensuring Poland's security. Such an approach is developed within the *Solidarity Fund PL* (until February 2013 known as the *Polish Foundation for International Cooperation for Development "Knowing How"*). While implementing its tasks of international co-operation for development (*Statut*, 2014: Par. 8.1), the Foundation disseminates Polish experiences of transformation and aids democratic transformations in third countries. The Foundation is financed by the State Treasury and subordinated to the Minister of Foreign Affairs (*Statut*, 2014: Pars. 3, 8.2), therefore it is clear that it performs the tasks indicated by the Minister and work towards the implementation of tasks considered to be the priorities of Poland's foreign policy. Consequently, its activities are focused on supporting the states covered by the Eastern Partnership, countries of Central Asia and Myanmar (Burma) and Tunisia. For instance, out of the 88 projects submitted within the Support for Democracy 2015 contest for subsidies, only the projects from Belarus (5 projects), Georgia and Moldova (7 projects), Tajikistan (3 projects) and Tunisia (3 projects) won financing.

The six-month presidency of the European Union Council, and the necessity of taking a standpoint in relation to the events in North African states did not bring about changes to the assumptions, objectives, priorities and directions of the foreign policy of Poland. In spite of declared support for the transformation processes in the states of the Arab Spring, Poland did not intensify its activities, and the expressions of interest observable in the second half of 2011 have not been continued.

BIBLIOGRAPHY

Czachór Z. (2011), *Prezydencja w Unii Europejskiej i jej priorytety. Analiza politologiczna*, in: *Priorytety prezydencji Polski w Radzie Unii Europejskiej*, eds. Z. Czachór, T. Szymczyński, Poznań.

Informacja ministra spraw zagranicznych o założeniach polskiej polityki zagranicznej w 2008 r. Sprawowdanie stenograficzne z 15. posiedzenia Sejmu Rzeczypospolitej Polskiej (2008), Warszawa.

Informal meeting of the Justice and Home Affairs Ministers, 18–19 July 2011 (2011), Sopot.

Jankowski D. (2011), *Po "arabskiej wiośnie" – "zima" dla europejskiej obrony*, "Bezpieczeństwo Narodowe", No. 2 (18).

Jańczak J. (2011), *Polish Presidency of the European Union and the Arab Spring*, in: *The Arab Spring*, ed. B. Przybylska-Maszner, Poznań.

Kaczyński P. M. (2011), *Polish Council Presidency 2011. Ambitions and Limitations*, Sieps – Swedish Institute for European Policy Studies, Stockholm.

Polish Presidency of the Council of the European Union. 1 July–31 December 2011. Final Report – preparations, achievements, conclusions (2012), Council of Ministers, Warsaw.

Priorytety polskiej polityki zagranicznej 2012–2016 (2012), Rada Ministrów, Warszawa.

Programme of the 6-Month Polish Presidency of the EU Council in the Second Half of 2011 (2010), Warsaw.

Program przygotowań Rzeczypospolitej Polskiej do objęcia i sprawowania Przewodnictwa w Radzie Unii Europejskiej. Dokument przyjęty przez Radę Ministrów 13 stycznia 2009 r. Tekst ostateczny (2009), Warszawa.

Przybylska-Maszner B. (2014), *Uwarunkowania reorientacji polityki Unii Europejskiej wobec Afryki Północnej po roku 2011*, "Przegląd Politologiczny", No. 1.

Sasnal P. (2011), *Bliski Wschód bliższy niż Wschód: Polska wobec arabskiej wiosny ludów*, "Polski Przegląd Dyplomatyczny", No. 1.

Statut Fundacji Solidarności Międzynarodowej (2013), http://solidarityfund.pl/en/fundacja1/statut-i-sprawozdania/7-statut-fundacji-solidarnoci-midzynarodowej, 10.03.2015.

Strategia RP w odniesieniu do pozaeuropejskich krajów rozwijających się (2004), Warszawa.

Szpak K. (2012), *Polityka zagraniczna na forum Unii Europejskiej*, in: *Główne kierunki polityki zagranicznej rządu Donalda Tuska w latach 2007–2011*, ed. P. Musiałek, Kraków.

Szpak K. (2012), *Założenia programowe polityki zagranicznej koalicji rządowej PO-PSL w latach 2007–2011*, in: *Główne kierunki polityki zagranicznej rządu Donalda Tuska w latach 2007–2011*, ed. P. Musiałek, Kraków.

The Constitution of the Republic of Poland, 2 April 1997, Official Journal 1997, No. 78, Item 483 as amended.

Ustawa o działach administracji rządowej, 4 września 1997, Official Journal 2013, Item 743, 27.06.2013.

We support. European Endowment for Democracy (2015), http://www.democracyendowment.eu/we-support, 12.03.2015.

Wyniki otwartego konkursu grantowego "Wsparcie demokracji 2015" (2015), Fundacja Solidarności Międzynarodowej, http://www.solidarityfund.pl/pl/nowosci-2/135-news-projekty/wsparcie-demokracji-2015, 10.03.2015.

SELECTED BIBLIOGRAPHY

ACADEMIC BOOKS

Adib-Moghaddam A. (2014), *On the Arab Revolts and the Iranian Revolution: Power and Resistance Today*, New York.

Ahmadi H. (2014), *The Third Wave of the Arab Awakening; the Anatomy of the Recent Uprisings in the Arab Countries*, The Institute for Middle East Strategic Studies (IMESS), Tehran.

Al-Aswany A. (2011), *On the State of Egypt: What Caused the Revolution*, Edinburgh.

Albareda A., Barba O. (2011), *Sub-Regionalism in North Africa and the Middle East: Lessons Learned and New Opportunities*, Barcelona.

Althani M. A. J. (2012), *The Arab State and the Gulf States: Time to Embrace Change*, London.

Amin G. (2011), *Egypt in the Era of Hosni Mubarak 1981–2011*, Cairo.

Antonius G. (2010), *The Arab Awakening: The Story of the Arab Nationalism*, London.

Ayad R., Gadi S. (2011), *The Future of Euro-Mediterranean Regional Cooperation: The Role of the Union for the Mediterranean*, Barcelona.

Behr T., Colombo S., Ebeid H., Guliński S., Sasnal P., Sławek J. (2012), *Still Awake: The Beginnings of Arab Democratic Change*, Warszawa.

Ben-Meir A. (2014), *Spring or Cruel Winter? The Evolution of the Arab Revolutions*, Washington D.C.

Bradley J. R. (2008), *Inside Egypt: The Land of the Pharaohs on the Brink of a Revolution*, Basingstoke.

Bradley J. R. (2012), *After the Arab Spring: How Islamists Hijacked the Middle East Revolts*, Basingstoke.

Burke E., Echagüe A., Youngs R. (2010), *Why the European Union Needs a Broader Middle East's Policy*, Madrid.

Cambanis T. (2015), *Once Upon A Revolution: An Egyptian Story*, New York.

Coppedge M. (2012), *Democratization and Research Methods*, New York.

Dabashi H. (2012), *The Arab Spring: the End of Postcolonialism*, London.

Dawisha A. (2013), *The Second Arab Awakening: Revolution, Democracy, and the Islamist Challenge from Tunis to Damascus*, New York.

Fiedler R. (2010), *Od przywództwa do hegemonii. Polityka Stanów Zjednoczonych wobec bliskowschodniego obszaru niestabilności 1991–2009*, Poznań.

Filiu J. P. (2011), *The Arab Revolution: Ten Lessons From the Democratic Uprising*, London.

Fuller G. E. (2014), *Turkey and the Arab Spring: Leadership in the Middle East*, Bozorg Press.

Gelvin J. L. (2012), *The Arab Uprisings: What Everyone Needs to Know*, Oxford.

Ghoraba H. (2013), *Egypt's Arab Spring. The Long and Winding Road to Democracy*, Pau.

Ginat R. (1997), *Egypt's Incomplete Revolution: Lufti al-Khuli and Nasser's Socialism in the 1960s*, London.

Herrera L. (2014), *Revolution in the Age of Social Media: The Egyptian Popular Insurrection and the Internet*, London–New York.

Howard P. N., Hussain M. M. (2013), *Democracy's Fourth Wave?: Digital Media and the Arab Spring*, Oxford.

Kandil H. (2012), *Soldiers, Spies and Statesmen: Egypt's Road to Revolt*, New York.

Khosrokhavar F. (2009), *Inside Jihadism. Understanding Jihadi Movements Worldwide*, Boulder–London.

Kozłowski K. (2012), *Kolory rewolucji*, Warszawa.

Lipa M. (2013), *Autorytaryzm na arabskim Bliskim Wschodzie. Egipt w latach 1981–2010*, Warszawa.

Lynch M. (2013), *The Arab Uprising: The Unfinished Revolutions of the New Middle East*, New York.

Muasher M. (2013), *Year Four of the Arab Awakening*, Carnegie Endowment for International Peace.

Muasher M. (2014), *The current Arab Awakening and the Battle for Pluralism*, New Haven.

Ramadan T. (2012), *The Arab Awakening: Islam and the New Middle East*, London.

Rosenberg J. M. (2012), *Aftermath of the Arab Uprisings: The Rebirth of the Middle East*, Lanham.

Rutherford B. K. (2008), *Egypt After Mubarak: Liberalism, Islam, and Democracy in the Arab World*, Princeton.

Sedky A. R. (2013), *Cairo Rewind: The First Two Years of Egypt's Revolution 2011–2013*, Victoria.

Seib P. (2008), *The Al Jazeera Effect: How the New Global Media Are Reshaping World Politics*, Washington.

The Arab Spring (2011), ed. B. Przybylska-Maszner, Poznań.

Zahid M. (2012), *The Muslim Brotherhood and Egypt's Succession Crisis: The Politics of Liberalisation and Reform in the Middle East*, London.

Zdanowski J. (2011), *Bliski Wschód 2011: bunt czy rewolucja?*, Kraków.

Zielonka J. (2007), *Europa jako imperium. Nowe spojrzenie na Unię Europejską*, Warszawa.

ACADEMIC ARTICLES

Bania R. (2014), *"Arabska Wiosna" – doświadczenia arabskich monarchii subregionu Zatoki Perskiej*, "Przegląd Politologiczny", No. 1.

Beliakov V. (2013), *The Road that Took a Quarter of a Century: On the History of Soviet-Egyptian Relations*, "International Affairs: A Russian Journal Of World Politics, Diplomacy & International Relations", Vol. 59, No. 5.

Black A. (2011), *Egypt's Muslim Brotherhood: Internal Divisions and External Challenges in the Post-Mubarak Era*, "Terrorism Monitor", Vol. IX, Issue 29.

Colombo S. (2012), *The GCC Countries and the Arab Spring. Between Outreach, Patronage and Repression*, Istituto Affari Internazionali, "Working Paper", No. 12.

Dalacoura K. (2013), *The Arab Uprisings Two Years On: Ideology, Sectarianism and the Changing Balance of Power in the Middle East*, "Insight Turkey", Vol. 15, No. 1.

Dzisiów-Szuszczykiewicz A. (2011), *"Arabska wiosna" – przyczyny, przebieg i prognozy*, "Bezpieczeństwo Narodowe", No. 18.

El Fegiery M. (2012), *Crunch Time for Egypt's Civil-Military Relations*, "Policy Brief – Fride", No 134.

Elshahed M. (2014), *Road Rage*, "The Cairo Review of Global Affairs", 24.08.2012.

Fiedler R. (2014), *Arabska Wiosna – szanse i wyzwania dla polityki USA wobec Bliskiego Wschodu*, "Przegląd Politologiczny", No. 1.

Heydemann S. (2014), *America's Response to the Arab Uprisings: US Foreign Assistance in an Era of Ambivalence*, "Mediterranean Politics", Vol. 19, No. 3.

Huber D. (2015), *A Pragmatic Actor – The US Response to the Arab Uprisings*, "Journal of European Integration", Vol. 37, No. 1.

Ibish H. (2012), *Was the Arab Spring Worth It?*, "Foreign Policy", July/August 2012.

Jankowski D. (2011), *Po "arabskiej wiośnie" – "zima" dla europejskiej obrony*, "Bezpieczeństwo Narodowe", No. 2 (18).

Kader A. B. (2014), *Contradictory Paths: Islamist Experiments of Egypt and Turkey*, "Turkish Review", Vol. 4, No. 4.

Kelly S., Ross Smith N. (2013), *The EU's Reaction to the Arab Spring: External Media Portrayals in China, India and Russia*, "European Foreign Affairs Review", Vol. 18, No. 2.

Khondker H. (2011), *Role of the New Media in the Arab Spring*, "Globalizations", Vol. 8, Issue 5.

Laz E. (2014), *Sustainable Democracy and the Paradox of the Arab Spring: The Egypt Experience*, "Alternatives: Turkish Journal of International Relations", Vol. 13, No. 1/2.

Lim M. (2012), *Clicks, Cabs, and Coffee Houses: Social Media and Oppositional Movements in Egypt, 2004–2011*, "Journal of Communication", Vol. 62.

Magen Z. (2013), *Russia and the Middle East: Policy Challenges*, "Memorandum", No. 127.

Marshall R. (2013), *The Coup That Wasn't: When Policy Overrides the Facts*, "Washington Report On Middle East Affairs", Vol. 32, No. 7.

Matthiesen T. (2012), *A 'Saudi Spring'? The Shia Protest Movement in the Eastern Province 2011–2012*, "The Middle East Journal", Vol. 66, No. 4.

Nasira H. (2011), *After Mubarak: Egypt's Islamists Respond to a Secular Revolution*, "Terrorism Monitor", Vol. IX, Issue 8.

Nasira H. (2011), *Al-Qaeda's Egyptian Ideologues Planning Caliphate's Return to Egypt*, "Terrorism Monitor", Vol. IX, Issue 27.

Omidi A. (2012), *A Comparative Analysis of the Turkish and Iranian Foreign Policy Towards the Arab Revolutions*, "Discourse: An Iranian Quarterly", No. 3–4.

Osiewicz P. (2014), *Zmiany społeczno-polityczne w państwach arabskich po 2010 roku: krytyczna analiza stosowanych pojęć*, "Przegląd Politologiczny", No. 1.

Parsi T., Marashi R. (2011), *Arab Spring Seen From Tehran*, "Cairo Review", No. 2.

Pohl A. (2014), *Arabia Saudyjska wobec Arabskiej Wiosny*, "Przegląd Politologiczny", Vol. 19, No. 1.

221

Przybylska-Maszner B. (2014), *Uwarunkowania reorientacji polityki Unii Europejskiej wobec Afryki Północnej po roku 2011*, "Przegląd Politologiczny", No. 1.

Purat A. (2014), *Znaczenie Bractwa Muzułmańskiego w polityce Egiptu oraz w wydarzeniach Arabskiej Wiosny 2011 roku*, "Przegląd Politologiczny", Vol. 19, No. 1.

Sarıhan A. (2012), *Is the Arab Spring in the Third Wave of Democratization? The Case of Syria and Egypt*, "Turkish Journal of Politics", Vol. 3, No. 1.

Sasnal P. (2011), *Bliski Wschód bliższy niż Wschód: Polska wobec arabskiej wiosny ludów*, "Polski Przegląd Dyplomatyczny", No. 1.

Shirky C. (2011), *The Political Power of Social Media*, "Foreign Affairs", Vol. 90, Issue 1.

Wejkszner A. (2014), *Ewolucja zagrożenia dżihadystycznego a przemiany demokratyczne w państwach Maghrebu*, "Przegląd Politologiczny", Vol. 19, No. 1.

CONTRIBUTORS

ROBERT CZULDA, Assistant Professor (Adjunct) at the Department of Theory of Foreign and Security Policy (Katedra Teorii Polityki Zagranicznej i Bezpieczeństwa) at the University of Lodz (Uniwersytet Łódzki), participant of the Young Leaders Dialogue of the US Department of State (2010–2011), fellow of the Lanckoroński Foundation in London (2014), visiting lecturer at universities in Lithuania, Ireland, Turkey and Slovakia, as well as the National Cheng-chi University in Taipei, within the framework of the Taiwan Fellowship programme (2013). He works as a freelance journalist and freelance contributor to IHS Jane's.
Contact: rczulda@uni.lodz.pl.

RADOSŁAW FIEDLER, Professor at AMU, working in the Section for Strategic Studies in the Department of Political Science and Journalism. Author of numerous papers and monographs on the issues of the Middle East. His research interests are focused on the determinants of instability in the Middle East, the policy of the US and EU towards North Africa and the Middle East, the proliferation of nuclear weapons in the context of Iranian nuclear programme and the role of NGOs in promoting civil society. He is in charge of two research programmes financed by the National Science Centre: Iranian nuclear programme versus the non-proliferation regime (concluded in 2013) and The EU towards the transformation processes in Egypt after 2011. He has also been granted a research subsidy within the EU Partnership and International Cooperation in Jordan. He coordinates the Erasmus+ programme in his Department. He is the President of the Fundacja Fiedlerów foundation which fosters cross-cultural dialogue and the initiatives of local communities.
Contact: radoslaw.fiedler@amu.edu.pl.

MOHAMMAD HOUSHISADAT, Assistant Professor of Middle East Politics at the University of Tehran, Faculty of Law and Political Science. He has received his Ph.D. from the Institute for Middle Eastern and Islamic Studies at Durham University in England. He is the Head of the Middle East Office in the Iranian Parliament (Islamic Consultative Assembly) Research Center and the author of several books and academic papers in Persian and English.
Contact: s.m.houshisadat@ut.ac.ir.

PRZEMYSŁAW OSIEWICZ, Associate Professor at Adam Mickiewicz University in Poznan, graduated in political science in the field of international relations from AMU. He holds a Ph.D. in political science. The Secretary of Research Committee RC-15 of the International Political Science Association (IPSA). Member of PTNP and PTSM. Previous studies/guest researcher: Södertörns Högskola (Stockholm, Sweden); Eastern Mediterranean University (Famagusta, Cyprus); Chinese Culture University (Taipei, Taiwan); National Taipei University (Taiwan); Selçuk Üniversitesi (Konya, Turkey); the Policy Research Center of Ningbo (the People's Republic

223

of China); Mersin Üniversitesi (Turkey); Linnaeus University (Vaxjo, Sweden) and University College Ghent (Belgium), the Ministry of Interior (Cyprus, 2012), the Institute for Political and International Studies (Iran, 2013), University of Nicosia (Cyprus, 2014), University of Cairo (Egypt, 2014), Georgetown University (USA, 2015). He lectured in Cyprus, Turkey, Iran, Belgium, Sweden, Germany and Taiwan. So far he has published three books as well as over 60 academic articles. The main academic interests include the Middle Eastern political studies, geopolitical codes, unrecognised states, the Cyprus question, EU – Turkey relations, Iran's foreign policy and the Turkish foreign policy.
Contact: przemyslaw.osiewicz@amu.edu.pl.

ARTUR POHL, Ph.D. candidate at the Faculty of Political Science and Journalism of Adam Mickiewicz University in Poznań. His research interests focus on the international relations and security policy in the Middle East, particularly with references to Iran, Israel and Turkey.
Contact: a.pohl@amu.edu.pl.

ANNA POTYRAŁA, Adam Mickiewicz University Professor, political scientist and lawyer. Her scientific interests include the EU Justice and Home Affairs, migration and refugee questions, as well as the problem of international crimes and international responsibility. Author of numerous monographs (among others: *Contemporary refugeeism*, 2005; *State cooperation with international criminal tribunals and sovereignty*, 2010; *The EU towards international criminal tribunals. Genesis, concept and practice of cooperation*, 2012; *The UN towards the refugee problem. Genesis, concept and practice of activity*, 2015) and lexicons concerning the European integration (2008 and 2009). Assistant Editor of the "Przegląd Strategiczny" (Strategic Review) academic periodical.
Contact: anna.potyrala@amu.edu.pl.

MAREK REWIZORSKI, Ph.D. in the field of Political Science, lawyer, Assistant Professor at the Institute of History and Political Science of the Pomeranian University in Słupsk. Member of the Polish, British and European International Studies Association and the Polish Association of Political Science. He taught at the Institute of Political Science and Management at the University of Tallinn. The author of eight books, as well as over 60 papers and studies in the field of international relations. His recent publications include: *From Washington to St. Petersburg. Development of the G20 as a New Centre of Global Governance* published by Logos Verlag Berlin in 2014. Research interests: international political economy, global governance, G7/G20, BRICS, emerging markets, the EU institutional system, economic security.
Contact: marcuser@o2.pl.

MICHAŁ SKORZYCKI, Ph.D., is a graduate of the University of Łódź (master's degree in international relations and doctoral degree in sociology), holding the positions of Assistant Professor and Vice Dean of the Faculty of Social Sciences and Humanities at the University of Social Sciences in Łódź. His research interests involve the fields of sociology of politics and international relations, particularly external relations of the European Union, problems of nationalism and national identity, as well as internal politics and democratic transformation of the Czech Republic (the latter has made him a scholarship holder of the International Visegrad Fund).
Contact: skorzycki@gmail.com.

MARCIN STYSZYŃSKI, Ph.D., is an Assistant Professor in the Faculty of Arabic and Islamic Studies at Adam Mickiewicz University in Poznan, Poland. He also served as the cultural and scientific attaché in the Embassy of Poland in Egypt (2009–2012) and the second secretary and the Consul in the Embassy of Poland in Algeria (2012–2014).
Contact: martin@amu.edu.pl.

MARCIN TARNAWSKI, Jagiellonian University, holds a Ph.D. in political studies and currently lectures at the Institute of Political Studies and International Relations at the Jagiellonian University. He is the author of works and publications focused on the issue of international security, international economics, energy security and the foreign and security policy of the Russian Federation. He is an expert of the Kosciuszko Institute.
Contact: needlemt@wp.pl.

ARTUR WEJKSZNER, AMU Professor, graduated from AMU in Poznań. His academic interests encompass the issues of modern international terrorism, international NGOs and European integration, with particular emphasis given to EU common foreign and security policy.
Contact: artur.wejkszner@amu.edu.pl.

SEBASTIAN WOJCIECHOWSKI, Professor at Adam Mickiewicz University in Poznań and the Institute for Western Affairs in Poznań. Head of the Strategic Studies Department of the Faculty of Political Science and Journalism of Adam Mickiewicz University in Poznań. Former Dean of the Faculty of Political Science and International Relations at the Higher School of Humanities and Journalism in Poznań. Awarded scholarships by the Foundation for Polish Science and the US State Department. Recipient of the Scholar's Award from the Prime Minister of the Republic of Poland and an award for a scholarly publication in a European Union-wide contest. Editor-in-chief of the "Przegląd Strategiczny" academic periodical. Security expert of the Organization for Security and Co-operation in Europe.
Contact: sebastian.wojciechowski@amu.edu.pl.

Appendix 1.

PROJECT QUESTIONNAIRE

"The European Union's attitude to the transformation processes in Egypt after 2011"
Grant no 2012/05/B/HS5/00510

Part I – BRUSSELS

Information about the interviewee

First and last name
Position . . . .
Institution . . . .
Date of interview . . . .

Issue I
The role a given institution plays in co-creating EU policy towards Egypt

1. What, in your opinion, is the role of the institution you work for in developing policy/attitudes towards Egypt?
2. Which EU institution's activities have, in your opinion, the greatest significance in creating EU policy towards Egypt?

Issue II
The influence individual states (institutions) have on EU policy

3. Which EU member states are, in your opinion, most interested in developing EU instruments concerning Egypt, and why?
4. What is the formal and informal influence of these states on the creation of EU policy towards Egypt?

Issue III
Assessment of current EU policy towards Egypt

5. What is your assessment of current EU policy towards Egypt?

6. Is the EU facilitating transformation processes in Egypt? If so, how?
7. Has current EU policy towards Egypt proved effective?
8. Which instruments of EU policies towards Egypt do you consider to be most effective?
9. Could you indicate some examples of effective EU activities?
10. Could you indicate the main problems facing the implementation of EU policy towards Egypt?

Additional

11. Do the latest post-Lisbon changes in EU structures, including the establishment of the External Action Service of the European Union, facilitate the implementation of EU policy towards third countries such as Egypt?

Part II – CAIRO

Issue I
Political, economic and social reasons for changes in Egypt

1. What were the most important political reasons for changes in Egypt after 2010?
2. What were the most important economic as well as social reasons for these changes?
3. What was the role of social media for changes between 25th January and 18th February 2011?
4. Which term suits the political changes in Egypt best: the Arab Spring, the Arab Revolution, the Arab Awakening or maybe the Islamic Awakening?
5. What is your overall assessment of the political changes in Egypt after 2010?
6. Was the political change of July 2013 unavoidable? Was it an example of a coup d'état or rather a necessary action to protect the state?

Issue II
Political changes in Egypt and their international dimension

1. Were the political changes in Egypt significant as far as international security and stability were concerned?
2. Which Middle Eastern states backed changes in Egypt? For what reasons?
3. Which Middle Eastern states opposed the removal of President Hosni Mubarak from power?
4. How do you assess Egypt's bilateral relations with various Middle Eastern states after the political changes of July 2013?
5. Did the Egyptian Muslim Brotherhood pose any serious threat to other Arab states, for example, Arab monarchies in the Persian Gulf region?

Issue III
Political changes in Egypt and their influence on EU energy security

1. What was Egypt's energy balance before and after 2011?
2. What was the level of deliveries of energy sources from Egypt to the EU before 2011?
3. What is the level of deliveries of energy sources from Egypt to the EU after 2011?
4. How do you assess Egypt's share in the EU's energy supplies? Is it significant or not?
5. What are the prospects for EU-Egypt cooperation as far as energy sources are concerned?

Appendix 2.

LIST OF INSTITUTIONS INTERVIEWED

Embassy of the Arab Republic of Egypt, Warsaw

European Commission, Brussels

European Endowment for Democracy, Brussels

European External Action Service, Brussels

European Parliament, Brussels

European Union Delegation to Egypt, Cairo

European Union Delegation to Jordan, Amman

International Committee of the Red Cross Brussels Delegation

Permanent Representation of the Republic of Poland to the European Union, Brussels